D0519213

Regency Library Cupboard in Rosewood
Michael Brett
MAJOR C. A. BRETT, M.B.E.
PORCELAIN, PLATE, ANTIQUE &
EARLY VICTORIAN FURNITURE
1 Market Square
& 25 High Street
Stony Stratford, Bucks.
Member B.A.D.A.
Phone 3112
ON THE WATLING STREET

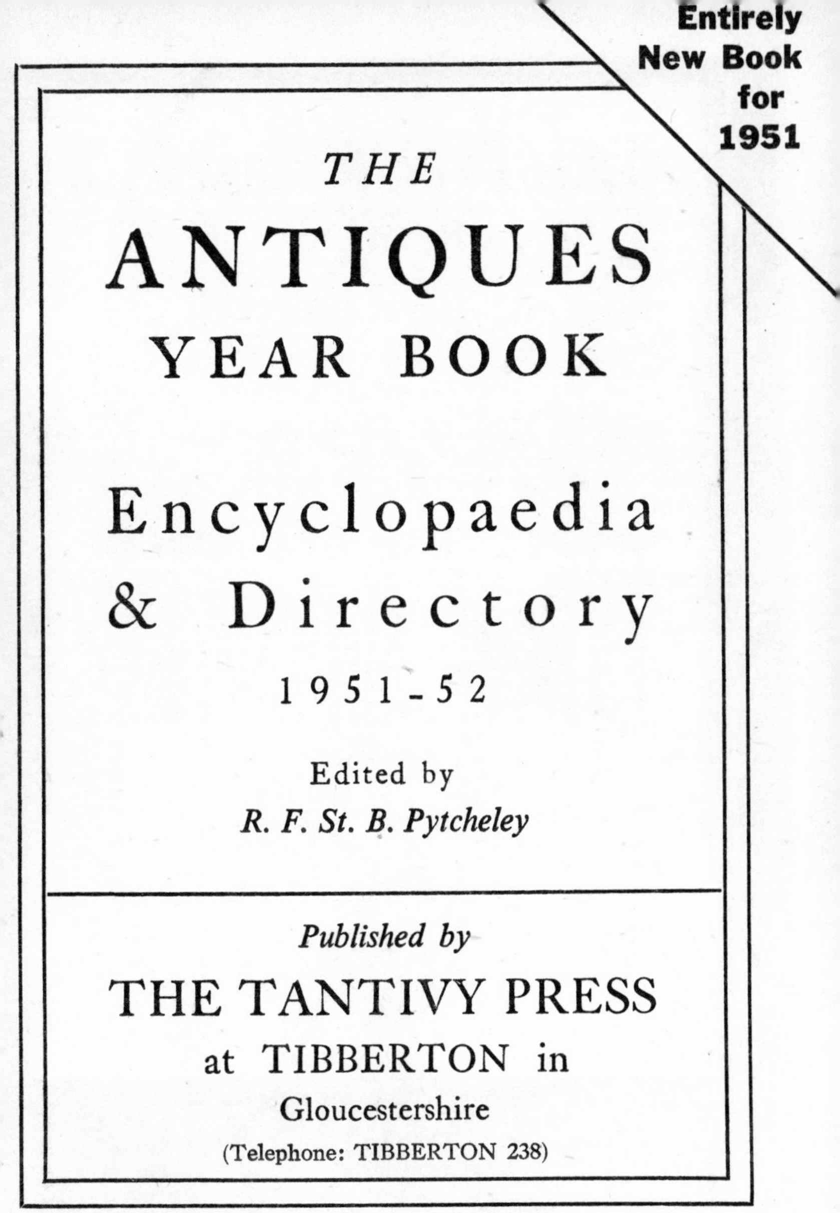

Entirely New Book for 1951

THE

ANTIQUES YEAR BOOK

Encyclopaedia & Directory

1951-52

Edited by

R. F. St. B. Pytcheley

Published by

THE TANTIVY PRESS

at TIBBERTON in

Gloucestershire

(Telephone: TIBBERTON 238)

WHOLLY MADE AND PRINTED IN GREAT BRITAIN.

Contents

Illustrations

ILLUSTRATIONS

Introduction

ENTIRELY new in contents, this 1951–52 Festival of Britain edition follows the great success of our previous years' books with not only a record demand from the public, who like to have the annual volume for the unique reference and pictorial material it contains, but also outstandingly heavy support from the antiques trade.

The new contents comprise a fresh version of our 1949 *Dictionary of Antiques*, which has been largely re-written by one of our greatest living authorities on the subject, additional silver marks in cycles (including Glasgow), numerous other features, an increased number of fine illustrations, itineraries for antiques tours widened and covering most of the country, not to mention the *Directories*.

These tours and *Directories* have to be completely re-set at considerable expense each year, such are the changes constantly taking place in the ownership, specialities and status of antique shops. We are here conscious of performing an arduous public service of unique scope in the history of collecting.

Visitors to Britain for the Festival will be able to use our book as a constant companion in their search for the lovely relics of our history.

The price of the book has been increased slightly because the costs of production have nearly doubled in twelve months, but in compensation the size of the volume has been greatly enlarged.

Unfortunately the quality of the paper used, though actually more expensive, has declined, and inferior art paper for the illustrations was obtained at great cost in the teeth of a famine caused by the cold war preparations.

But our struggle to give you this book has been worth while if once again you appreciate it as you did the previous volumes (never have we known in publishing history such a spate of complimentary letters received, from the highest to the lowest in the land). It is our constant endeavour to justify these kind words of our friends, to help collectors find what they want, and to continue fostering the interests of those among us who like to see the heritage of the past kept in circulation.

Under the patronage of

H.M QUEEN MARY

THE ELEVENTH

ANTIQUE DEALERS'

FAIR

AND EXHIBITION

JUNE 6th - 21st, 1951

(Except Sundays)

GROSVENOR HOUSE, PARK LANE, W.1

OPEN 11.0 A.M. TO 7.30 P.M. (Opening Day from 5 p.m.)

◆

ADMISSION 3/6. SEASON TICKETS 15/-

(including Tax)

Round the Antique Salons of London

AN INFORMAL SERVICE FOR THE INTEREST AND GUIDANCE OF COLLECTORS AND TOURISTS.

LONDON has so many fine salons devoted to antiques, as well as large and small specialists, not to mention ordinary shops by the hundred, and these are spread over such a wide area, that it would be quite impossible to describe all in a single section. Nor would it be helpful to the reader, who is best served, we feel, by careful guidance to interesting addresses in each of the main streets and areas devoted to antiques. We give you, then, a cross-section of London, which will be cut at different angles in succeeding years.

BOND STREET

Bond Street, traditionally one of the smartest shopping thoroughfares in the world, properly houses in itself and the immediate area some of the leading antiques salons. Go there first for the best, and find the firm of H. Blairman and Sons, Ltd., who occupy lovely premises at Number 23, Grafton Street, turning off Bond Street near the Piccadilly end towards Berkeley Square. Messrs. Blairman deal in the finest of 18th century objects of art, specialising in English furniture and very fine 18th century Chinese mirror paintings. They also have a number of pieces of Regency furniture of the highest quality.

That is the fine furniture salon. Now turn back into Bond Street proper for the leading representative of yet another kind of business, the world-famous Asprey and Co., Ltd., of 165–9 New Bond Street. Asprey is really indefinable—save in so far as the policy might be to sell only the best of everything—but here we have the foremost of those shops which give us lovely antique silver in one department, rare porcelains in another, superb jewellery next, or fine old bindings here and some beautiful furniture there: all glossed with the same subtle patina of accurate taste.

It is a remarkable congerie of fashion and olden charm, the Asprey building (which extends for some distance with restrained

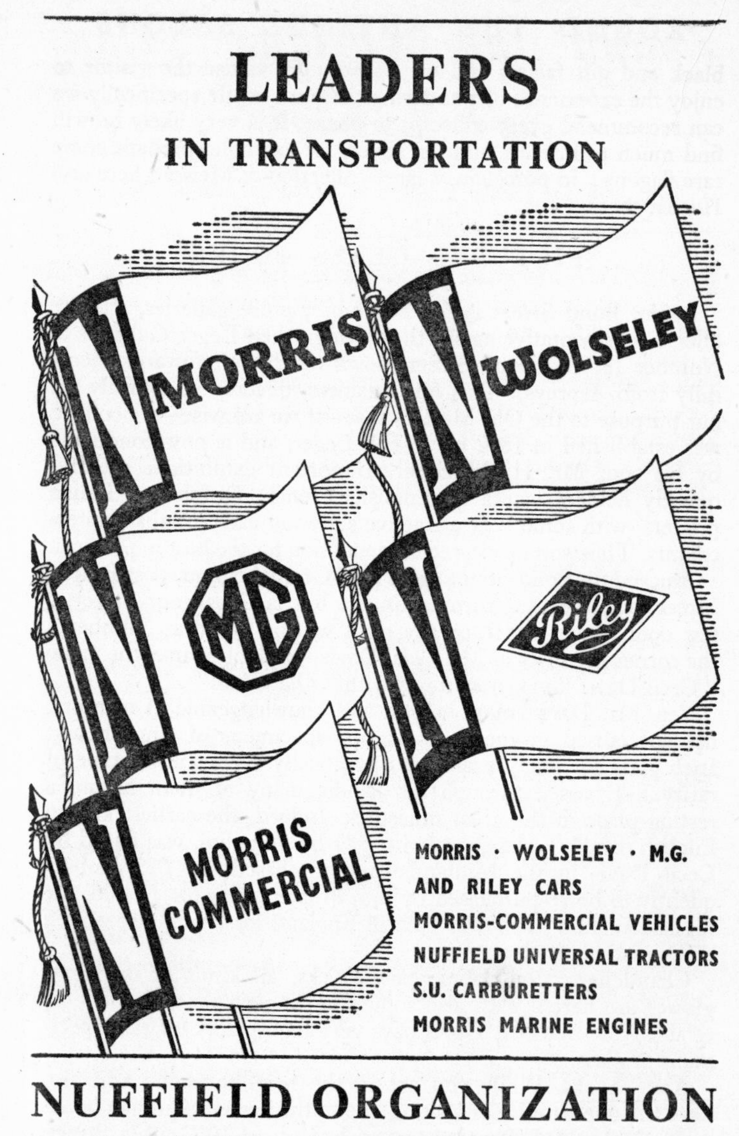
LEADERS
IN TRANSPORTATION
MORRIS
WOLSELEY
MG
Riley
MORRIS
COMMERCIAL
MORRIS · WOLSELEY · M.G.
AND RILEY CARS
MORRIS-COMMERCIAL VEHICLES
NUFFIELD UNIVERSAL TRACTORS
S.U. CARBURETTERS
MORRIS MARINE ENGINES
NUFFIELD ORGANIZATION
Overseas business: Nuffield Exports Ltd., Cowley, Oxford and 41 Piccadilly, London, W.1

black and gilt facias) and we do strongly advise the visitor to enjoy the experience of wandering therein : while specifically we can recommend every collector to pause. It is very likely he will find much to interest him. In silver, for example, perhaps some rare flagons ; in porcelain, a large collection of Meissen here and Hochst there. . . .

PICTURES—GLASS—BOOKS

Again, Bond Street is the home of picture galleries, and we offer a representative again, the distinguished Leger Galleries at Number 13, Old Bond Street (down on the left towards Piccadilly from Aspreys). This fine business, devoted so usefully for our purpose to the Old Masters that—if we are wise—we collect, was established in 1892 by Joseph Leger, and is now conducted by his son, Mr. H. L. Leger. Important exhibitions are frequently held of works by English, French, Dutch and Italian masters, with some very attractive shows of early English water-colours. Thus you have a recommendation for the best in pictures.

Proceed up Bond Street again past Grafton Street, past Bruton Street, and the next turning on the left is Grosvenor Street, a few doors down which on the right will be found at Number 3 the corner premises of Mr. Cecil Davis—and, of course, the name " Cecil Davis " is synonymous with " *Old Glass*."

Yes, Mr. Davis, most helpful and knowledgeable of mentors, has specialised in the finest-known specimens of English and Irish glass for many years, and practically every known type of rarity has passed through his hands, many of them finding a resting-place in the great museums. Indeed, the earliest known English drinking-glass, made in 1577 by Verzelini, was found by Cecil Davis in the Midlands and purchased for £15—subsequently to be re-purchased by him in later years for £1,400, the highest auction price ever paid in England for a single specimen of English glass.

Chandeliers, candelabra, candlesticks, all kinds of drinking-glasses are here : with also some fine English pottery and porcelain. Note that Mr. Davis pays very high prices for rare specimens of glass.

And—books. While you are in the neighbourhood you also have the opportunity of visiting one of the best antiquarian booksellers in London, Bernard Quaritch, Ltd., at 10 Grafton Street. Note that they carry a very large stock of books on fine art subjects: and collectors will always be certain of finding a book on their own particular antiques subject.

Return to Bond Street and cross over to Clifford Street, finding at Number 14A yet another fine firm of booksellers, Messrs. Truslove and Hanson, with new and old books but especially the latest volumes on antiques. (And they have the speciality of being able to print fine Court stationery.)

CHINESE ART

Now proceed down Hay Hill into Berkeley Square and strike across to Mount Street at the top left hand corner, a comparatively peaceful thoroughfare leading to another famous district of antiques salons, from which we single out for special mention the firm of John Sparks Ltd., Number 128 Mount Street.

The reader interested in Chinese antiquities, oldest and most fascinating of antiques, will find at Messrs. Sparks not only one of the outstanding collections in the world of porcelains, jades and Chinese works of art generally, but also knowledge, probity and courtesy, those three essentials in art-dealing. We can unreservedly recommend our readers who wisely buy Chinese both for pleasure and for a sure investment, to visit and experience the charm of these quiet salons. Mr. Peter Sparks, the Managing Director, who is antiquary of Chinese Art to Her Majesty Queen Mary, is a foremost authority on his subject. Exhibitions have been held by his firm in the United States and other parts of the world. This should be, for our readers, an essential port of call, as all who are wise in the collecting of antiques come gratefully to Chinese at last. There is no other acquisition that yields quite the same ultimate satisfaction.

So for a suitable introduction to the Mayfair area, fittingly completed by mention of a smaller, general establishment, that of Christy's of Kent Ltd., at 104 Mount Street, a few doors along. Here are sold pleasant old furniture, *bijouterie*, bygones generally, something of everything but with the West End touch, just back of Grosvenor Square. American visitors are specially catered for here.

And to complete the picture, if you come from overseas and are particulary interested in antique books, pictures, drawings and *literary portraits*, call at Number 79, Duke Street, across Grosvenor Square, where Messrs. B. F. Stevens and Brown,

Ltd., Library and Fine Art Agents for the American Market since 1864, have their West End showrooms.

PORCELAIN AND POTTERY

There is now an opportunity of visiting a firm of leading specialists in old porcelain and pottery, Messrs. D. M. & P. Manheim, than whom few experts to-day are so reliable or so pleasant to deal with. (This is a very universal opinion in the antiques trade.)

Their charming establishment can easily be reached by proceeding up Duke Street across Oxford Street and Wigmore Street, then across Manchester Square (where the Wallace Collection may be visited profitably.) At Number 7 Manchester Street in a shop adapted from a genuine Adam's house will be found anything from a quaint early 19th century figure, trifling in cost, to an exquisite pair of Chelsea figures. Indeed, this business is just as representative of all the different factories as a museum collection. Derby, Chelsea, Bow, Worcester, Rockingham—all are here—together with a magnificent pottery section, comprising Staffordshire, Toby jugs and figures, Leeds, Wheildon, lustre, delftware in profusion. Every article is guaranteed genuine of the period, and dates and factories are given wherever there is a certainty, a very great comfort to the beginner as well as to the more experienced collector.

Messrs. D. M. & P. Manheim are actually a sister and two brothers who have been in business together for almost thirty years. Throughout the country, collectors and traders speak highly of their knowledge. We do recommend them most confidently—and their American branch at 46, East 57th Street, New York, notable for the brilliant display of its fine stock.

LONDON'S ANTIQUE SHOP—PEWTER—MAPS

Hereabouts is, moreover, what we always feel should be described as one of London's only real antique shops, in the sense of a fine establishment with all kinds of antiques but not just for the specialist alone. Find it by retracing steps to Wigmore Street, where at Numbers 59 to 61 the famous old firm of Charles Woollett & Son still preserve the popular atmosphere—yet sell

some very excellent pieces indeed, particularly first-class porcelain, of which Captain Woollett can always show some fine specimens in figures. The writer of these notes, with some experience, can unhesitatingly advise the visitor to patronise this wonderful old firm and wander around the four large showrooms packed with the most attractive treasures of byegone days presided over by really pleasant people.

Then if the interest continues to be porcelain, but *especially if the interest be pewter*, inquire the way carefully to Chiltern Street hereabouts, where at Number 19 Mr. Richard Mundey specialises in the last-named. One of the few specialist pewter dealers in London, he takes care to stock pieces that can be bought by the beginner and modest collector as well as by the advanced connoisseur. The fact that Mr. Mundey already does a considerable export trade should recommend him to visitors. All export details are attended to by the firm—and, in addition to the pewter, there is a good stock of English and Continental porcelain, as well as silver and Sheffield and Victorian plate.

And maps : you are now near to Marylebone High Street, where at Number 83 is the fine old firm of Francis Edwards, not only outstanding among London dealers in old maps and atlases, but renowned antiquarian booksellers, whose speciality is old works on colonial subjects. The overseas visitor could not browse in a more fascinating shop for material relating to their own lands : also prints.

PHILLIPS OF HITCHIN

Now to visit one of the finest salons for antiquities in all the London area—at Hitchin in Hertfordshire, which is reached by a quick car or train journey : Hitchin which has always been associated with the name of Phillips of Hitchin, Ltd. Here, in a beautiful 18th century mansion with panelled rooms known as The Manor House, will be found the very finest antique furniture of the 17th and 18th century periods. Indeed, this business is world-famous, and if any of our readers were unable to spare time for a tour of England, he would be more than consoled by a visit one afternoon to The Manor House at Hitchin. In the post-war years seven antiquities have been acquired from the Antique Dealers' Fair at Grosvenor House by the Victoria and Albert Museum, and *no less than six of these have come from Messrs. Phillips of Hitchin.* It might well be said that this is the most important trade collection of genuine antique furniture in England. The Manor House is built with two wings so that it is possible to walk from room to inter-connecting room until even the sceptic is convinced that he has never seen anything like this before. (Heavily-starred.)

BACK TO TOWN

And after visiting Hitchin a valuable route back to town can be taken via Hertford where, in an ancient building at the Old Cross, will be found the old firm of Beckwiths, specialities: pottery and old oak—Beckwith's recent discovery of an historic Meal Ark is described elsewhere in this book—but also porcelain and old mahogany and walnut furniture, besides many other interesting items.

Then remember as you pass through Waltham Cross that at Harold House, Number 73, High Street—on the right—is the headquarters of J. de Haan and Son, Ltd., not a firm for the casual sightseer but one of our largest exporters of antiques, specialising in furniture, barometers, glass, china, etc., with American wholesale business a speciality.

After which it is suggested that the day be rounded off with three calls in North London, the first at the establishment of Mary Adair, Ltd., Number 3 Heath Street, Hampstead. Do not miss this, because an ordinary shop has been converted cleverly by the two lady proprietors into an abode of charm and beauty. Porcelain, pottery and glass are the interests—and not for nothing has some of their pottery been illustrated in *The Saturday Book.*

Then we have Highgate nearby, and in Highgate, at Number 76 of the fine old High Street, there is the shop known as Nicholas, especially interesting because the proprietor is an unusual personality (who actually constructed his magnificent period shopfront with his own hands). To meet him is an experience and a pleasure. His stock of antiques has been accumulated to suit purchasers who wish to furnish with fine small pieces of the past at low cost—often lower than the cost of new furniture. China and glass of individual character are provided for the buyer of discrimination.

And on the way back to town make sure that you obtain accurate directions to *Camden Town*, and that you find in Camden High Street at Number 230 the firm of Charles L. Nyman & Co., whom we single out in this area because of their interest in

genuine antiques often offered at bargain prices, combined with a wholly individual speciality—Webb cameo glass. Nymans have a lovely collection of this unusual product—and are always interested to acquire specimens. They have a branch at Epping, described elsewhere.

ST. JAMES'S

But we must return to the centre of things and investigate the other, Piccadilly side of Bond Street, which becomes St. James's, traditional home of specialists in antiques. We could devote pages to the various experts hereabouts, but must mention two as representatives who will be particularly useful to our readers.

The first is a furniture specialist, Mrs. L. Loewenthal, of Number 4, St. James's Street, down on the left at the foot of this thoroughfare of clubs and gentlemen's shops leading to the perfect Tudor palace of St. James. Mrs. Loewenthal has an excellent business based upon taste and knowledge and upon the kind of courtesy and fair-dealing to customers which makes lasting friends. Her speciality is the best 18th century furniture. We always like her fine chairs, and note that she wishes to purchase good specimens, particularly arms, of the Chippendale school. Then there are glass and silkwork pictures (which are again urgently required to purchase as well as sell).

The second is a fine representative picture gallery of St. James's, that of M. Bernard at Number 21, Ryder Street, a turning on the right if you proceed up St. James's Street towards Piccadilly. This is a most attractive salon, wherein you cannot wander long without desiring to possess an Old Master or two of the type so tastefully chosen for value and colour. There is always on view a large selection of paintings and drawings of most schools and subjects, also engravings ; and it is worth noting that Messrs. Bernard are pleased to hear from owners or their agents with a view to purchasing for cash fine drawings and paintings of all schools either single pictures or complete collections. This is a dealer that comes increasingly to the forefront of the profession, and we hope that our readers will take our advice to visit Number 21, Ryder Street.

Turn left into Bury Street. On the way up do pause at the little, lovely shop of Miss Vesta Kittelsen, called " Old and New," at Number 26, Bury Street. Here a young lady of taste and enter-

prise purveys pleasant pieces of period porcelain, glass and antique jewellery : she has Norwegian connections and can sometimes get interesting Scandinavian glass and silver.

Then in Piccadilly Arcade—between Jermyn Street and Piccadilly—is the establishment at Number 10 of Gered (Antiques) Ltd., most usefully specialists in Wedgwood alone. We know no similar shop in all our experience where the serried arrays of those blue and whites, those basalts and jaspers, all kinds from plaques to diminutive salts produce such brave effect. It is readily seen that Wedgwood like some garden flowers should be massed alone. Our American friends particularly will want to remember this address, for Messrs. Gered cater for them. As usual please mention *Antiques Yearbook*, as we have had many letters from readers asking for the name of a purely Wedgwood specialist in London.

Finally repair to Princes Arcade, another connection between Jermyn Street and Piccadilly, where at Number 4 will be found the interesting shop of Richard Ogden—interesting for antique jewellery (unusual stock of garnet, topaz, turquoise) and for fine antique silver.

CHESSMEN

Elsewhere in this book we review with enthusiasm Mr. Alex Hammond's new and unique work on *Chessmen*. Now is an opportunity not only to meet the author, but also to inspect his collection of chess-sets, one of the most famous in the world, yet including many on sale to the public and much that will enable you inexpensively to start your own collection.

Cross Piccadilly to Burlington Arcade (itself among the sights of London, with its own ordinances and trade customs, almost a little self-governing republic of fashion) and find Mr. Hammond's salon at Number 16, under the name " Emil." The proprietor is one of the personalities of London, renowned equally among his friends as a chess-player, and to a large part of England for his television displays of chess-sets. He will give you advice and place your feet properly on the path of the connoisseur, being expert, enthusiastic and completely reliable. Do visit him, because, even if you are not interested in chessmen, his stock is a revelation of historic beauty, and somehow, once you have seen it, you begin to be interested in chessmen . . . also in backgammon and mah jongg sets, ivories : and fine antique jewellery.

SILVER AND FORWARDING

Burlington Arcade leads from Piccadilly to Burlington Gardens, where you can turn right and proceed to Vigo Street. At the corner of Vigo Street and Sackville Street will be found the premises of Hancocks and Company, famous diamond merchants and silversmiths since 1848. This is one of the leading and most fashionable centres for the purchase of fine jewels and beautiful silver, having Royal Warrant to the Crown, and at various times Appointments to the Russian, Italian, Belgian, German, Austrian and Portuguese Royal Families.

Mr. Hancock made the first Victoria Cross in 1857, and the firm has been entrusted with the execution of this decoration ever since. The Oxford and Cambridge Boat Race of 1867 was timed by Hancocks' Chronograph Watch (Oxford won); some days later a Director of the firm took an assortment of plate and jewellery to Queen Victoria at Windsor; at the Paris Exhibition His Imperial Majesty Napoleon III purchased from Hancocks' collection a silver jug, a gold collar and other pieces of jewellery; in 1947 the firm supplied several of the articles given as wedding presents to H.R.H. Princess Elizabeth.

So we can here recommend, if you collect antique silver and jewellery, a firm upon which you can rely completely. They always have a superb stock and treat the customer of whatever size with the utmost consideration and courtesy. Do call—as an experience which will probably be converted into a lasting connection.

Moreoever you are conveniently situated, if from overseas and requiring to have antiques packed and shipped home, to visit Messrs. Bolton & Fairhead, Ltd., the famous forwarding agents nearby. They are to be found at Number 106 Regent Street, entrance in Glasshouse Street, next door to the renowned Oyster Bar. This firm *specialises* in the forwarding of antiques, from the smallest package to the largest case, but even more than that pay comforting attention to the personal side, looking after the overseas buyer of antiques from the moment he enters the country and relieving him of most of his problems and worries. Complete itineraries are arranged. The Directors, Mr. C. K. Bolton and Mr. R. C. Kent, are both personally acquainted with the United States. Very good terms are given by this firm for bulk work, and once again our warm recommendation is extended.

COINS TO CAMEOS

It is recommended next that a course be set eastwards temporarily via Oxford Street (noting Great Portland Street on the left where at Number 65 the remarkable firm of B. A. Seaby, Ltd., handle some 100,000 antique coins a year : they are really worth visiting) and turning right at Charing Cross Road to call at the world's largest bookshop, W. & G. Foyle, Ltd., Numbers 119–125, who also have an antique coins department, as well as large sections for collectors' books, stamps, prints, old maps. . . .

Regain New Oxford Street and proceed until Museum Street is reached on the left. There is a firm here, at Number 26, Museum Street, which is daily visited by persons of taste and fashion from the West End. We have ourselves seldom seen such a good business done as by Mr. Mosheh Oved at this delightful " Cameo Corner," where he has a very fine stock of cameos and intaglios ; Renaissance and Stuart jewellery and an interesting collection of Roman jewellery ; snuff boxes ; Georgian silver ; some Russian silver ; also a large collection of Georgian and Queen Anne jewellery. We single out this remarkable business because it is really good for the items enumerated—and completely reliable. (Look in the shop also for several pieces of Mr. Oved's own sculpture in bronze, work of importance and rare beauty.)

After which you may care to visit at New Ruskin House, 28–30 Little Russell Street, turning on the right, the headquarters of B. F. Stevens & Brown, Ltd., the library agents with American connection previously mentioned for Duke Street. Here they are dealing with the wants of private collectors and libraries in all parts of the world, wants ranging from a single copy of *The Times* to a First Folio Shakespeare.

CITY SILVER

Continue citywards via High Holborn and turn down Chancery Lane on the right to notice the Chancery Lane Safe Deposit on the left a short way down. At the foot of the stairs find the glittering cavern wherein Mr. William Walter has his splendid stock of antique silver. These "Silver Vaults," as they are

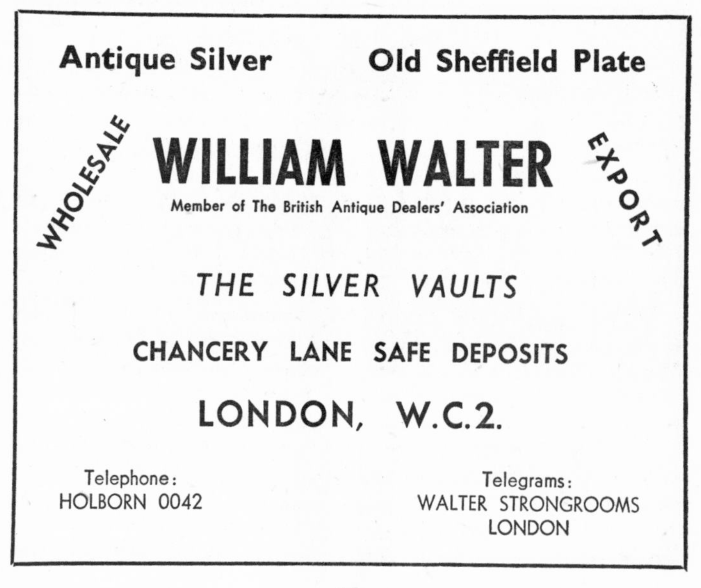

called, are undoubtedly one of the sights of London, and Mr. Walter is a leading wholesaler, with fine pieces at very reasonable prices. He and his daughter are authorities on Hester Bateman and can always offer excellent specimens of this popular silversmith's work.

So back to High Holborn and along to Cheapside for what we have pleasure in presenting as the representative firm of City of London silversmiths, Messrs. Hicklenton & Phillips at Number 83 Cheapside—between St. Paul's and the Mansion House. Their modest shop hides a considerable history of selling and making fine silver—the silver which comes from the City of London and still reigns supreme the world over. They are homely folk, as ready to satisfy the humble requirements of the passer-by as to produce the connoisseur's dream: but we do say, note their name and go to them for City silver, particularly of the 18th century. (And, by the way, Messrs. Hicklenton and Phillips are jewellers to the Lord Mayor of London and the Court of Aldermen, as well as consultants on City Plate to the old Guilds and Livery Companies.)

So for two kinds of antique silver firms, the first wholesalers and specialists, the second a leading shop for the best 18th century and particularly London silver. Now we draw attention to yet another kind of business, N. Bloom and Son, Ltd., 15, Norton Folgate (continuation of Bishopsgate past Liverpool Street).

Blooms are largely exporters of antique silver and old Sheffield plate to the United States. They have branches both at 42–44 W.48th Street, New York, and at 328–329, Coristine Building, Montreal. We mention them here because they are very big buyers in this country of antique silver, and our readers, both private persons and antique dealers, might well like to know that Blooms pay exceptionally good prices for old silver and plate of every description, not only 18th century but also 19th century specimens. We believe many of our readers might well care to get in touch with this large firm, which operates on wholesale proportions and may be relied upon to give a square deal.

PARK LANE

So back to the West End for a final voyage of exploration, this time in the Sloane Street and Brompton Road areas, but not without first visiting Park Lane.

We suggest that the journey back should follow High Holborn and the Oxford Streets again to the Marble Arch, where you turn left down Park Lane and then take the first turning on the left, Park Row, where at Number 12 is the London salon of Mr. Alfred Bullard, Anglo-American expert on 18th century furniture. He has a branch at 1604 Pine Street, Philadelphia, and well appreciates the requirements of American buyers. His furniture is uniformly fine and sober, with the accent on mahogany, and we cannot recommend too highly both his goods and his attitude towards the selling of them, which is pre-eminently fair, courteous and helpful. Our readers will be grateful to us if they make a point of calling on Mr. Bullard.

Park Lane is now a lovely thoroughfare with the magnificent block half-way of Grosvenor House, hotel of transatlantic standards for antiques visitors and home of the annual Antique Dealers' Fair.

And before leaving the Lane call at the small but tasteful salon of Lansborough Ltd., Number 32, towards the Piccadilly end. Here a connoisseur offers small porcelain, *objets-d'art*,

English furniture, Battersea boxes—all chosen for loveliness and well-worth the attention of discriminating buyers.

FRENCH FURNITURE—DECORATIONS—SWANS

To reach the exceedingly bountiful antiques area of Sloane Street and Brompton Road turn right from Park Lane and proceed from Hyde Park Corner down Knightsbridge till Sloane Street is a main turning on the left. Down Sloane Street at Number 44 will be found the fascinating salons of Meubles Francais, fascinating because here a foremost expert on the subject concentrates on French furniture alone. It is illuminating to be with him and appreciate fine points so often ignored by English dealers. Some of the loveliest French furniture in the country, especially for furnishing purposes, is to be found here at exceptionally reasonable prices.

On the opposite side of Sloane Street now, at Numbers 164–169 will be found the firm of Charles Hammond, Ltd., which is another of London's almost indefinable specialists, this time in decorations and fabrics primarily. We know that hundreds of firms undertake decorations for antique schemes, but there is only one Charles Hammond. For several generations they have struck a wholly distinctive note of taste in their work, and you will find here the best in appurtenances to antiques, the final word in furnishings if you desire to have rooms laid out in consonance with the objects of antique beauty therein. We can once again take pride in a wholly reliable recommendation.

Continue down Sloane Street and turn into Pont Street on the left, finding at the far end, Number One, the excellent shop of A. J. Reffold and Partners, Ltd. The visitor will much appreciate the courteous attention he will receive here. The firm has all kinds of Regency and decorative furniture, but readers will carefully note their very interesting speciality—china swans. Reffolds have been known for these swans a long time and are always searching the country to keep up a good selective stock: an ever-changing stock of approximately one hundred of the finest specimens always.

(And while in this area it might be worth reminding the reader that Mr. Leslie S. Scott at 18, Motcomb Street, just off Belgrave Square, is an expert at the repair and restoration of chandeliers, candelabra and lustres: very reasonable prices.)

ROUND THE ANTIQUE SALONS

FINE FURNITURE—POTTERY

The journey down Sloane Street should be continued until the establishment of Saint of Sloane Street is found on a corner at the left-hand side. We are always trying to find unusual firms which can be recommended for the best in various specialities. The outstanding feature here is extremely meticulous concentration alone upon only the first quality 18th century furniture, particularly small pieces of fine colour. For example, Saints can nearly always show some perfect specimens of wine-coolers, of such a colour as is rarely found. Do make the acquaintance of this careful firm.

A short distance further down, on the opposite side of Sloane Street, is the establishment of U. H. King Smith and Co., Ltd., Number 133. Some remarkable work has been done by this firm for clients across the world in the provision of antique furnishings, electrical fittings and similar appurtenances. We refer readers to page 49 of this book, on which will be found the illustration of a suite of furniture made by Messrs. King Smith for a Turkish client and shipped to Turkey. Those who require similar work done should communicate with Messrs. King Smith referring to this illustration. A wide variety of old porcelain and glass is offered also.

So to Sloane Square itself, and, of course, William Willett Ltd., whose large galleries, dominating one side of the Square, have long been regarded as one of the principal antiques centres of London, particularly for the collector who wishes to buy for the home. William Willett was, of course, the promoter of the original Daylight Saving Act, a notable figure indeed. In these spacious galleries find a choice selection of Georgian chairs, wing and easy chairs, settees, dining tables, bureaux, tallboys, chests, Persian carpets and rugs, mirrors, clocks, ornamental china, ivories, glass—indeed, all that can be desired.

An interesting experience thereafter awaits he who walks the short distance up the King's Road on Willett's side of the Square to the second turning on the right, Eaton Terrace. Here at Number 40 will be found that connoisseur and friend to collectors, Colonel G. B. Drury, whose firm Drury and Drury occupies a delightful corner shop of period interest itself, and sells—resist lustre ware.

Here we have one of the foremost specialists in a type of pottery that has become increasingly popular and valuable in recent years. There is always a splendid display of lustre of all kinds, but also fine pottery of other schools, together with small pieces of period furniture. Experts here undertake specialist repairs to fine pottery and porcelain. This business, in our guide to collectors, is undoubtedly a heavily-starred " find."

WELSH DRESSERS—CLOCKS—MONKEY BANDS

We must next proceed to the Brompton Road, but first inquire the way in Sloane Square to Sloane Avenue, and take that route, as the firm of Leonard Wyburd, Ltd., is to be found at Number 73 in Sloane Avenue. It is an excellent firm, outstandingly one of the great pleasures of the tour, as they have the unusual speciality in London of Welsh dressers, and what lovely specimens they glean, the best from the provinces here presented almost as museum pieces but at prices often lower than in Wales! There are, of course, other types of fine country-made 17th and 18th century furniture, distinguished by superb colour, which is the special predeliction of that well-known expert Mr. Wyburd. (And the firm is famed for carrying out suitable decorative schemes and undertaking really good restoration work: busy vans ever-plying between the workshops and customers.)

Continue to the end of Sloane Avenue and inquire again the way to Beauchamp Place, traditional little thoroughfare of antiques wherein we can recommend foremostly two firms, of which the first is R. G. A. Wells, Ltd., at Number 50. Quite a lot is said about this firm in Tour 3, where the renowned St. Catherine's House at Guildford is described. Here we take the opportunity of drawing our readers' attention to one of the foremost trade experts in antique clocks. Mr. Wells, whose progress in a few years has been almost meteoric, is specially recommended by us because of his enterprise, flair, and superb mechanical sense. He has a very large staff of finely-trained repairers, and his stock of antique clocks at Beauchamp Place is indeed remarkable.

The second firm, nearly opposite, is the London headquarters (10, Beauchamp Place) of Geoffrey Van of Brighton. Here is an excellent showroom of porcelain and shipping goods, Dresden, Meissen, most of the Continental and English factories, together with small furniture. But Mr. Van has himself a curious sub-speciality, namely monkey-band figures, of which he usually has a unique stock. This is a most enterprising younger dealer.

ROUND THE ANTIQUE SALONS

BROMPTON ROAD

Proceed into the Brompton Road, one of the most famous thoroughfares of all for antiques, and find opposite the imposing frontage of Messrs. Perez, whom we outstandingly recommend in all London as carpet specialists. It is an education to visit the seemingly endless showrooms of this unique concern, and probably to be guided round by a foremost expert on the subject. Prayer rugs, tapestries, needlework, fine modern carpets are offered in addition to the finest Orientals and, of course, *Persians*. Prices are about the lowest in the trade.

The next recommended business is that known as " Gloria Antica," next door at Number 170, because here some interesting historical pieces are to be found, as well as unusual old oak, and English and Continental pottery and porcelain. Call with our name.

This is the thoroughfare of specialists indeed. Further down the road on the same side at Number 186, in the corner just before buildings protrude outwards, is the wonderful old firm of Messrs. C. J. Pratt, Royal-appointed specialists in antique mantelpieces, grates, fireirons and the like—also furniture and fittings of similar periods—absolutely reliable and very highly recommended.

Now continue to Number 194 where it will not be necessary for any advice to be given to stop. The " Old Metalcraft Shop " of Mr. Harold Casimir has one of the most attractive windows in London for the connoisseur of antique pewter and other early metalwork. Here is a leading expert and an assortment of wares normally encountered only in a few museums, yet also including the occasional small piece that can be acquired by the new collector as the starting-point of a lifelong interest and investment.

Furniture, carpets, jewellery, mantelpieces, pewter—so the Brompton Road runs as the veritable Harley Street of antiques. Over the road, at Number 229, for example, is yet another kind of specialist, the silver firm of Messrs. Jones and Son, wherein you will find Georgian silver, really fine antique jewellery, all with the guarantee behind it of some 150 years of trading (formerly in Long Acre). Messrs. Jones have served half the titled families of England in their time, yet their principle is to sell silver " to use and not just to look at."

Such a firm is worth knowing if you are a stranger to London—and it so happens that a few steps further on is another silver

LEGER GALLERIES
WE DESIRE TO PURCHASE OLD MASTER PAINTINGS OF THE DUTCH, ENGLISH, FRENCH AND ITALIAN SCHOOLS, ALSO EARLY ENGLISH WATER COLOURS
EST. 1892 13, OLD BOND STREET, W1. REG. 2679
Old Metalcraft Shop
HAROLD CASIMIR, MEMBER B.A.D.A.
Finest Collection of Antique Metalware in the Country
194 BROMPTON ROAD, LONDON, S.W.3.
Tel.: KENsington 5001

FILKINS & CO.

ENGLISH & CONTINENTAL PORCELAIN

9a THURLOE PLACE
LONDON, S.W.7.

RICHARD
GROSE

for
OLD ENGLISH
FURNITURE

8 EXHIBITION ROAD
SOUTH KENSINGTON
LONDON, S.W.7
Kensington 2128

ALFRED BULLARD

12 NORTH ROW, PARK LANE, LONDON, W.1.

ALSO A BRANCH AT 1604 PINE STREET, PHILADELPHIA PA

SPECIALITY

Antique Pewter

English & Continental
PORCELAIN

SILVER ; SHEFFIELD
& VICTORIAN PLATE

Overseas Buyers welcomed
We attend to all Export details

RICHARD MUNDEY

Tel.: Wel. 5613

19 CHILTERN STREET, LONDON, W.1.

For Fine and Genuine

18th Century Furniture

come and see Miss Saint who will be very happy to assist you in finding rare and beautiful pieces.

SAINT OF SLOANE STREET, LTD.,

158 Sloane Street, LONDON, S.W.1.

Cables: Saintiques *Tel.: SLO 5000*

By appointment
Fireplace Furnishers

to the late
King George V

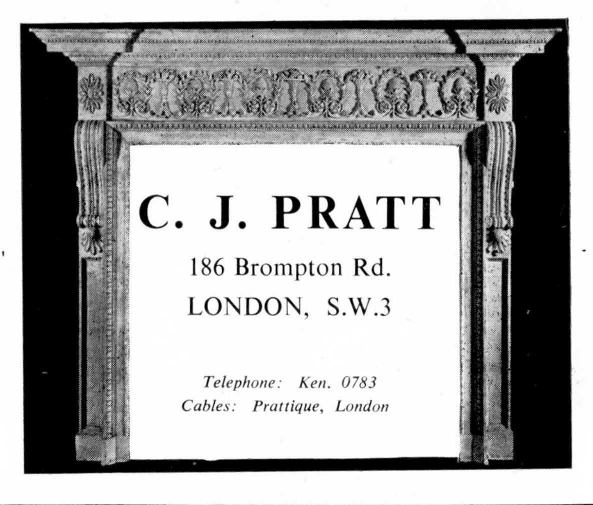

26 GLOUCESTER ROAD,
near Kensington Gardens

LONDON, S.W.7.
Tel.: WESTERN 0865

Antique Silver by Hester Bateman is particularly required.
We offer you fabulous prices for interesting pieces.

firm of equal standing and high reputation, namely that of Messrs. James Hardy and Company, at Number 235. Hardy's have not only been established longer in the Brompton Road than any other firm devoted to their interests, the best Georgian silver and the most superb antique jewellery, but their clientele is world-wide. To enter this establishment is usually to found a lasting interest in good silver and to remember always on leaving the courtesy and profound knowledge of the proprietors and staff. *Silver models a speciality.*

Now continue to Number 245, a landmark of the Brompton Road which cannot be missed, namely the fine frontage of Messrs. Maurice H. Turner & Co., Ltd. Probably more visitors have got their initial idea that the Brompton Road is good for antiques from glancing at these windows than from any other displays. But Turners, of course, are *the* specialists in period furnishings and decorations. The fact that they do such a large trade testifies to their taste and exemplary workmanship. How many fine homes in all parts of the country owe their superb decorations to Turners! The firm is very good for period upholstery also, and, of course, stocks some fine articles of furniture, particularly good wing chairs.

Next, before proceeding to South Kensington, take the opportunity to run down the Fulham Road and make the acquaintance of Mr. F. H. Webber at Numbers 185–187, a small firm that is extending its business thanks to fair dealing and an always-interesting stock of small articles. *American dealers* are specially catered for.

SOUTH KENSINGTON

Return to the Brompton Road and continue a few steps along Thurloe Place where, at Number 9A, nearly opposite the Brompton Oratory, is the establishment of Messrs. Filkins and Co., who are chosen as dealers in English and Continental porcelain. Furniture is sold, but the porcelain is outstanding, and this important firm should prove a find to discriminating collectors who desire the best at sensible prices.

Which brings us along Thurloe Place (most conveniently situated for the Victoria and Albert Museum), to Exhibition Road, wherein, at Number 8, will be found the outstanding black and white frontage of Mr. Richard Grose's establishment, possibly one of the most pleasing antique shop frontages in the

world. And, as clean cars usually have good engines inside, so Mr. Grose's stock is very lovely and most suited to those readers of this book who wish to have genuine, fine antique furniture but not at inflated collector's piece prices. There are three floors, the stock is in splendid condition always, and the service is pre-eminently friendly and helpful.

From Exhibition Road gain Cromwell Road, which continues Brompton Road, and proceed to the far end nearly and Number 124 where Mr. F. B. Royer-Collard has his very individual horological business. He sells and repairs all kinds of antique clocks, and is one of the good horologists of London, particularly good for complex movements. What an excellent French Rolling Clock and other novelties we saw in his showroom!

Retrace steps a little to Gloucester Road which cuts across Cromwell Road, and at Number 26, conveniently at the Kensington Gardens end, is the new salons of Denys Wrey Ltd., a most knowledgeable younger firm which will undoubtedly occupy a considerable place in the antiques world. They specialise in 18th century furniture, and carry a fine selection in their showrooms at very reasonable prices.

THE END—AND CROWTHERS

We could turn into Kensington and explore the smaller shops of Kensington Church Street—recommended are the firms of Sylvia Sheppard, Numbers 71, and Vera Bird, Number 174A, both for American buyers particularly, shipping goods being the interest hereabouts—but prefer to direct the reader for a final outstanding call of interest in London proper to Crowthers, the famous mantelpiece, panelling and garden ornament people. The firm, T. Crowther and Son, Ltd., occupy what was once evidentaly an old country house at Number 282 North End Road, Fulham. We turned the car in that direction ourselves on a memorable morning, right down the Fulham Road to Walham Green Station, then, at the fourways junction, proceeded up North End Road till we became involved in an exciting street market. On the left we saw Crowthers' unique habitat, and, entering, soon left the hubbub behind.

The house contains many rooms with a huge stock of general antiques. There are some magnificent examples of 18th century dog grates with decorative brass paterals polished as new and a revelation of what can be done with such old pieces, then genuine Adams statuary marble mantelpieces ; after which you enter a carved panelled room of stripped pine with magnificent overmantel, glorious chandelier, and period furniture suitably arranged as for a great industrial boardroom (an idea for industrialists, who want to do the thing properly : consult Crowthers, and get only the best).

The house has an interior garden courtyard like an oasis in this drab London, with sufficient pieces of statuary and ornaments to stock a hundred great parks. Really, it is as interesting to visit Crowthers as to explore the Victoria and Albert or be guests at some fine country seat of the past. And it is a fitting finale to this tour of central London.

Always Travel With ANTIQUES YEAR BOOK

Period Timetable

Louis XIV, 1643 to 1715.
Louis XV, 1715 to 1747.
Louis XVI, 1747 to 1793.
Gothic, 1475 to 1509.
Elizabethan, 1558 to 1603.
Jacobean, 1603 to 1624.
Charles I, 1624 to 1648.
Cromwellian, 1648 to 1659.
Charles II, 1640 to 1684.
James II, 1685 to 1688.
William and Mary, 1689 to 1702.
Queen Anne, 1702 to 1714.
Georgian, 1714 to 1820.
Chippendale, 1754 to 1800.
Hepplewhite, 1775 to 1800.
Sheraton, 1775 to 1800.
R. & J. Adams, 1762 to 1800.
Empire, 1804 to 1814.

(By Courtesy of Messrs. B. A. Seaby, Ltd., 65, Great Portland Street, London, W.1.)

ANCIENT COINS

Top. *Gold Daric of Persian King Artaxerxes I* (359–338, *B.C.*). Second. *Silver Tetradrachm of Chalcis in Macedonia* (*circa* 370, *B.C.*). Third. *Silver Denarius of the Emperor Tiberius, A.D.* 14–37 (*the " Tribute Penny " of the Bible*). Fourth. *Bronze. Sestertius of the Emperor Titus, A.D.* 79–81, *commemorating the Capture of Jerusalem.*

Ancient Coins: An Explanatory Note

(By H. A. Seaby)

THIS term usually means the coins of the Greek cities and states, of the Roman republic and empire, and of the neighbours of both in Europe and Asia. For it was by the Lydians of Asia Minor or by the Greeks of Ionia that coining was invented and by trading the custom spread to all the civilised nations, though by no means the same weight or metal standards were observed.

Figure 1 opposite shows a close copy of the Lydian original in a Persian gold *daric* of Artaxerxes II, 359–338 B.C., which has a design on the obverse only in the Lydian fashion. The type represents the king in a warlike crouching attitude bearing spear and bow, and though this coin is of archaic design it was struck later than the much more advanced—in fact stylistically decadent—silver *tetradrachm* of the Chalcidian League (Macedonia) of the period 392–358 B.C., illustrated by Figure 2. This piece has the head of Apollo for its obverse type and one of his attributes, the lyre, on the reverse.

Struck in vast quantities during the early empire, the *denarius* was the standard silver coin of the Romans and the type of Tiberius shown as Figure 3, circulating in Judaea, was the occasion of Jesus Christ's pronouncement: "Render unto Cæsar the things that are Cæsar's. . . ." Later the Jews rendered not tribute but revolt, which led to the capture of Jerusalem by Titus, commemorated on the bronze sestertius ($\frac{1}{4}$ denarius) illustrated by Figure 4. This progress from archaic invention to standardisation is the story of the ancient coinage.

Forde House, Newton Abbot, Unique Historical Antiques Galleries.

Come to the Fairs

1951, FESTIVAL OF BRITAIN YEAR, IS OUTSTANDING FOR *ANTIQUES FAIRS*, NOT ONLY THE PRE-EMINENT DISPLAY AT GROSVENOR HOUSE, LONDON, BUT ALSO PROVINCIAL OCCASIONS, ORGANISED IN RESPONSE TO THE SUGGESTION MADE BY US LAST YEAR. FIRSTLY, THEN :

LONDON

From June 6th to June 21st.

AMONG the important social fixtures at the height of the brilliant London Season is the Antique Dealers' Fair every June, and the Fair of 1951, it is fully anticipated, will be one of the outstanding attractions of the Festival of Britain Year. It will as usual be held in the famous Great Hall of Grosvenor House, Park Lane, London, W.1., magnificent venue in one of the great caravanserais of the world.

The Fair, which is the eleventh of the series, is under the patronage of H.M. Queen Mary, herself a connoisseur. The indications are already that the Fair will even exceed in interest its predecessors which attracted world-wide attention, and that the total estimated value of antiques to be seen during the run will be in the region of £4,000,000. All the objects of art on the exhibitors' stands are for sale, and each article must have been made prior to the year 1830.

Every article, large or small, which is exhibited has to be submitted to experts drawn from fourteen panels appointed to ensure that as far as possible, each article shown was made prior to the year 1830, and is an authentic antique of the period it is represented to be. Every morning before the Fair is opened to the public, articles brought in as replacements of the previous day's sales are submitted to this examination before being passed for exhibition.

The year 1830 is chosen as representing the dividing line between the hand-craft age, and that of the machine era. While there will be seen important exhibits which the connoisseur and the collector will desire to add to their treasures, there will be many lovely objects of art well within the power of the moderate purse to acquire. Each year the total sales have been of considerable magnitude.

The Fair as a spectacle of beauty in hand-craftsmanship has won the admiration and appreciation of visitors from the United States of America, South America, the Dominions, Europe and the East. Stands are simple. Ornate treatment is not given to them. It is the varied reflection of light on the patina of lovely old furniture, the gleam of glass, of silver and of porcelains, as well as the elegance and the rich colour of objects of art which hold the attention and please the eye.

WINCHESTER

From June 5th – 9th.

IT is with particular pleasure that we proceed with an account of provincial antique dealers' fairs planned for 1951, as we can justly claim to have suggested these originally both in the pages of this *Year Book* and during conversations with many leading members of the trade throughout the country.

Firstly, the Hampshire Antiques Dealers' Fair at Winchester. This event, initially held in July 1950 at the Guildhall, was the pioneer of its kind to be held in Great Britain, and its unqualified success encouraged not only its repetition in the same place between the 5th and 9th of June, 1951, but also the organisation of similar events in other provincial centres.

The Guildhall at Winchester was a miniature Grosvenor House for the occasion, the twenty-four tastefully-arranged stands being replete with the polished beauty of the past : albeit most of the articles offered were within the purses of the 3,278 people who crowded the aisles in enthusiastic public attendance. The Fair was probably a financial success after the first twenty-four hours, for buyers from London and overseas attended early to contribute part of the £20,000-odd takings.

Throughout the Fair the familiar little yellow " Antiques Year Book " stand was a constant centre of interest, and copies of the book were sold so quickly that it was difficult for the assistants to keep pace with sales.

Mr. G. H. Bell, Chairman, Mr. J. W. Blanchard, Secretary, and Mr. A. Alliston, Treasurer, made this Fair possible by their

BRIGHTON &
DEALERS

President:
WILLIAM TEELING, M.P.
Chairman:
E. H. STEWART-BROWNE

List of

BRIGHTON

The Lanes

Otter and Moore, 6 Brighton Place, The Lanes. Tel.: 24692
Furniture—China.
Leonard Fewell, 45 The Lanes. Tel.: 28749
Porcelain—Fine Ormolu—Chandeliers—Small Furniture.
Geoffrey Van, 47 The Lanes. Tel.: 22523
Porcelain—Pottery—Small Furniture.
Margaret Trevor—Antiques, (Michael Trevor Venis), 52 The Lanes. Tel.: 26712. Also 15a Ship Street Gardens.
Porcelain—Pottery—Furniture—Specialist in Export.

Ship Street and Adjacent Streets

Dragonwyck, (M. N. McKibbon, Mrs. D. R. Collins), 59B Ship Street. Tel.: 28887
Porcelain—Pottery—Curios
Margaret Cadman, 25 Ship Street and 12 Marine Square. Tel.: 28485 and 29627
Porcelain—Pottery—Enamels—Furniture, etc.
Peter Carmichael, 14 Ship Street Gardens. Tel.: 28072
English and French Furniture—Chandeliers—English China.
Ward of Brighton, 5 Prince Albert Street. Tel.: 24159
Silver and Plate.
H. A. Davis, 10 Duke Street, Tel.: 25953
Antique Silver—Old Sheffield Plate—Antique Jewellery.
Goodleys, 24 Market Street. Tel.: 28767
Antique and Reproduction Furniture—China—Glass.

North Street

John Fileman, 4 Upper North Street. Tel.: 25521
Glass—Chandeliers—Candelabra—Porcelain—General Dealer.

New Road

Friar Tuck, 26 New Road.
Jewellery—Clocks—China—Curios.
Cynthia Asquith, Ltd., 25 New Road. Tel.: 27436.
Small Antiques—Objets d'Art.

HOVE ANTIQUE ASSOCIATION

Hon. Treasurer:
MICHAEL T. VENIS
Secretary:
MISS B. PORTE, 47 The Lanes, Brighton. Tel.: 22523

Members

Kensington Gardens

E. A. Coleman, 35 Kensington Gardens. Tel.: 27050
Porcelain—Glass—Chandeliers—Furniture.

Edward Street

C. Arnold and Son, 62-3-4 Edward Street. Tel.: 21340
Early Victorian and Reproduction Furniture.

Kings Road

Curio Corner (S. Mitzman), 20-21 Kings Road. Tel.: 21858
Objets d' Art—Jewellery—China, etc.
A. Herbert Kisch, 34 Regency Square. Tel.: 256541. By appointment.
Period Jewellery—Objets d'Art.

HOVE

Ashleys (L. Strawbaum Ltd.), 42 Lansdowne Place. Tel.: 38489
Decorative Glass—China—Jewellery—Silver.
The Treasure Chest (F. Ward), 146 Church Road. Tel.: 31148
Jewellery—Porcelain—Silver—Silverplate.
Phillip Moore, The Grosvenor Gallery, 1 Victoria Terrace, Kingsway. Tel.: 38900
Oil Paintings—Porcelain—Furniture—Picture Restorer and Valuer.
W. C. Wilkinson, 23 St. Aubyns. Tel.: 34770. By appointment.
Porcelain—Furniture—Silver.
H. Choretz, 65 Langdale Gardens. Tel.: 39659. By appointment.
Antique and Modern Silver—Sheffield Plate.
H. Buckler, 51 Palmeira Avenue. Tel.: 35569. By appointment.
Silver and Plate.
D. F. Ward, 90 Furze Croft, Furzehill. Tel.: 36840. By appointment
English and Continental Porcelain.

TELSCOMBE

Ernest A. Grey, The Telscombe Antique Shop, South Coast Road, Telscombe Cliff. Tel.: Rottingdean 822745
Old English and Continental Porcelain and Pottery.

hard work and enthusiasm.

Trade buyers from everywhere should visit the 1951 Fair in June ; the general public will find the event most interesting—and should visit it during a planned antiques tour of Hampshire aided by the itinerary (Tour One) in our book.

BRIGHTON

From July 16th – 21st.

THE second provincial fair of the year will be held by the Brighton and Hove Antique Dealers' Association at the Corn Exchange, Brighton, from 16th July to 21st July—in conjunction with the Regency Exhibition which is to be held in the adjacent Royal Pavilion.

The Regency Exhibition, organised by the Regency Festival, London, has Her Majesty the Queen as gracious patron, and it is hoped that not only the Queen but also Queen Mary and Princess Elizabeth will honour the exhibition by their attendance.

This will be "the spotlight period," when the eyes of the world will be transferred from the London festivities to those of Brighton.

Much credit is due to the new Brighton and Hove Antique Dealers' Association for organising the antiques fair, which will be different from others in that Brighton of all towns outside London has an unequalled store of antiques, particularly porcelain and the small items we all nowadays want. Then there will be the unique Regency atmosphere. And Brighton is so near London. A very large attendance can be expected. English and overseas trade buyers should be especially interested.

EXETER

From July 23rd – 28th.

AFTER Brighton—Exeter. The following week, 23rd to 28th July, the first West Country Antique Dealers' Fair will be held at the Rougemont Hotel, Exeter. All leading West Country dealers from the counties specifically of Devon, Dorset and Cornwall will be exhibiting. Once again, as with the other fairs, the fine display of antique articles for sale will first have been "vetted" by a panel of experts and guaranteed—so far as is humanly possible—to be (furniture) dated before 1830, and (china, etc.) prior to 1851.

The West Country Fair will have this outstanding interest—that it will represent the fresh outlook and treasures of a part of England that has antique shops as rich, homely and lovely as the red, green and blue land and seascapes of Devon itself. So, when the London days grow hot and long, come to the West.

HARROGATE

From September 17th – 22nd.

FINALLY, at that period of the summer's end when the beautiful floral resort of Harrogate is so pleasant to visit, with the prospects of walks among the surrounding moors and dales and excursions to so many famous Yorkshire beauty spots, there will be an Antiques Fair in the North.

COME TO THE FAIRS

The date of this event at Harrogate will be 17th to 22nd of September, and the magnificent resources of The Royal Hall will be made available for the occasion. Different from the others, this fair will be organised by the Entertainments Department of the Town Council, but of course with the active co-operation of the antique dealers, of whom there are an outstanding number in this town.

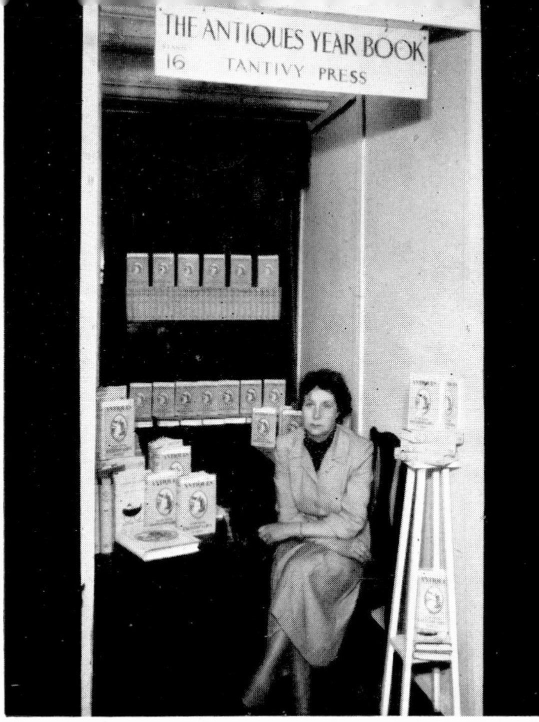

At the first Hampshire Antique Dealers' Fair, Winchester, Where so Many Visitors Bought their Copies of The Antiques Year Book.

The Medieval Mint House at Pevensey, Sussex, with its 28 Showrooms of Antiques.

A ROOM AT MR. J.W. BLANCHARD'S HOUSE AT WINCHESTER, SHOWING SOME OF HIS PRIVATE COLLECTION OF FINE REGENCY FURNISHINGS

*(By Courtesy of Messrs. R. G. A. Wells,
56 Beauchamp Place, London, S.W.3.)*

Remarkable 18*th Century Musical Clock, with Pyrotechnic and Waterfall Display, made by Robert Philp in* 1780 *for the Emperor of China.*

" Somebody will make Mr. Wigington a Bold Offer for that Block one day and Build a Fortune thereon "—the Fascinating Business

A Typical London Antiques Salon: that of Mrs. L. Loewenthal,
4, St. James's St., London, S.W.1.

From a Set of Chairs made for the Earl of Peterborough at Drayton House, one of which has been acquired by the Victoria and Albert Museum from Messrs. Phillips of Hitchin, Ltd.

The Antiques Dictionary

WE HEREWITH PRESENT A NEW SHORT VERSION OF OUR ANTIQUES DICTIONARY, WHICH HAS UNDERGONE EXPERT REVISION AND ADDITION IN THE LIGHT OF THE LATEST KNOWLEDGE.

A

ACACIA : The pseudo-acacia (*Robinia pseudo-acacia*) was introduced into England in the 17th century ; the timber shows a contrast between the pale yellow sapwood and the dark heartwood.

ACANTHUS : An ornament derived from the stylised foliage of the acanthus on Greek and Roman decoration, as dandelion leaf, much favoured by Chippendale school.

ADAM (ROBERT), style of : The architect Robert Adam introduced from about 1760 a classical revival in England. In the *Works of Architecture* (by Robert and James Adam) they claim to have brought about "a kind of Revolution in the whole System" of architecture. With classical detail in Adam's decoration elements from the Italian *cinquecento* are coalesced. The style in furniture and ceramics is characterised by severe classical motifs. The Adams made no furniture themselves.

ADAMS POTTERY : The Adams family was one of the oldest potter families in Staffordshire, of which the most famous member was William Adams (1745 to 1803), a modeller and potter, who followed in the footsteps of Wedgwood. Specialities: jasper, Egyptian black.

AGATE WARE : An imitation of veined agate (in which clays of different colours were kneaded together) introduced by the potter Thomas Whieldon (1750 to 1770).

ALMERY : (A form of the word *aumbry*.) A safe for food, clothing and other objects. In churches and cathedrals it was fitted with a door in which the sacred utensils were kept.

AMBOYNA : A name applied to certain burr woods imported from the Moluccas and Borneo. These are brown, tinged with yellow, marked with small knots and curls.

AMPHORA : A vessel used by the Greeks and Romans for holding wine and other liquors. It has two handles, and is usually tall, slender and narrow-necked.

ANDIRONS : (Fire-dogs.) A pair of metal stands consisting of a horizontal bar raised on short legs, and affixed to an upright standard.

ANTHEMIUM : Honeysuckle ornament used in sculpture and decorative work, of Greek and Roman origin.

ARABESQUE : Ornament of capricious character consisting of fanciful figures, monsters, fruit and flowers combined or grouped.

ARMOIRE : A large cupboard usually enclosed by doors from base to top, parent of the wardrobe.

APOSTLE SPOONS : See *Spoons*.

APRON : Masking piece under the front edge of a table or seat.

ARRAS : Tapestry, a name derived from the town of Arras, in the Pas de Calais, France.

ASH : A tough, elastic timber, used chiefly for seat furniture. It is white in colour, veined with streaks in the direction of its growth.

ASTBURY (JOHN AND THOMAS) : John Astbury (died 1743) set up a factory for red earthenware, and improved white ware by fixing flint in its body. This improvement is also attributed to John Astbury's son Thomas, who in 1725 set up a factory at Felton.

ASTRAGAL : (1) A small convex moulding used between the capital and shaft of the classic order (with the exception of the Greek Doric), and in other positions in later architecture. (2) A bar containing the panes of glass of a window, or of a glazed cupboard or bookcase.

AUBUSSON : A centre of tapestry weaving in France during the 17th and 18th centuries, marked by technical inferiority to the Beauvais and Gobelins *ateliers*.

AVENTURINE : A term applied to small fragments of gold wire, sprinkled over the surface of lacquer.

AXMINSTER : A centre of carpet weaving founded by Thomas Whitley, a cloth weaver, in 1755. In 1779 it was "a considerable manufacture."

B

BALUSTER : A small pillar (made in various forms, but during the Renaissance period, commonly vase- or urn-shaped) used in a series to support the railing of a balustrade.

BANDING : Strip inlay contrasting in colour with background.

BANISTER-BACK : Chair-back of slender balusters or rods.

BANJO-CLOCK : Invented by the American, Simon Willard, in 1801.

BARBOTINE : A slip technique in which patterns in clay are

squeezed through the fingers and worked in detail after being applied.

BAROMETER: An instrument for indicating impending changes of temperature, recorded by a column of mercury which registers variations in atmospheric pressure. The barometer originated in the experiments of Toricelli in 1643.

BAROQUE: Italian ornate style in art which led to French *rococo* and English late Carolean design. Ornamentation without restraint for ornamentation's sake, succeeding sometimes by sheer excess of splendour.

BASALT: (Or "Egyptian black"). A stoneware produced in Staffordshire, and further developed by Wedgwood who, employed it for panels and plaquettes, also portrait medallions, seals and intaglios, vases.

BATTERSEA ENAMEL: A factory was set up about 1750 by Stephen Theodore Janssen at York House, Battersea, which was advertised for sale in 1756, after its promoter had become bankrupt. Objects decorated in this manufacture had a copper base, which was coated with tin enamel, on which decorative detail was painted or transfer-printed.

BEADING: Strip of half-round moulding.

BEAKER: Tall cup without handle.

BEAUFAIT: (Buffet.) A term used in the 18th century for a recess for the storage and display of glass and china. It is defined in the *Cabinet Dictionary* (1803) as a piece of furniture with cupboard doors in the lower portion, and tiers of shelves above.

BEAUVAIS: A centre of tapestry-weaving in France, using only the *basse-lisse* method, founded about the same time as the Gobelins factory.

BEECH: A timber of light-brown colour, tough but easily worked. It takes stain well, and was much used for stained, painted and gilded furniture.

BERGÈRE: French name for wide-seated arm-chair with upholstered sides and back.

BERLIN: A factory was started in 1752 in Berlin but abandoned in 1757. Another factory, which was set up in 1761, was sold to Frederick the Great in 1763, and has remained State property till the present day. Its best period is from 1763 to 1786.

BEZEL: (1) A slope, a sloping face. (2) The groove, flange, or lip by which the crystal of a watch, or the stone of a jewel is contained in its setting.

BIEDERMEIER : A name given to a style of decoration and furniture in Germany lasting from the Wars of Liberation (1815) until about 1848. The distinguishing feature of Biedermeier style in seat furniture is a preference for curved supports and chairbacks, and curved supports in tables and case-furniture.

BILLIARD TABLE : A table with top covered with cloth and having raised padded sides, for a game of which the origin is uncertain. Billiards is mentioned in 1429 in France as an indoor recreation.

BILSTON : A town in South Staffordshire in which decorated enamelware imitating Battersea was produced from about 1760 until the early 19th century. In this ware, the enamel was laid upon a metal base.

BIRCH : A timber which takes staining well and was much used in the 18th and early 19th century for painted, japanned, and gilt furniture.

BIRD CAGE CLOCKS : A name for lantern clock, a clock composed entirely of metal, the case being rectangular, with a framing of turned angle pillars. The spaces between these pillars are filled in by back and front plates and side doors.

BISCUIT : Porcelain, stoneware, and pottery after the first baking, and before the application of glaze.

BLEEDING DISH : Silver or pewter graduated vessel to contain blood.

BLOBS : Pimples of glass applied in molten state as decoration to glassware. Also known as seals, mascaroons, prunts.

BLOCK FOOT : Leg ending in a rectangular base.

BLOCK FRONT : A front projecting beyond the surrounding body.

BOG OAK : Wood obtained from trees found submerged in peat bogs in Ireland.

BOHEMIAN GLASS : Glass of Bohemia, made from silicate of potash and lime ; often coloured on the surface and cut through the colour to reveal clear substance beneath.

BOLECTION : A moulding projecting above the surface of the framework enclosing a panel.

BOMBÉ : A French term applied to furniture with a swelling outline towards the base.

BONE CHINA : Hard porcelain rendered soft, or half soft by an admixture of bone ash, which became the standard body in

England from the close of the 18th century to the present day.

BOOKCASE : The bookcase was not made in England in large numbers until there was a reading public that demanded it. In the late 17th century, bookcases were provided in college libraries, and for a few book-lovers, such as Samuel Pepys. In the early Georgian period the winged bookcase appears, and its architectural character was often emphasized by an order, and a crowning pediment. During the second half of the 18th century, there was a demand for a bookcase in which the upper stage was glazed. During the Regency period, the dwarf bookcase (consisting of two or three tiers of shelves) was introduced.

BOULLE WORK : Marquetry in metal (copper, brass and tin) and horn or tortoiseshell was practised in France in the 17th century, and was developed (especially after 1680), by the *ébéniste* André Charles Boulle (1642–1732) and his sons. The process was transferred from Boulle to other French workshops, and was carried on throughout the 18th century. It was also practised by Parisian cabinet makers in the 19th century.

BOW : Porcelain made at Bow in East London, founded in 1744. The output of the factory was mainly table-ware, but some attractive figures were produced, and it has been stated that the Bow factory and its moulds and models were removed to the Derby works, but no date or evidence is given for this.

BOW FRONT : Convex or swell front.

BOXWOOD : A hard wood of light yellow colour, with close, compact grain, and fine uniform texture, used in marquetry and inlay.

BRACKET CLOCK : See Clocks.

BRACKET CORNICE : Cornice supported by brackets.

BRASS : Alloy of copper with tin, zinc or other base metal.

BRASSES : (Furniture.) Handles, handle - plates, and escutcheons.

BREAKFRONT : The front line of furniture as broken by projections and/or recesses.

BRISTOL :

(1) A manufacture of porcelain was established by William Cookworthy at Plymouth and removed to Bristol about 1770. In 1781, the patent rights of the firm were sold, and the manufacture of simpler ware carried on in 1782 at Shelton.

(2) The manufacture of faience (or Delft) originated in the village of Brislington near Bristol in the middle years of the 17th century, and was given up towards the middle of the

18th century. A factory was set up in Bristol in 1683 and others in the 18th century. Its existence was put an end to by the output of the great lead-glazed ware industry.

(3) Glass was made at Bristol in the late 17th century, and one manufacturer, Jacob Little (died 1752), is associated with opaque white glass. The making of opaque white and coloured glass was carried on in Bristol during part of the 19th century.

BRITANNIA METAL : An alloy consisting of tin (90 per cent) and antimony (10 per cent) having a white silvery appearance. A cheaper alloy containing 94 per cent tin and 5 per cent antimony has a small addition of copper, which gives it a slightly yellow colour.

BRITANNIA STANDARD : Adopted for silver in 1697 when the standard of purity was raised to 11 oz. 11 dwt. pure silver to each pound troy. The old standard was resumed in 1720.

BRONZE : An alloy of copper and tin, in varying proportions, but averaging nine parts of copper to one of tin.

BRUSSELS : (Carpet.) A term used for a carpet with a looped pile, made like an uncut (a terry) velvet.

BUREAU : A French term that appears in England in the late 17th century, and has not been clearly distinguished from other terms (such as *scrutoire*) used for writing desks or cabinets. In the *Cabinet Dictionary* (1803) the term is said to be generally applied to common desks with drawers under them.

BURRS : (Burls.) Wood taken from the outside of the trunk of a tree (or from the stump of a tree), which shows a mottled figure, valued for veneering.

BUTTERFLY TABLE : A table in which the supports for the drop tops are not the legs but hinged pieces of wood roughly resembling a butterfly's wing.

C

CABINET : A case for the storage of papers and valuables, probably originating in Italy and appearing in France in the early 16th century. The cabinet was made in a variety of forms and sometimes was mounted upon a stand.

CABINET-MAKER : Cabinet-making had become a distinct industry in the middle years of the 17th century, and by the last quarter of the century the term was in common use. By about 1750 there had been formed a separate society of cabinet-makers.

CABOCHON : A precious stone, which is polished but not cut

into facets, or shaped into a regular figure.

CABRIOLE : A " leap like that of a goat," term applied to the curve of legs for furniture, which appeared in England in the early 18th century.

CAMBRIAN : The factory at Swansea made all kinds of Staffordshire ware, and the so-called " opaque china " (a white variety of cream earthenware).

CANAPÉ : The French term for a sofa.

CANDLESTICK : A support for a candle, but used formerly to include chandeliers.

CANDELABRUM : A support for more than one candle.

CANE : A pliant material made from a class of palms known as rattans, introduced into England by the East India Company early in Charles II's reign. When first used the mesh was large, but was reduced in William III's reign. In 1803, Shenstone speaks of the revival of caning for seat furniture.

CANTERBURY : A music stand ; also a supper tray with partitions for plates and cutlery.

CAPITAL : The head (or top) of a column or pilaster.

CAPO-DI-MONTE : A factory for porcelain set up in 1743 at Capo di Monte, near Naples, which remained in operation until 1759, when Charles III took with him to Spain some of the best workmen of the factory. The factory was revived in 1771, but transplanted to Portici and (in 1773) to Naples. The factory was closed in 1821. During the first period, it produced soft paste, but in the later period, both soft and hard paste.

CARCASE : The basis in main structure of a piece of furniture, on which veneer is applied.

CARD-CUT : A term applied (1) in silver for designs cut in thin sheet-metal and applied to the body, an ornament introduced in Charles II's reign, but fully developed in the first quarter of the 18th century ; (2) in furniture to flat ornament applied to or carved on the piece (in fashion during the middle years of the 18th century).

CARD-TABLE : A table designed for card-playing appears in rare instances in the late years of the 17th century, but was developed in the early 18th century. It took the form of a table with folding top covered with cloth or velvet, having sometimes sinkings for counters and candlesticks.

CARPETS : The term carpet was used until the mid-eighteenth century for coverings for furniture as well as for the floor. There are different methods of carpet-weaving. In tapestry (or smooth-faced) carpets, a loom is used. For pile carpets, rows of knots are tied on the warp thread of a loom, and the ends cut down close to the knots, thus forming a pile. After each row is finished weft threads are run through the knots to secure them. Persia and Asia Minor are and have been the great carpet-producing countries. Other important centres are China and Spain. In England the chief manufacturing centres were Axminster and Milton.

CARTOUCHE : A term used originally for a roll or case of paper ; also applied to an ornament in the form of a tablet representing a sheet of paper with the ends rolled or curled over.

CARVER CHAIR : A name given to a heavy, square type of American chair of turned oak, named after Governor Carver's chair at Pilgrim Hall, Plymouth.

CARYATID : A standing figure used to support an entablature.

CASSONE : Italian chest.

CASTER : A receptacle for containing sugar and dry condiments, such as pepper, having a perforated lid.

CASTOR : Small wheel or roller fitted to a piece of furniture to enable it to be moved without lifting. Castors were at first made of wood, but later of leather in the form of a single roller. In the mid-18th century the single roller was succeeded by a system of leather discs. During the late 18th and 19th centuries, brass wheels were employed.

CAUDLE-CUP : Cup used for serving a drink composed of thin gruel, and sweetened and spiced wine or ale. The term appears in 16th century inventories, but it is uncertain to which form of two-handled cup it should be applied.

CAUGHLEY : A pottery existed at Caughley, Shropshire, after 1750. In 1772 Thomas Turner became the owner of the works, and porcelain was made there shortly after this sale. In 1799 John Rose, proprietor of the Coalport works, purchased the Caughley factory, which continued to make biscuit porcelain, which was glazed and decorated at Coalport. In 1814 the Caughley plant was transferred to Coalport. " Willow pattern " a feature.

CELADON : Chinese porcelain with a pale bluish or greyish green glaze, dating from the Sung period. Imitations of this ware were made in China in the 18th century.

CELLARET : A case for bottles, fitted with partitions.

CHAISE LONGUE : A French term for a couch or daybed

with an upholstered back.

CHAMFER: Edge removed by bevel.

CHANDELIER: The term chandelier has been applied to a number of lighting fittings, but is now confined to lights suspended from the roof or ceiling. The early " candlebeams " remained in use until ousted by metal chandeliers made chiefly in the Low Countries. Brass chandeliers with S-shaped branches were made in Holland and England in the late 17th and 18th centuries. The use of glass for chandeliers became an important English industry from the early Georgian period until the early 19th century.

CHANNELING: Pattern of parallel grooves cut into woodwork.

CHARGER: A large plate or dish.

CHECKER: Inlay of light and dark woods in alternate squares.

CHELSEA: No date is known for the foundation of this factory for porcelain, but a jug, inscribed " Chelsea," is dated 1745. It is probable that a silversmith, Nicholas Sprimont, was connected with the factory from the first. After a considerable success, the factory was sold in 1769 and in the following year it was resold to William Duesbury and John Heath of Derby.

CHERRY: A fruit wood of close compact grain and reddish colour, used for inlay, and also for making small pieces of furniture.

CHESTNUT: There are two varieties of this tree, the " horse " and the " Spanish " chestnut, both having almost white wood, which was used as a substitute for satinwood in the late 18th century.

CHINTZ: Originally used for painted and stained calicos, imported from India, later for cotton cloths, fast-printed with designs.

CHIPPENDALE: (Style of furniture.) Corresponding in design to the illustrations in the *Director* issued by Thomas Chippendale in 1754, 1755 and 1762.

CLAW AND BALL FOOT: (Or Ball and Claw): A form derived from Chinese designs of a dragon whose claw grasps a ball or pearl. It appears in English furniture in the 18th century, succeeding the club foot, but was outmoded, by the date of the *Director* (1754).

CLOCK: There is evidence that mechanical weight-driven clocks were known in the late 13th century. A spring-driven clock was invented by Peter Henlein of Nuremberg about

1500–10, in which an expansive spring coiled within a drum was the motive power, and spring-driven clocks were made in numbers during the second half of the 16th century at Augsburg and Nuremberg. The first individual English type of weight-driven chamber clock (the lantern-clock) had a frame, dial and side-doors of brass, and was surmounted by a bell. The long-case (later called the " grandfather ") clock was made in England as early as the first pendulum clocks (1658).

CLOCK-JACK : Contraption for meat-turning.

CLUB-FOOT : Type of plain foot on furniture used throughout 18th century.

COALPORT : Porcelain from a factory founded by John Rose, who started a factory at Jackfield about 1780, and returned soon afterwards to Coalport. Rose acquired the Nantgarw, and Swansea moulds and stock in 1822–3. The firm was still in existence lately, but the factory had been removed to Stoke-on-Trent. About the middle of the 19th century the firm specialized in copies of Meissen, Sèvres and Chelsea porcelain, which had the marks of these factories.

COCK-BEADING : Narrow beading round edge of drawers, introduced about 1730.

COMMODE : A French term, applied to a low case of drawers, described as a new word in 1708. The commode was adopted in England in the reign of George II and illustrated in the *Director* (1754 and 1762). Japanned, inlaid and painted commodes were a feature of late Georgian furniture.

CONSOLE :

(1) A bracket (usually of scroll shape in profile).

(2) A side-table partly supported by and fixed to the wall.

CORBEL : A projection jutting from a wall, serving to support a weight.

CORNER CHAIR : See *Round about* chair.

CORNICE : The uppermost member of an entablature in classical architecture; but also used for a horizontal moulding crowning a building or part of an interior, or a piece of furniture.

COUCH : A piece of furniture intended for reclining, usually having a back and head piece.

COURT CUPBOARD : A term used in the Elizabethan and Jacobean periods for a stand for the display of plate and for the vessels in use during meals.

CRACKLE :

(1) Crazing of the glaze on porcelain, as a result of the unequal contraction of the glaze and body.
(2) In glass, an effect produced by the sudden cooling of the surface of glass when still not completely blown.

CRANE: (Chimney.) Iron bracket for swinging over fire and holding pots.

CREAMWARE: Pottery (made of plastic clay with flint or quartz pebbles, to which a certain amount of Kaolin was added), which became white on firing, and was glazed with transparent tinted glaze.

CREDENCE: The term belongs to a small table by the altar side on which bread and wine were set before consecration. In the reign of Henri III of France *credences* were introduced for the arranging of meals and drinks for the royal table. English examples of the domestic *credence* are extremely rare.

CROSS-BANDING: Banding of veneer placed so that grain runs across that of the ground.

CURULE (Chair.) A seat shaped like a camp-stool, used by Roman magistrates. A chair of different form with semi-circular back and elongated seat is illustrated in the *Cabinet Dictionary*, 1803, as a curule chair.

CYMA: A moulding, of which the outline consists of a concave and convex line.

CYPRESS: Fine grain wood of reddish colour and great durability.

D

DAMASK: A fabric woven with the ornament contrasting in the weave with the ground.

DAVENPORT: (Ware.) Earthenware and porcelain from the works of John Davenport of Longport in Staffordshire, from 1793 to 1882. Some porcelain dating from the first half of the 19th century is imitative of Derby.

DAVENPORT: A desk resting upon a small case of drawers, on which the desk portion extends on a train.

DEAL: A term applied to the timber of the Scots pine.

DECANTER: " Crystal " decanters (then called bottles) were made in 1677; the word decanter appears in 1701 and is defined in 1715 as a bottle made of clear flint glass for the holding of wine, etc., to be poured off into a drinking glass. The ordinary form between 1675 and 1750 has a narrow neck and globular body. Shortly before 1720 a form with sloping shoulders and shorter neck was introduced. The finest decanters were made between 1790 and 1820.

DELFT : A tin-enamelled faience made at Delft in Holland before 1600, and in great demand during the 17th and 18th century. English delft was made at Lambeth, Liverpool, Bristol and Wincanton.

DENTIL : A small rectangular block, placed in series under the bed-mould of the cornice of the Ionic, Corinthian and composite orders.

DERBYSHIRE CHAIR : (See *Yorkshire Chair.*)

DERBY : Porcelain was made in Derby as early as 1750 (on the evidence of marked and dated pieces), and in 1756 William Duesbury is mentioned as partner in a firm for making " English china."

DESK : A piece of furniture with a sloping front, which serves to support writing materials.

DIAPER :

(1) A fabric woven in a small pattern consisting of lines crossing diamond-wise enclosing a space filled with simple ornament.

(2) A similar pattern used in decoration.

DISHED CORNER : Depression near corner of table top to hold counters, or candle-stick.

DISH-TOP : Table top with raised rim.

DIVAN : Low, cushioned seat of Eastern origin.

DOULTON : Wares produced by the works at Vauxhall, and then Lambeth, founded by John Doulton.

DOWEL : A headless pin or peg, which serves to fasten two pieces of timber by piercing some distance into the connected pieces.

DRESDEN : Search for the secret of making porcelain was carried on in Dresden from 1706 onwards, and the success of these experiments led to the foundation of the Royal Saxon factory at Meissen (q.v.).

DRESSER : Originally a board or table on which food was *dressed*, later, (1) a table from which dishes were served, and (2) a provincial side table, usually surmounted by rows of shelves.

DRESSING TABLE : Dressing tables are listed, as a distinct variety in inventories of the middle 17th century. In the early

Georgian period, tables of knee-hole pedestal type often had a drawer fitted with compartments and a mirror, and in the *Director*, and late Georgian period small tables with a hinged box lid were made in quantities.

DRINKING GLASSES: The making of glass drinking vessels was a speciality of Venice. In 1575 a Venetian, Giacomo Verzelini, who set up the industry of making drinking glasses in London, secured a patent and imported a staff of foreign glass workers. Drinking glasses fall into two main classes: (1) stemmed glasses, for wine, ale and cordials, consisting of a bowl, stem and foot, in the form and decoration of which there are many varieties; (2) beer glasses, roughly cylindrical in form. The decoration of the stems of glasses by enamel work was in fashion about 1740 to 1777, and cutting an English speciality in the second half of the 18th and in the early 19th centuries.

DROP-HANDLE: Pear-shaped handle of late 17th century.

DROPPED SEAT: Chair seat shaped to fit the body.

DUMB WAITER: A stand with tiers of trays from a central stem, introduced in the 18th century.

E

EARTHENWARE: Pottery of baked clay too porous for use in biscuit state and requiring glaze.

EGG-AND-DART: Moulding of alternate egg-shapes and dart- or anchor-shapes.

ELERS WARE: Pottery made by the brothers Elers, who emigrated to Staffordshire from Holland soon after 1688, and manufactured red, unglazed pottery, and sometimes ornamented in relief. The term is applied generally to all early, unglazed hard red ware made in England.

EMPIRE: The French furniture of 1790–1830, based on styles of antiquity, with much use made of wreathes and pateras, urns, winged figures, clawed feet, brasses, mahogany, rosewood.

ENAMEL: The art of fusing a paste of powdered glass on to a base of metal usually copper, bronze, or gold. When this moistened paste has been spread over the metal base, the object is fired in a kiln, until the heat melts the paste, which adheres to the ground. Enamel on metal has been ascribed to Greek and Etruscan origin between the 6th and 3rd centuries B.C. Of the techniques used in enamelling the most important are: (1) *Cloisonne*, in which the design is divided by metal strips, soldered on to the ground, forming small compartments or *cloisons* (which were filled with enamel); (2) *Champleve*, in which small compartments were hollowed out of the ground, to keep the enamels separate during firing; (3) *Painted enamels*, in which pictures or designs were painted upon an undercoat of white enamel.

ENCAUSTIC: Burned-in colour.

EPERGNE: A centre dish for the table, often having branches which support small dishes or baskets for pickles or sweet-meets.

ESCALLOP: An enrichment based on the shell of the escallop (or scallop), usually showing a single valve.

ESCUTCHEON:

(1) A shield-shaped surface on which a coat of arms, cypher or other device appears.

(2) A metal plate pierced for a keyhole.

F

FAIENCE: (*Maiolica, delftware.*) A kind of lightly-fired earthenware coated with an opaque white glaze composed of fine sand, calcined lead and tin oxides, with an addition of an alkali such as soda or potash.

FAENZA: A town in Italy (from which the term faience is derived), a leading pottery town in the early 16th century.

FAN BACK: Windsor chair back, flared like a fan.

FARTHINGALE CHAIR: Chair without arms; with narrow, high back; so-called because they were built to accommodate females in farthingales, for whom any other kind of seat was an impossibility.

FAUTEUIL: French term for an arm-chair.

FEATHER-BANDING: See "Herring-bone."

FESTOON: A garland of flowers, leaves, fruit, etc., loosely suspended between two points, and hence a representation of similar ornaments in carving, stucco and painting.

FINIAL : An ornament projecting from the apex of a roof or gable ; and hence applied to a similar ornament heading a canopy or piece of furniture.

FIRE-DOG : See *Andiron.*

FIRE-SCREEN : See *Screen.*

FIRING-GLASSES : Short, stubby drinking glasses so made to withstand rapping at toasts on tables.

FLAGON : Originally used for a bottle to hold liquor, later for a tall drinking vessel with a handle, and usually a lid.

FLAMBÉ : (A French term meaning singed, passed through flame), which is applied to certain colour effects in the glaze obtained in the process of firing in Chinese porcelain.

FLUTES : A term for the channels cut in the columns of the classical orders, divided by a sharp fillet.

FORK : The fork was known in the Middle Ages, but was not in ordinary table use in England until after the Restoration (1660). The use of forks in Italy is commented on by an English traveller in 1608, where it is stated that they were not used by any other nation.

FORM : The terms bench and form (which are interchangeable) describe a seat with supports or legs which has remained essentially the same throughout its history. In early times the form was sometimes a plank resting on trestles.

FRIEZE : Member of entablature coming between architrave and cornice.

FROG MUGS : Mugs made mostly at Sunderland, but also at Leeds, Nottingham and elsewhere, containing a model of frog.

FUDDLING-CUPS : Number of cups cemented together with openings one to the other, Lambeth 17th century, and early Staffordshire.

FULHAM : Stoneware from the factory of John Dwight, who obtained in 1671 a patent in making stoneware vulgarly called Cologne ware. He started his operations at Fulham about 1685, and made a small number of busts and statuettes. Dwight died in 1703, but the factory was carried down to 1862.

G

GADROONING : (Also *nulling*, and lobing.) A series of convex and concave forms carved on the edge of furniture, and used as an enrichment of silver. There are two varieties, the upright and the waved.

GALLIPOT : Small jar, usually with handle, employed by apothecaries.

GARNISH : Complete set of dozen platters, dozen bowls, and dozen small plates of pewter.

GATE-LEG : Term applied to table with drop leaves and extra legs on hinges at either side which swing out to support leaves when raised.

GESSO : A preparation of chalk worked up into a paste with parchment size, used as priming before colouring or gilding furniture. In the late years of the 17th and early 18th centuries the gesso coat on mirrors, side-tables (and more rarely seat furniture) received low relief carving before gilding.

GILDING : The extreme malleability of gold permitted it to be a skin so that it would adhere to a plaster ground. The two chief methods of gilding with gold leaf are (1) Water, (2) Oil gilding. Water gilding was applied over a ground of size and whiting, to which a paste of red clay and parchment size had been added. When dry, the surface was wetted and the gold leaf applied. In oil gilding the piece is painted with gold size, left on for some hours, and the gold leaf applied when still "tacky." The surface is then spirit-varnished with size.

GIMMAL : A finger-ring, constructed so that it can be divided into two (or occasionally, three) rings.

GIRANDOLE : A French term for a wall-light or elaborate candlestick, first advertised in 1768. In trade catalogues of the second half of the 18th century, elaborate wall-lights (often with a mirror back-plate) are described as girandoles.

GOBELINS : A tapestry make, uniting several Parisian factories inaugurated in 1662, under State patronage, and continuing almost without interruption to the present day, employing the *haute lisse* method of weaving.

GRANDFATHER CLOCK : The invention of the anchor escapement (attributed to Dr. Hooke about 1670, and to William Clement, a London clockmaker) altered the escape to take place within a small angle, and thus the pendulum could be used in a narrow space such as that of the long-case (grandfather) clock, which was increasingly made as a result.

GRANDMOTHER CLOCK : A small long-case clock.

GUERIDON : A French term, for a stand for lights.

GUILLOCHE : An ornament consisting of two (or more) intersecting curved bands, twisting over each other and repeating the same figure in a continued series.

(*By Courtesy of Messrs. Leger Galleries*, 13, *Old Bond St., London, W*.1.)

Portrait of the Artist, by Angelica Kauffmann. Canvas 30 *in. by* 25 *in.*

(By Courtesy of Mrs. Mary Bellis, Hungerford.)

Above: *Late 16th century Polychromed Carving, "Death of the Virgin."* Below: *Fine Gothic Stool, 16th century.*

(By Courtesy of Mr. T. Leonard Crow, Tewkesbury.)

Important Worcester Vase, Dr. Wall Period circa 1770, *formerly in Drane and Hughes Collections.* 14 *in. high. Painted in Colours with Scene from Aesop's Fable of " The Two Bears," by J. H. O'Neale, in a heart-shaped panel on ground of Bleu-de-Roi relieved by Fine Quality Gilding. Marked with Fretted Square in Underglaze Blue.*

(*By Courtesy of Messrs. John Sparks, Ltd.*, 128, *Mount St., London, W*.1.)

An English Lacquer Cabinet in Chippendale Style, the two Doors with Fine Chinese Mirror Glass paintings of the Ch'ien Lung Period, A.D. 1736–95, *stretcher modern, Height* 5 *ft*. 11 *in*.

H

HALL-MARKS: Were introduced in England in 1300, and Wardens of the London Goldsmiths were ordered to assey and mark with a leopard's head all plate before it left the goldsmith's hands. In 1363 it was decreed that all goldsmiths should have a mark. Date letters were introduced in London in 1478.

HAREWOOD: Sycamore, stained with a solution of oxide of iron, used as a veneer in the late 18th century.

HARPSICHORD: A stringed instrument furnished with two keyboards and extra strings which can be operated by stops. The instrument is enclosed in a case in outline like the later grand piano. An early example, dating from James I's reign is at Knole.

HEPPLEWHITE: (Style of.); The style of Hepplewhite can be assessed from the illustrations in his *Cabinetmaker and Upholsterer's Guide*, first issued in 1788. A third edition (with some alterations) was issued in 1794. In this work, the neo classic style is seen with its more conspicuous classic ornament eliminated, and adapted to current English cabinet-making.

HERRINGBONE: A banding of veneer formed of two strips, of which the grain, running diagonally, produces a "herring bone" or a "feather" effect.

HIGHBOY: A term of comparatively recent origin given to a chest of drawers resting on a stand or frame.

HOLLY: White wood used in marquetry and inlay.

HOOD: Round arch surmounting article of furniture.

HORSE TRAPPINGS: Ornamental brasses used on horse harness as charms against evil, valuable if old and genuine, but sometimes manufactured lately for use without horses.

HOUR-GLASS: A contrivance for measuring time consisting of a glass vessel divided into two parts by a narrow neck, through which a quantity of sand (sometimes mercury) is timed to run in an hour.

I

INLAY: The insertion of pieces of wood, mother of pearl, ivory, metal, etc. into a ground of contrasting colour.

INTARSIA: (Tarsia.) Inlay in coloured woods (either natural or dyed) which reached its climax in the work of Fra Giovanno da Verona (1459–1525), in which landscapes, human figures, and vistas of cities are represented. Intarsia became less popular in the second half of the 16th century. Parent of marquetry.

J

JAPANNING: (On wood.) The imitation of Oriental *lacquer* (q.v.) for which recipes were given in Stalker and Parker's *Treatise on Japanning and Varnishing* (1688). The ground of the piece to be decorated was coated with layers of " varnish," and polished when dry. The ornament (in the oriental style) was drawn on the ground with gold size or vermilion mixed with gum water, and the raised portions put in with a paste composed of whiting and gum arabic. The taste for japanned furniture extended from the late 17th to the last years of the 18th century.

JAPANNING: (On metal.) About 1660 Thomas Allgood of Pontypool, discovered a substance which could be applied under heat to the surface of metal, and this process was developed by his son Edward Allgood. This process was also carried on in London and in Birmingham.

JASPER WARE: Made by Wedgwood, after experiments, towards 1775; containing barium sulphate. It was vitrified, and white in colour, but could be stained with metallic oxides. To this coloured ground white reliefs were applied.

JOINER: Furniture-maker before the days of pride and cabinet-makers (i.e., before the Dutch invasion of early 18th century). Originally known as an arkwright. The change in the use of the terms is valid in fact, as the joiners did join wood by mortise, tenon and dowels or wood pins, whereas the cabinet-makers placed pieces cunningly together according to a new technique which involved the use of different joins and metal fasteners such as nails and screws, also glue.

K

KAOLIN: China Clay.

KETTLE FRONT: Furniture with swelled sides giving shape of a kettle.

KIDDERMINSTER: A factory to manufacture carpeting was set up in 1735 at Kidderminster. In 1749, the first loom for making " Brussels " carpets was set up, and the industry prospered in the 18th and 19th centuries.

KINGWOOD: A wood imported from South America, of a rich violet-brown shading into black, and showing distinct streaky markings. It was much used in parquetry and veneer in the late years of the 17th century.

KNEE: The broad upper part of a cabriole leg.

KNIFE: (Table.) Originally knives carried by the owner in a case offered a means of display, especially in the materials and decoration of their handles (which included steel, carved ivory and bone, faience, silver and agate). When the use of the fork became general from the late 17th century onwards, knives and forks were made in sets, with handles of simpler form, chiefly of horn, bone or silver.

KNIFE BOX: A case with its interior divided into small compartments in which knives and forks and spoons were inserted, handles and bowls upwards. Wooden knife boxes of the late 18th century are finished pieces of cabinet work, fitted with a lock and handles. In the late 18th century, a new form, the knife-vase, was introduced, in which the partitions are arranged around a central tube or stem to which the lid or cover is attached. The lid is kept up, when required, by a spring.

L

LACQUER: The art of lacquering (which was known in China as early as the Shang-Yin period) originated in the discovery of the protective properties of the sap of the lacquer tree (*Rhus vernicifera*) which can be used to coat almost any material and forms a hard semi-transparent film. Chinese lacquer falls into three groups, in the first, the ornament was raised in low relief, in the second, painted upon the surface, in the third cut or incised. The trade in Chinese lacquered goods was very extensive in the early 18th century, and patterns of cabinet work were sent out to China in the reign of Charles II to teach the Chinese what manufactured goods were required for the English market.

LACQUERED FURNITURE: (European. See *Japanning*.)

LADDER-BACK: Chairback with horizontal rails like ladder.

LANCASHIRE CHAIR: An oak type, with solid back panel surmounted by a lunette-shaped cresting.

LANTERN CLOCK: First type of domestic clock in general use. (See *Clocks*.)

LEEDS: A factory for pottery founded about 1760 by the brothers Green; later owners were Humble, Green & Co., 1770–5, who were joined from 1775–81 by William Hartley. From 1781 to 1825 the firm was Hartley, Green & Co. Its best product was a cream-coloured ware in which much use was made of pierced patterns in the body.

LIGNUM VITAE: West Indian, hard, greenish-brown wood, used in the 17th century.

LIMEWOOD: A wood of light straw colour and close, compact grain, much used for ornamental carving.

LINENFOLD: The decorative device for panel enrichment (variously termed *drapery* and *parchment-scroll* pattern) appears in all the works of French and Flemish artists about the middle of the 15th century. The resemblance to folded linen is very slight in early examples. Later variations show a tendency towards complexity, and the upper and lower edges are sometimes fantastically cut and shaped.

LION'S MASK: Decoration on knees of cabriole legs from about 1720 to 1740.

LIVERY CUPBOARD: A cupboard which during the 16th and first half of the 17th century, served to contain the "liveries" (consisting of food, drink, and candles) given out at night-time to members of a household, and guests.

LONGCASE CLOCK: See *Clock* and *Grandfather Clock.*

LOPERS: Slides to support drop-fronts of bureaux.

LOUIS XIV: (Style of.) The period between 1660 and 1715, known as the *Grand Siècle* characterised by State intervention in the production of works of art. Decoration was characterised by sumptuousness and massiveness; large use was made of modelled stucco, and gilt metal ornaments, and marble for wall-linings. Metal marquetry was developed by *Boulle* (q.v.).

LOUIS XV: (Style of.) 1715–1774. After a short period of transition (the Régence) the style shows a greater suppleness in the general design of decoration and furniture, in a reaction against the symmetry of the preceding reign. During this reign the *rococo* (or as it was known, the *goût moderne*) was established, with its accent on asymmetry. Seat-furniture became lighter, and more comfortable, and small bureaux and tables were designed.

LOUIS XVI: (Style of.). 1774 to 1793. During this period the straight line was recalled to structure in decoration and furniture. Under the influence of the classical revival vertical and horizontal lines predominate and detail moves in the direction of refinement and delicacy until about 1790.

LOWBOY: An American term for a small dressing table with drawers often made en suite with the highboy.

LOWESTOFT : A small factory for soft-paste porcelain which was set up in 1754 and closed down about 1802. In early editions of Chaffers, some Chinese porcelain (hard paste) was ascribed to this factory, but this exception has long been discredited.

LUNETTE : Half-moon.

LUSTRE : Earthenware in which the surface is covered with a thin coating of tin enamel, and painted in metallic colours with pigments containing sulphide of copper or silver. Lustre ware produced in Spain, known as Hispano-Moresque ware, dates from the 14th century. The majority of surviving pieces are, however, not earlier than the 15th century. By 1600 the ware had lost its artistic interest. Lustre pottery was revived with some success by William de Morgan.

LYRE-BACK : Chair-back in shape of lyre.

M

MAHOGANY : Three varieties of mahogany were used in the 18th century. Spanish (or St. Domingo) was used from about 1725 to the *Director* period (1754). After the latter date two other varieties appear, the " Cuban " and the " Honduras." Some of the Cuban timber is finely figured and marked with a curly or wavy grain. Honduras timber (from British Honduras) is inferior in colour and figure to the two other varieties, but is lighter in weight and softer in texture.

MAIOLICA : Earthenware enamelled with oxide of tin, which gives a brilliant white surface, and incorporates colour decoration at one firing. This ware was made at the greater Italian factories from the latter part of the 15th century, and reached its highest artistic development in the first quarter of the 16th century.

MARQUETRY : The process of cutting and assembling a veneer of various woods (or metals) and applying it to a ground. Floral marquetry was in fashion during the late 17th century in England, France and Holland. During the first years of the 18th century a type of veneer in which two contrasting woods only were employed, called arabesque or seaweed marquetry came into fashion. A revival of marquetry took place in the second half of the 18th century.

MAZER : Bowl of maple-wood sometimes mounted on and/or with silver or pewter.

MEDALLION : A circular or oval disc decorated with objects

in relief; also a portion of a decorative design (as in carpets) which is specially treated.

MEISSEN: A factory twelve miles from Dresden, founded in 1710 and active for more than two centuries. Its first Director was Böttger, and under him hard red stone ware and white porcelain was produced. The factory was reformed in 1720, when a variety of decorated wares were made. Remarkable plastic work was produced by the talented modeller, Kändler, notable for their baroque movement and brilliant colouring. In 1764 an "academic period" of design was inaugurated and a French sculptor, Acier, was installed as a *modelmeister*.

MILLEFIORI: (Italian for "a thousand flowers.) A term for a technique of Roman glass mosaic, in which bundles of slender glass rods of varied colours were fused together into a cylinder, which was drawn out while still plastic. It was afterwards cut into transverse sections. This process was revived in the 15th century, and in France and England about 1840. See *Paperweight*.

MINTON: A factory set up at Stoke-on-Trent in 1796, under the directorship of Thomas Minton, which remained in this family until, in 1883, it was converted into a Limited Company.

MIRROR: Mirrors in China, and in classical antiquity, were of polished metal. The centre of mirror-making (of glass, backed with a metallic substance) was Murano, near Venice, where two craftsmen perfected the manufacture of glass mirrors, in 1507 and secured a monopoly. Craftsmen from Murano were imported into England early in the 17th century to instruct the natives in the making of looking-glass plates. In 1663 a considerable manufacture was set up at Vauxhall, and the industry developed in the 18th and early 19th centuries in various glass houses.

MITRE: Angle cut in wood moulding to form joint.

MORTAR: Vessel for use with pestle.

MORTISE: Receptacle of the tenon in a joint.

MOULDINGS: Strips of different shapes and patterns applied to or carved from furniture.

MOUNT: Metal work such as handle or escutcheon.

MUNTIN: Upright between panels.

N

NANTGARW: (And Swansea.) A factory for porcelain was started in 1813 at Nantgarw in Glamorganshire by William

Billingsley and Samuel Walker, which produced a glassy soft-paste porcelain containing a large proportion of bone-ash. The factory was transferred in the following year to Swansea. Alterations were made in the composition, and in 1817 a body containing soapstone was introduced. About 1822 porcelain ceased to be made at Swansea.

NEO-CLASSIC : Of the 18th century classical revival.

NULLING : See *Gadrooning*.

O

OAK : A hard and heavy wood, of which the most common species in England are the common oak and the sessile-fruited oak. Native and imported oak was almost the " universal timber " for furniture till the Restoration and remained in use in country districts throughout the 18th century for " yeoman " and farmhouse furniture.

OGEE : A moulding consisting of a double curve, convex above and concave below.

OLIVEWOOD : A close-grained wood of greenish yellow colour, used in parquetry during the late Stuart period.

ORMOLU : A French term for brass of high purity, containing an admixture of zinc, cast in ornamental forms and gilded.

ORRERY : A mechanism representing the motions of the planets about the sun, invented by George Graham, about 1700, and named after Charles, Earl of Orrery, for whom a copy of this invention was made.

OTTOMAN : Backless, upholstered seat of Turkish origin.

OVOLO : A convex moulding (also called " quarter-round ") of which the section is a quarter-circle.

OYSTERED : Veneer from cross-sections of small branches of finely-grained wood.

P

PAPERWEIGHT : (Glass.) Specimens of *millefiori* glass (q.v.) were shown at an exhibition in Paris in 1844. In 1845 glass paperweights were described as " a new item of trade, the round shaped *millefiori* paperweights of transparent glass in which are inserted quantities of small tubes of all colours and forms assembled to look like a multitude of florets." The manufacture of these paperweights centred in France at St. Louis and Baccarat. In England the centres of manufacture were the glass-making towns of Bristol, Stourbridge and

"MINTON" YE OLDE BOX TREE COTTAGE. 37 & 39 CHURCH ST ILKLEY, YORKS TEL 1509 ILKLEY

Charming "Minton," One of the Most Attractive Antique Shops in the North, at Ilkley.

London, between 1840 and 1855. Paperweights produced from about 1865 to 1880 are inferior in colouring and quality.

PARQUETRY:

(1) Mosaic of wood applied to a ground in simple geometrical forms in furniture.

(2) A flooring of small blocks of wood arranged in geometrical patterns.

PARTRIDGE WOOD: Red-brown Brazilian wood used in marquetry and veneer.

PATERA: A saucer or disk used for libations or sacrifices by Greeks and Romans, and hence a shallow disc or roundel used as ornament.

PATINA:

(1) The surface condition of bronzes, oxydised by exposure.

(2) The surface condition of furniture produced by natural means, rubbing, polishing, etc.

PEAR WOOD: Reddish wood with fine grain, used in marquetry and inlaying.

PEDIMENT: A triangular structure, like a low gable, surmounting the front of a building in Greek architecture.

PEMBROKE TABLE: Small table with drop-leaf sides, supported by brackets, and with a drawer.

PEWTER: An alloy of tin, with an admixture of another metal (usually lead). (In some cases brass or a copper is used instead of lead.) This alloy can be worked by casting and also by turning and hammering. There was a large production of pewter in France, Germany and Switzerland from the 14th century onwards. It was also used in the 13th century in England, and was popular in Elizabeth's reign. The use of pewter was widespread until the close of the 18th century, and though it declined in the 19th century, it is still employed for measures and tankards.

PIANOFORTE: A keyboard instrument in which the strings are struck, not plucked. Invented by Cristofori of Florence about 1718. The first piano was made in England about 1762.

PINCHBECK: A metal alloy (chiefly of zinc and copper) of a gold colour, invented by the clockmaker, Pinchbeck, "the only maker of the True and genuine metal." A long list of goods made by Edward Pinchbeck, printed in 1732, states that this metal is not to be distinguished by the nicest eye from real gold.

PILASTER: A rectangular pillar engaged in a wall, and projecting only a fraction of its breadth.

PINEWOOD : Timber from a genus of resin-producing trees, having a straight grain, and easy to work. Little was used before the Restoration, when it was employed for carcase-work in veneer furniture, and for certain carved and gilt furniture such as picture frames and cabinet-stands. It was freely used in the 18th century for carvers pieces.

PIPKIN : Brass or iron coal-scuttle, from middle 18th century, when coal fires came into general, domestic use.

PLANEWOOD : The timber of the Maple-leaved plane, which is stated in the *Cabinet Dictionary* (1803) to have been used instead of beech for painted chairs by country furniture-makers.

PLAQUE : An ornamental plate affixed to furniture, chimney-pieces.

PLATEAU : A stand resting on short feet or a plinth, serving as a centre ornament for the dinner table, in fashion during the late years of the 18th and early 19th centuries.

PLINTH : In architecture, the square member at the base of a column, and by analogy, the base of a piece of furniture when this is not supported on feet.

PLUMWOOD : Yellow wood, red of heart, and very hard, used in country furniture.

PONTIL MARK : The mark under old blown glass made by pontil rod held by maker during process of manufacture. (Not seen in glass made after 1850.)

POPLAR : A timber ranging in colour from whitish yellow to grey, used in inlay in the 16th and early 17th centuries.

PORCELAIN : A translucent ware made of " white refractory clay produced by the decay of feldspar," fused at a high temperature with the help of less decayed feldspathic material (china stone) and which acts as a cement. It is coated with a glaze.

POTTERY : Clay baked to a certain degree of hardness, which varies with the duration and intensity of the firing. Certain elements, such as sand or calcined flints, are added in certain wares. When the clay is fused to a hard, vitrified mass, it becomes stoneware. As against porcelain, pottery is heavy and opaque.

PRESS BED : A folding bed, made to pack into a concealing press or cabinet.

PRICKET : The spike for holding a candle, used in candlesticks before the introduction of the socket or nozzle.

PUNCH BOWLS : These bowls appeared in silver after the Restoration. The earliest known examples are shallow. Those dating from between 1690 and 1700 are larger and usually have removable rims or " collars." Large bowls were made to order by English factories during the 18th century for farmers, and these also formed a profitable branch of Chinese export art.

Q

QUARREL : (Quarry.) A pane of glass, used in glazing lattice windows.

R

RABBET : See *Rebate.*

RACK : (Pipe.) Various types of racks for holding clay pipes were in use, (1) a metal frame for cleaning pipes on a hot oven (also known as a pipe-kiln) ; (2) a wooden stand, fitted with a pierced disc (on a central standard), through which the stems of pipes passed ; (3) a hanging rack of wood, constructed to hold pipes in a horizontal position supported on indented uprights ; (4) a wooden fixture with a backboard fitted with two narrow cross bars pierced to receive the pipes.

RACK : (Spoon). The most common form consists of a backboard fitted with pierced cross-bars, with a box or open receptacle below for knives and forks.

RAIL : A constructional member in a horizontal position.

REBATE : (Rabbet.) A recess formed along the edge of a piece of timber to meet and fit a corresponding piece.

REEDING : A group of two (or more) beads in parallel lines.

REFECTORY TABLE : A term (now disused) for a long table, such as might have been used in the refectory of monasteries. It was applied to long oak tables from the halls of domestic buildings.

REPOUSSÉ : The decoration in relief of metal by hammering.

ROCOCO : A version of the French form of decoration known as ***rocaille***, a form of asymmetrical ornament dating from the Régence, and developed during the reign of Louis XV. In its introduction in England in the middle years of the 18th century it was known as " the French taste." Designs in the rococo style were published by Chippendale, Matthias Lock, Thomas Johnson and Ince and Mayhew.

ROMAYNE WORK : Medallions of heads derived from Italian

Renaissance forms.

ROSETTE : Stylised rose form.

ROSEWOOD : The name given to several distinct kinds of ornamental timber of a dark blackish brown colour, finely marked, which is chiefly used in veneering. The wood was known in the late 17th century, and used sparingly in the middle years of the 18th century, but it was much in demand in the Regency period.

ROUNDABOUT CHAIR : (Also Corner Chair.) An arm-chair in which a round back (with two splats) is carried round two sides of the seat. Was a much favoured type in England from about 1720 to 1770. As a writing and reading chair, it allowed the occupant to turn without shifting in his seat. Two-tiered chairs of this type are known as barbers' chairs, as the added high back served as a rest for the head when the sitter was being shaved.

ROUNDEL : Bull's-eye glass or bottle glass in early windows and door lights.

RUNNER : Piece of wood on either side under drawers to support its movement. (Also another name for lopers on which drop-fronts of bureaux are supported.)

RUSH BOTTOM : Seat of chair made from dried rushes, chiefly found on country furniture.

S

SAD WARE : Flat articles of pewter.

SALT CELLAR : The important position of the great salt-cellar on the dining-table in the Middle Ages and during the Renaissance periods accounts for the elaborate workmanship bestowed on it. Existing examples of the hour glass form date from between 1490 and 1522. During the early Renaissance the salt assumed a different form, either square or circular in plan, the cover raised on brackets, and often surmounted by a figure. The salts known as " bell salts " which, as the name implies, expand towards the base, appear towards the close of the 16th century. The appearance of small open salts (trencher salts) in sets dates from the reign of Charles II, when the ceremonial use of the great salt had died out.

SALT-GLAZE : Salt-glazed ware was made since the Middle Ages in the Rhenish provinces and Cologne, and was familiar in England in the 16th and 17th centuries. Salt-glazed ware was produced in England in the last half of the 17th century, but the term is usually applied to the white salt-glazed stoneware produced in the Staffordshire potteries in the early part of the 18th century. The characteristic glaze is minutely pitted in a manner resembling orange peel.

SALTIRE : Stretchers of tables and chairs which cross in X-form, usually with a finial at the crossing.

SATINWOOD : Two varieties of satinwood were employed in cabinetwork, the East Indian (introduced in the late 18th century) and the West Indian, used both as a veneer and in the solid early in George III's reign. Both woods are yellow in tone, and vary from plain grain to a mottled figure.

SCAGLIOLA : A composition composed of ground plaster of paris, mixed with a solution of glue, and coloured to imitate marble. The art was revived in Italy by Guido del Conte (1584–1649) ; and slabs of scagliola were frequently imported from Italy in the 18th century for the tops of tables and commodes.

SCONCE : A term applied in the late 17th and 18th centuries to a fixed wall-light consisting of a candle-branch (or branches) or socket, or sockets, and a back-plate. The back-plate of metal or mirror-glass served as a reflector.

SCREEN : A piece of furniture to ward off the heat of fire, and draughts. There are three chief forms of screen : (1) the folding screen, made up of leaves hinged (or otherwise connected) and covered with paper, lacquered wood, or textiles ; (2) a frame standing on a base and feet (cheval screen) ; (3) a frame supported on a standard or a pole (pole-screen). The three types were made in considerable quantities during the 18th and 19th centuries.

SCREW : The use in cabinet work of metal screws with slotted heads dates from the late 17th century. The early hand-wrought screws with irregular threads were superseded by machine-cut steel screws in the 18th century.

SCRUTOIRE : Form of French escritoire or bureau.

SERPENTINE FRONT : An undulating front, in which the centre is usually convex and the two ends concave. In case-furniture dating from the middle years of the 18th century this shaping was used to display the figure of veneers ; a serpentine-shaping was also freely used for the friezes of tables, and rails of seat furniture.

SETTEE : A seat with back and arms for two or more persons.

SETTLE : A long seat (accommodating two or more persons),

having a back and arms, and frequently a seat with a lid, (used for storage).

SÈVRES : After an experimental period at Vincennes (in which some samples of soft-paste porcelain were produced in 1745) the factory was reorganised in 1753 and removed to Sèvres, near Paris, where a new factory was built in 1756. The porcelain produced is famous for its range of colour and the artistry of its decoration during the great period between 1756 and 1780. Under new management in 1800, the direction turned its attention to the production of hard-paste porcelain after 1804 ; but collectors are not interested in Sèvres produced after about 1800.

SHAGREEN : (From the French *chagrin.*) A term used for (1) the skin of sharks (and other fish) prepared as covering for boxes, knife cases, etc. ; (2) unstained leather, in which a granular surface was obtained by pressing seeds into the material while soft and flexible. This leather when dyed and dried was also used for box and case-coverings.

SHEFFIELD PLATE : a process invented by Thomas Boulsover, 1742, consisting of plating with silver on copper, superseded in 19th century by electro-plating.

SHERATON : (Style of.) Thomas Sheraton was a formative influence in design during the last decade of the 18th century, and his *Cabinet Makers' and Upholsterers' Drawing Book* (1791–1794) gives a summary of the style, exhibiting, as he writes, "the present taste in furniture." The draughtsmanship is excellent, and the full notes to the plates reveal the author's technical experience. Some six hundred cabinet-makers and joiners were among the subscribers to this work. His *Cabinet Dictionary* (1803) shows a definite decline in taste.

SIDEBOARD. The sideboard proper, as distinguished from the dining-room side-table dates from the early years of George III's reign. At first detached pedestals, supporting urns, flanked the side-table ; a little later the pedestals became connected with the board, and drawers were fitted to the frieze. During the Regency period the pedestal type returned to fashion but the proportions were ill-considered.

SIDE-TABLE : A table designed to stand against the wall. The pier table and console table (q.v.) are a variety of table fixed to the wall.

SKIRT : The apron, or strip of wood beneath the front of the seat of a chair.

SLEIGH BED : Bed of Empire period without posts but with head and foot boards rolling over.

SNAKE FOOT : Foot splaying out like a snake's head.

SNAKEWOOD : Red Brazilian wood with black markings like snakeskin, for marquetry.

SNUFF BOTTLE : Chinese bottle to contain snuff or medicine with stopper-spoon, most finely made in Chien Lung period, 1736 to 1795.

SNUFFERS : An implement for shortening the wick of a candle, which (until the 19th century) was not fully consumed by the flame. Snuffers are mentioned in the 15th century. From the post-Restoration period onward they consist of two hinged blades, one fitted with a box, and the other with a plate which is pressed into the box when the candle is snuffed.

SOFA : The term appears in the late years of the 17th century ; and was used for " a couch for reclining " (1692). It was applied to a long, upholstered piece of furniture. In the Regency and Empire period, a version of the classical couch was designed, described as a " Grecian sofa."

SPANDREL : The space between the outer curve of an arch and the rectangle formed by enclosing moulding.

SPANDREL PIECES : Cast brass ornaments affixed to the spaces outside the hour-ring in clock faces, dating from the Restoration period to the middle years of the 18th century.

SPINDLE : Fine rod or baluster.

SPINET : A stringed musical instrument in which, like the virginal and harpsichord, an upright piece of wood (the jack) rests on the end of the key lever. On the top of the jack is inset a pivoted slip of wood bearing a point (quill or leather). When the end of the key-lever rises this point " plucks " the strings. The Spinet (known in Italy as *spineta traversa*) was an instrument of "trapezond, pentagonal, or wing-shape"; while the word virginal was restricted to one of rectangular form.

SPINNING WHEEL : A machine (generally constructed of wood) with a revolving wheel operated by a treadle, for converting wool flax or cotton into thread.

SPIRAL TURNING : Turned work in form of twist.

SPLAT : Centre of chair back from top rail to seat.

SPODE : A factory at Stoke-on-Trent founded by Josiah Spode, and carried on by the second Josiah, whose contribution to ceramics was the combination of bone-ash with purified feldspar (extracted from china stone), and the fixing of the respective proportions in which they were allied to certain other materials. By this development Spode "produced a porcelain which had no equivalent in all that had been produced before."

SPOOL TURNING: Turned work in form of a succession of spools.

SPOON: The spoon usually consists of three parts, the bowl, the stem, and the end, or knop, though a form like the "Puritan" and the "slipped tops" have no knop or finial. The types interesting to collectors are: (1) the *Maidenhead* spoon, which appears at the close of the 14th century; (2) the *acorn-knop*, mentioned as early as 1346, which continued to be made until the early 17th century; (3) the *diamond point*, which appeared in the mid 14th century and continued to be made until the early 17th century; (4) *slipper top* (i.e., without a knop) mentioned in 1498 and still made in the second half of the 17th century; (5) the *seal top*, introduced about 1525 and continuing to be made in late Carolean times; (6) the *Puritan spoon* (which has no finial), introduced in the sixteen-thirties and in favour during the Commonwealth period and in Charles II's reign; (7) the *trifid* (or lobed end) spoon, introduced early in Charles II's reign and remaining in favour in the reigns of James II and William and Mary, but ceasing to be made a few years after Anne's accession; (8) *apostle spoons*, in sets surmounted by a figure of an Apostle as a knop. The earliest recorded example bears the hall-mark for 1478. Some sets of twelve are surmounted by figures of the twelve apostles, others in sets of thirteen include the figure of the "Master" (Christ).

SPOON-BACK: Chair back shaped to fit occupant.

STERLING: Term derived from the German tribe of the Easterlings, makers of fine silver in medieval times. Became applied to the standard of English silver, 925 parts fine.

STILE: The vertical member of a framework occupying an end position in that framework, into which the rails are tenoned.

STITCHED-UP: Term applied to upholstery completely covering seat to lower edge of frame.

STONEWARE: See *Pottery*.

STOOL: A term used in the Middle Ages for a seat for one person, especially one without arms or back (its usual significance from the Tudor period). In the *Academy of Armory* joint stools (so called because made by the joiner) are distinguished from turned stools made by the turner or wheel-

(By Courtesy of Messrs. D. M. & P. Manheim, 7, Manchester St., London, W.1.; and New York.)

Bristol Delft Bowl. On the Outside are Portraits of John Wilkes, the Arms of Jenings & Wilcox, and a Panel with Mansion in Rustic Setting. Inside, Masonic Emblems, and J. & W. 1770. *Decorated in Blue, probably by John Bowen,* $10\frac{1}{4}$ *in. diam.*

(*By Courtesy of Messrs. A. P. Càtherall, Chester.*)

Portrait by Rembrandt, formerly in the Collection of Lord Wakefield.

(By Courtesy of Messrs. M. Bernard, 21, *Ryder St., London, S.W.*1.)

Flowers in a Vase, by Jean Baptiste Monnoyer. Signed and Dated Baptiste 1677. *Canvas* 26 *in. by* 21 *in.*

F

(By Courtesy of Messrs. Meubles Francais, 44, Sloane St., London, S.W.1.)

Louis XV Bergère in fine Aubusson Tapestry, part of a Suite from the Collection of Lord Lonsdale.

wright. Until the second part of the 17th century stools were the normal seats for the dining table.

STRAPWORK : Carving, consisting of flat bands interlaced in various patterns.

STRAW MARQUETRY : Decoration with applied and dyed straw.

STRETCHER : Bracing piece of wood between legs of chair, table, cabinet.

STRINGING : Narrow inlay of colour contrasting with background.

SWANSEA : See *Nantgarw*.

SWELL FRONT : Bow front.

T

TABLE : The earliest form of table was of trestle construction (q.v.) in which the top, which rests upon two or more supports, can be readily dismantled. In the *joined table*, the main underframe is tenoned into the tops of the legs. In the *draw* table, the top can be extended by pulling out a pair of leaves from under the top. Various forms of extending tables were developed in the early 19th century. For varieties of table see *Gate-leg*, *Pembroke Table*, *Refectory*, etc.

TABOURET : A low seat or stool (so named from its drum-shape.

TALLBOY : A chest on chest.

TAMBOUR : Narrow strips of wood glued side by side to stout canvas, which served to form sliding doors in cabinets and sideboards, and " roll-top " covers to late 18th century writing tables.

TANKARD :

(1) A drinking vessel, originally made of wooden staves, hooped together.

(2) A one-handled mug, pewter or silver, usually fitted with a lid.

TAPESTRY : A hand-woven fabric in which the pattern is woven in a loom. Of the two weaving systems, in the *haute lisse* (high warp) the leashes are worked by hand ; in the *basse lisse* (low-warp) these are operated by heddles and treadles. Tapestry woven fragments have been found in Egypt in a tomb (1420–11 B.C.). In the Middle Ages, there were important centres in the Netherlands and France, and for two centuries Brussels dominated the field of tapestry production.

There were important centres in France at Beauvais, Aubus son, and the Gobelins (q.v.).

TEA-CADDY : Known as a tea chest till last quarter of 18th century. Often made of fine woods and delicately finished. Various shapes, inlaid, plain, and lacquered. Twin interior compartments lined with pewter, one for black and the other for green tea.

TEAK : Dark brown Indian wood much used in 18th century.

TEAPOT : The earliest known silver teapot (1670) is inscribed "tea pott" but resembles a coffee pot in form. During the last quarter of this century teapots in squat form copied from Chinese hot water pots of porcelain begin to appear. During the first quarter of the 18th century a pear-shaped body with a high domed lid was usual. A form with a rounded body and moulded base was made with little variations in design until the last quarter of the 18th century.

TEA POY : Defined as a small three-legged table on stand, not originally connected with the service of tea. In Smith's *Household Furniture* (1808) the tea poy illustrated is a stand with a tray top. But by 1866, the tea poy had acquired the meaning of a tea-chest on legs.

TENON : Projecting cut of wood for inserting into mortise for making of joint.

TESTER : A term used until the middle of the 16th century for the canopy of a bed ; in the case of fourpost beds the wooden ceiling supported by the headboard and posts.

THROWING : Early term for turning.

TOBY JUG : Probably made first by Ralph Wood, mid-18th century. Genuine old toby jugs have hollow legs and feet, weigh light.

TORCHÈRE : French term for candlestand.

TRAY : A tray is defined as "boards with rims round them in which to place glasses, plates, and a tea-equipage," in the *Cabinet Dictionary* (1803). Few trays exist of earlier date than the mid-eighteenth century. During the late 18th and early part of the 19th century *papier-maché* trays and trays of japanned metal were manufactured in quantities in Birmingham.

TREEN : Small articles of interest, of wood.

TRENCHER : Plate, of wood, and later of pewter.

TRESTLE : Supports for the top of tables consisting of solid shaped ends secured to massive feet and usually held in position by stretcher beams.

TRIPOD : Three-footed support, coming into general use in the early 18th century.

TRUCKLE BED : Small bed which could be pushed under a larger bed.

TULIPWOOD : West Indian light-coloured wood with pink stripes, used in marquetry.

TURNED CHAIR : Chair of which the members of legs and back consist of turned work.

TURNINGS : Lathe-turned wood.

U

UNDER-BRACE : Stretcher.

UPHOLDER : Old name for upholsterer.

UPHOLSTERY : Textile or leather covering, padded and/or sprung, for furniture. In early times confined to beds. Fringed upholstery a feature of Jacobean and Carolean periods when padded seats first came into use.

URN STAND : A small table, serving to carry the tea urn. (A small slide sometimes carries the teapot.)

V

VARNISH : Resinous solution applied to wood to give hard, shiny and transparent coat.

VENEER : Thin coating of finer wood on a coarse base. Originally one-eighth to one-sixteenth of an inch thick.

VERNIS-MARTIN : A term for a translucent lacquer used in France for the decoration of furniture, carriages, boxes and fans, its name being derived from the Martin brothers (Simon-Etienne, Julien and Robert), who though they did not invent this lacquer, developed, and improved it. There were three factories in Paris directed by them.

VIRGINAL : See *Spinet*.

W

WAG-ON-THE-WALL CLOCK : Or *Friesland Clock*. Of Dutch origin, for hanging on wall with long, exposed pendulum and weights.

WAINSCOT : (From the Low Danish *wagenshot*.) A term originally applied to oak as a timber, later to wall-panelling.

WALNUT : There are two varieties. The first is pale brown in colour, with dark brown and black veining. The second is a greyish-brown wood, with noticeable dark markings and veinings, and is harder and denser than the brown walnut. Walnut was largely used in the solid in France and Italy during the Renaissance; in England it was in general use from the Restoration to the reign of George II.

WARDROBE: A development of the oak cupboard or press during the age of mahogany. Early wardrobes are not usually made with doors the full height, but have a hanging section above a tier (or tiers) of drawers. Large wardrobes dating from the middle of the 18th century, are constructed in three sections, the centre forming a case of drawers or clothes press, the wings serving as hanging cupboards.

WARMING PAN: Originally a covered metal pan, enclosed in a wooden cage. Early in the 15th century the cage was dispensed with, and a long metal handle was attached to the pan.

WASHSTAND: Developed in the middle of the 18th century to hold basin and ewer.

WATCH: The invention of the portable watch goes back no further than the early 16th century. Nuremberg took the lead in watchmaking, and most of the few watches of this period are of Nuremberg make. Later the watchmaking industry was established in several centres in France, and Geneva took up the industry about 1585. "Nuremberg eggs," (watches of flattened oval form) were made in that city as early as 1600, and were in fashion for half a century. Elaborate watch cases enriched with enamels and gems were from the middle years of the 17th century protected by outer cases.

WEDGWOOD: Josiah Wedgwood (1730–95), a Staffordshire master-potter, began to work on his own account about 1758 or 1759. His partnership with Bentley resulted in the erection of the great factory of Etruria, near Stoke-on-Trent. Among his productions are the *cream ware* (also known as Queen's ware), the *rosso antico*, the *basalt* and jasper ware.

WILTON: A town in Wiltshire, noted for its carpet factory, established in 1740 by the efforts of the Earl of Pembroke. The carpets manufactured were of the "Brussels" make, in which the looped pile was cut.

WIG-STAND: A wooden standard, usually finishing in a knob at the top, an extremely rare survival.

WINE-COOLER: A vessel in which wine bottles were placed during meals, was in use in the 15th century, and vessels of metal are frequently mentioned in inventories. Wooden wine-coolers used with lead appear about 1730. In the late Georgian period, the most usual form was a tub of mahogany strengthened with horizontal brass hoops on the exterior.

WINDSOR CHAIR : A type of chair in which the back and legs are formed of spindles and turnings inserted in a shaped seat (usually of elm). The spindle back was surmounted by a top rail until about 1740, when a hoop back was substituted. This type of chair, centring chiefly in High Wycombe was widely used as a garden chair, and in inns and farmhouses.

WING-CHAIR : Upholstered chair with high back and projecting or winged sides, arms ending in a scroll or turnover.

WORCESTER : The " Worcester Tonquin Manufacture " was set up in Worcester in 1751. The name of Dr. Wall (who died in 1776) has been attached to the early and most attractive productions of the factory, and the " Wall period " is extended to about 1783, when the factory was bought by Thomas Flight for his sons (Joseph and John). After the death of John Flight, Barr was taken into partnership in 1792. In 1807 the firm's style was Barr, Flight and Barr, and Flight, Barr and Barr in 1813. In 1840 Robert Chamberlain's factory was amalgamated with the older company.

Y

YEW : Very hard wood, red-brown, used in country furniture and in veneering.

YORKSHIRE CHAIR : (Also Derbyshire.) A form peculiar to these counties, dating from about 1650–75, and distinguished by a back filled in by two shaped transverse bars.

Z

ZEBRA WOOD : Wood imported from Guiana during the late 18th century, light brown with prominent dark brown stripes, used for veneer.

How to Export

(Twelve questions answered by L. H. Fairhead, Director of C. R. Fenton & Co., Ltd.)

Do you have to obtain permission to take antiques overseas ?

Yes, it is necessary to comply with regulations of two Government Departments, the Board of Trade and Bank of England currency control. Both in the case of trade and private shipments, the currency control regulations must be complied with in connection with exports to all countries other than British Colonies, with the exception of Canada, which is designated as a dollar area.

In such cases how is permission obtained ?

Export Licence Form. Application for this document is readily obtainable from the Export Licensing Department of the Board of Trade, and should be completed by entering in appropriate columns the names and addresses of seller and purchaser, also full description of merchandise and value. Country and date of origin is also required. The method of payment should also be entered, and question as to whether the transaction is in accordance with exchange control regulations must be answered.

Currency Control. Form C.D.3 which is obtainable from any bank, should be completed, once again giving details as to names and addresses of seller and purchaser. Brief description of merchandise, total amount of transaction and method of payment by the overseas purchaser should also be given, together with vendor's bank and address.

The Special Conditions attaching to Exports to America ?

Briefly, it may be stated that all antique items produced prior to the year 1830 are admitted free of duty, the main exception being carpets and rugs, which to enjoy this privilege must have been produced prior to 1700. Also *original* paintings, sculptures and works of art are permitted to enter the country duty free. No actual import licences are required, but a consular invoice is necessary, and on this document should be entered, apart from the usual details on a commercial invoice, the country of origin and date of production of merchandise to be shipped.

Australia and New Zealand, Canada, South Africa ?

Antique items are permitted to enter these countries free of duty, provided that they are over 100 years old. Evidence, however, must be produced in the form of a certificate, which is granted by the British Antique Dealers' Association, after their representative has examined the merchandise prior to packing in the shipping agent's warehouse. The examiner applies a gilt transfer to each piece which passes to his satisfaction, and this, together with the certificate, guarantee free entry to all these countries.

Continental Countries ?

Most Continental countries admit antique items free of duty, but some of them may levy a purchase or luxury tax. The majority of them require an import licence, but in some cases this is readily obtainable subject to the purchaser having complied with their respective currency control regulations.

South America ?

The majority of countries on this Continent levy duty on merchandise entering their ports, and they also exercise rigid control as to the quantity entering, and, therefore, it is necessary to obtain import licences. Documentation in the case of shipments going to these countries is rather complicated and a reliable shipping agent should be consulted before embarking upon exports to these areas.

The cheapest way of shipping ?

Intending exporters should approach a reliable shipping agent of their choice for advice as to cost, and we are certain the services given by the majority of firms in the business are comprehensive and reasonable. Most charges are based on cubic area of a shipment and the expert packer is the one best able to conserve space and at the same time ensure that adequate protection is given to the valuable and fragile items to be shipped, and in this way is able to keep packing and freight charges to the lowest economic level.

The best way ?

Once again consult your shipping agent as to the method of dispatch and also the route by which the merchandise should be shipped. It may be possible to reduce the rates by adopting one or two or three possible routes, also in the case of small consignments, it is sometimes possible that shipment by air may be as reasonable as dispatch by ship.

Best way for large shipments ?

As far as large shipments are concerned, the most reasonable method of packing is to utilise as large a container as up to 14 feet or even 16 feet by 7 feet by 7 feet, for the reason that in a case of these dimensions it is possible to pack away many more small items and thus save expenses. It will be readily appreciated that by utilising one large container, the amount of timber is also reduced. Quite apart from these considerations, a container of this size must of necessity be handled by cranes whereas small containers may be pushed about and possibly sustain damage, whereas the larger one will probably merit more attention by those handling it, and, therefore, arrive more safely to its destination.

Have overseas visitors any privileges, i.e., as regards taking articles back with them personally ?

Yes, the visitors from the U.S.A. are permitted to take back to their own country dutiable merchandise to the value of $500 per head. Therefore, it will be appreciated that small items for personal or gift purposes which do not come within the category of antiques may be taken to their homes without duty being levied upon them.

Snags if you attempt to do the job for yourself ?

It is earnestly suggested to all intending shippers that before embarking on any export business, they would do well to either visit or request their shipping agent to call upon them in order that the matter may be fully discussed, in order that the shipment may be moved as smoothly as possible. The documents men-

Artist's Impression by Mrs. Benyon of Her Charming Antique Shop at 55, Gildredge Road, Eastbourne.

tioned above must be obtained, as has been stated, and whilst in themselves they do not present any great difficulties, there are sometimes some unusual condition or conditions which may arise, and possibly delay applications, when passing their Government departments. Furthermore, the expert packer with many years' experience behind him, will be in a much better position to advise just how items should be handled and protected all along their journey, and thus arrive in good condition when delivered to the purchaser. After all, it is of paramount importance that the purchaser be given full satisfaction in order that his goodwill may be gained.

From an economy viewpoint also, the advice of the shipping agent will be found of good service. He will have at his finger-tips the rates charged by various routes which may be open for dispatch, and he will know which is the best to be adopted.

With regard to currency control, there are a number of snags, most of them quite easily overcome, but nevertheless, advice on this most important matter may be very useful.

Facilities an expert forwarding agent can offer, and a rough idea of charges—and whether any of cost is customarily borne by dealers ?

An expert forwarding agent is able to offer advice on all the foregoing points and he is in a position to inform an intending exporter just how merchandise may be forwarded from the point of dispatch to the consignee's address, and he is well versed in all the necessary documentation, not only as far as this country is concerned, but as to the requirements of the countries to which the items may be dispatched. Furthermore, customs procedure and regulations of countries abroad are matters on which he will be in a position to give you good advice. In short, your shipping agent will take upon his shoulders all the worries which are part and parcel of the exporting business.

In respect to cost of packing and transportation, by far the greater percentage of these costs, as mentioned elsewhere, are governed by the cubic space taken up by the merchandise, and it is, therefore, hardly possible to give even a rough idea, but if the exporter is able to supply measurements, rates will be supplied with very little delay.

We would inform exporters that in the great majority of instances, all packing and shipping costs are borne by the purchaser, and in point of fact, we strongly advise that exporters sell on these conditions.

Period Pieces

by DONALD COWIE

REGENCY

Gilded cage and Chinese fret
Dancing in the light
Of a crystal waterfall
Through Egyptian night,
Where the clawing of the Sphinx
Fumbles frock of rosewood's minx.

Marble bosom, Greek design,
Adam's breed debased
In a pretty Paris line
Ormolu has raised,
With tall pillars at each side
Like stern brothers round the bride.

Tableau in Pavilion soft
Of a dying age,
Where a Sydney Smith has scoffed
At the moment's rage,
Then descending into junk
Piled upon the attic trunk.

Yet—remembered at a time
When our hearts are sick
For the ancient and sublime
As against the slick,
And, re-polished to beguile
Mass-production days awhile.

PEWTER PIECE

In grey the lady sat, where ashlar rose
To mingle with her modesty of clothes,
And skies all leaden with the northern hue
Around such sadness called desire away
Towards the dolour of a finished day ;
While still she wove her silken stuff bereft
Of gaudy colour on religious loom,
With warp of habit over sorrow's weft
To rise a wraith across the shadowed room :
Until, a beam of falling sun revives
One moment through the monochrome such shine
As never silver knew nor gold derives
Ecstatic from the unattainted mine.

CHANDELIER DROP

Facet-slung the light returns
And the spot at centre burns
As from glass held by a boy,
Or the pupil eye of joy,
And reflections dance together
In a minuet of pleasure,
As the couples in a hall,
Or the spears of waterfall ;
While the shape eternal pleases
Like the aftermath of sneezes,
Or the raindrop tearfully
Pulled by weight to symmetry :
Little frozen ape of life,
Cut from glass with cunning knife,
You can sparkle and delight—
Till a switch removes the light.

Tributes to Antiques Year Book

So many kind unsolicited encomiums of The Antiques Year Book 1950 *were received that it is only possible to give brief extracts from a few as typical samples, originals of which, of course, are in our files for examination.*

TRUTH, LONDON : **" The first number of this now annual production, which appeared last year, was warmly commended in these pages. The present volume lives up to the high standard of its predecessor. . . . The book should appeal to a wide range of collectors, and is extremely good value."**

AMERICAN READER, BALTIMORE, MD. : **" As I was looking through our largest city library I came across the ' Antiques Year Book.' Your book is filled with more information than I have ever had the pleasure of reading. I told my friends about the book, and we decided that we must have copies for our own libraries. Would you be kind enough to send me three copies of this wonderful book directly from your press? "**

EXETER READER : **" We have been so pleased with the enquiries we have received (and callers), as a result of our advertisement in the ' Antiques Year Book,' that we would like to increase our advertisement space for your next edition."**

SURREY COUNTY JOURNAL : **" What can now be regarded as an institution in the world of antiques, the ' Antiques Year Book. . . .'**

BLACKPOOL READER : **" I would like to compliment you on your book. I purchased one the other day, and after sitting in the car and looking through it, I immediately purchased a second one in case I lost it—it's really an excellent book, so very useful."**

DOCTOR READER, PLYMOUTH : **" I have much enjoyed ' Antique Year Book 1950 ' and would like to compliment you on its excellence."**

LEAMINGTON READER : **" May I heartily congratulate you on a most interesting and well-presented publication? I am sure that it will have a big sale and will be of interest to many thousands of people. It is most excellently compiled, printed and produced in every way."**

g Richard III House, Scar-
ugh. Wonderfully Preserved
Museum of Antiquities.

OCEAN TIMES, QUEEN ELIZABETH : **" A host of information can be obtained by those interested in antiques from the ' Antiques Year Book '."**

CHESTER READER : **" After reading your ' Antiques Year Book ' I wish to tell you how much I enjoyed it and found it a wonderful book for the price."**

BRIGHTON DEALER : **" I received an inquiry to-day from a private collector in America. He particularly mentioned that he saw my advertisement in the ' Antiques Year Book,' and I must say that I am very pleased indeed."**

STORE, TRADE MAGAZINE : **" This is a book which the stores that deal in antiques and executives who collect them for a hobby should not miss."**

FURNISHING, TRADE MAGAZINE : **" The volume is an invaluable guide and reference book."**

WILTSHIRE READER : **" May I say how useful and interesting I find your book, and it goes with me everywhere on my buying tours."**

Early 16th Century Furniture Discovery

IT is rare that a piece of furniture of the early 16th century is found, unrecognised and unhonoured. Messrs. Beckwith & Son had this pleasant experience recently, when, during a tour of the southern counties, they found an oak meal ark. This has since been pronounced by the highest authorities to be of no later date than 1520, for although bearing archaic features which might suggest an earlier date, the panelling of the front is of a type that was not introduced until the early 16th century.

The practice, in country districts, of using traditional methods of construction long after they have been superseded elsewhere, is illustrated in this ark by the simple "knuckle-and-socket" hinge device on which the lid swings, which had been prevalent two centuries earlier.

It is said that this piece stood for centuries in the vast domestic regions of Arundel Castle, being removed during a general clearance following the arrival there, many years ago, of a new bride. Its subsequent history cannot be traced, but as the ark was found within ten miles of the castle, and as so cumbersome a domestic piece could not have survived the centuries in a small household, the story is conceivably true.

We are very pleased to be able to report that this interesting relic has now been preserved for the nation, having been purchased by the Victoria and Albert Museum.

Messrs. Beckwiths' advertisement (on page 48) shows a small illustration of the ark, from a photograph taken while it was in their possession, and readers interested in this type of furniture will find some interesting information in *Early English Furniture and Woodwork* (Cescinsky & Gribble), in which a similar but earlier piece is shown on Plate 9 (Vol. 2).

Glasgow Silver Marks

TREE FISH & BELL | DATE

1681-2
1682-3
1683-4
1684-5
1685-6
1686-7
1687-8
1688-9
1689-90
1690-1
1691-2
1692-3
1693-4
1694-5
1695-6
1696-7
1697-8
1698-9
1699 1700
1700-1
1701-2
1702-3
1703-4
1704-5
1705-6

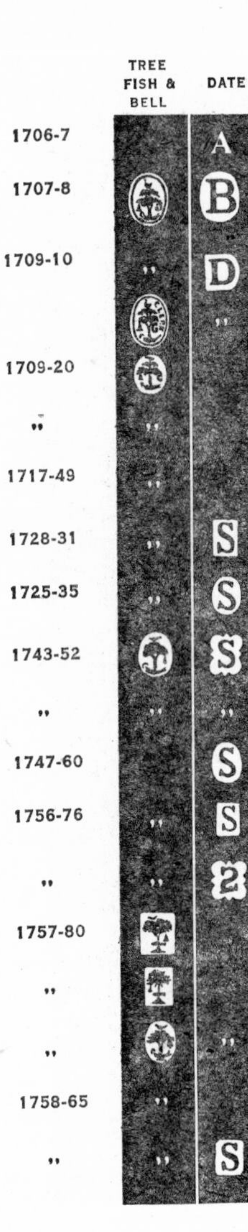

Glasgow Silver Marks

	TREE FISH & BELL	DATE
1763-70		
"	"	E
"	"	F
1773-80	S	S
1776-80		O
"		O
"		
"		S
1783		
"		"
1777-90	"	"
1782-92		
1785-95		S
"	"	O
1781 1800		S
	LION RAMPANT	
1811-3		

	TREE FISH & BELL	LION RAMP-ANT	DATE	KING'S HEAD
1819-20			A	
GEO. IV 1820-1		"	B	"
1821-2	"	"	C	"
1822-3	"	"	D	"
1823-4	"	"	E	"
1824-5	"	"	F	"
1825-6	"	"	G	"
1826-7	"	"	H	"
1827-8	"	"	I	"
1828-9	"	"	J	"
1829-30	"	"	K	"
WM. IV 1830-1	"	"	L	"
1831-2	"	"	M	"
1832-3	"	"	N	
1833-4	"	"	O	"
1834-5	"	"	P	"
1835-6	"	"	Q	"
1836-7	"	"	R	"
VICT. 1837-8	"	"	S	"
1838-9	"	"	T	"
1839-40	"	"	U	"
1840-1	"	"	V	"
1841-2	"	"	W	
1842-3	"	"	X	
1843-4	"	"	Y	
1844-5	"	"	Z	

HOW TO READ GLASGOW SILVER MARKS

Earliest Known Mark: 1681.

Town Mark: The burgh arms of a " fish, bell and tree " (sometimes including letter " G ").

Date Letter: Used between 1681 and 1710, then not regularly used again till 1819. Letter " S," often used between 1730 and 1800, possibly stands for " sterling."

Full Marks: Full marks not used till 1819 when Assay Office established in Glasgow, prescribing use of (1) Lion Rampant ; (2) City Arms ; (3) Maker's mark ; (4) Date letter ; (5) Sovereign's head.

Britannia: If figure of Britannia added to above marks it means the silver is above standard in weight.

(By Courtesy of Messrs. Hicklenton & Phillips, Ltd., 83, Cheapside, London, E.C.4.)

Above: *LONDON SILVER. A Mace, typical of a Thomas Maundy " Forme and Paterne." Maundy was granted Monopoly of Mace Making by Cromwell.* Below: *Silver Gilt Porringer marked* 1685–6, *Maker's Mark, I.C. with mullet below, Jackson's p.* 139, *James II (enlarged from Porringer with Mace above).*

London Silver Marks

	Britannia	Date	Lion's Head
1697			
March 27 to May 29 1697-8	"		"
1698-9	"		"
1699 1700			
1700-1	"		"
1700-2	"		"
ANNE 1702-3	"		"
1703-4	"		"
1704-5	"		"
1705-6	"		"
1706-7	"		"
1707-8	"		"
1708-9	"		"
1709-10	"		"
1710-11	"		"
1711-2	"		"
1712-3	"		"
1713-4	"		"
GEO. I. 1714-5	"		"
1715-6	"		"

	Britannia	Date	Lion's Head
1716-7		A	
1717-8	"	B	"
1718-9	"	C	"
	Leopard's Head Crowned		Lion Passant
1719-20		D	
1720-1	"	E	"
1721-2		F	
1722-3	"	G	"
1723-4	"	H	"
1724-5		I	
1725-6	"	K	"
1726-7		L L	
GEO. II. 1727-8	"	M M	"
1728-9	"	N	"
1729-30		O	
1730-1	"	P	"
1731-2	"	Q	"
1732-3	"	R	"
1733-4	"	S	"
1734-5	"	T	"
1735-6	"	V	"

G

London Silver Marks

	Leopard's Head	Date	Lion Passant
1736-7		a	
1737-8	,,	b	,,
1738-9	,,	c	,,
1739-40	,,	d	,,
1739-40		d	
1740-1	,,	e	,,
1741-2	,,	f	,,
1742-3	,,	g	,,
1743-4	,,	h	,,
1744-5	,,	i	,,
1745-6	,,	k	,,
1746-7	,,	l	,,
1747-8	,,	m	,,
1748-9	,,	n	,,
1749-50	,,	o	,,
1750-1	,,	p	,,
1751-2		q	
1752-3	,,	r	,,
1753-4	,,	s	,,
1754-5	,,	t	,,
1755-6	,,	u	,,

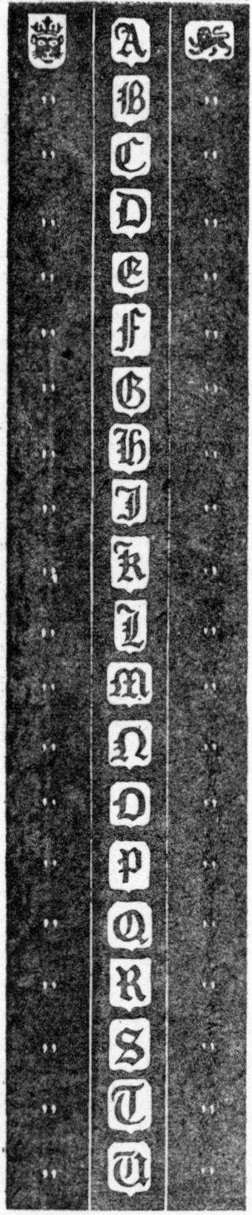

	Leopard's Head	Date	Lion Passant
1756-7		A	
1757-8	,,	B	,,
1758-9	,,	C	,,
1759-60	,,	D	,,
GEO. III. 1760-1	,,	E	,,
1761-2	,,	F	,,
1762-3	,,	G	,,
1763-4	,,	H	,,
1764-5	,,	I	,,
1765-6	,,	K	,,
1766-7	,,	L	,,
1767-8	,,	M	,,
1768-9	,,	N	,,
1769-70	,,	O	,,
1770-1	,,	P	,,
1771-2	,,	Q	,,
1772-3	,,	R	,,
1773-4	,,	S	,,
1774-5	,,	T	,,
1775-6	,,	U	,,

London Silver Marks

	Leopard's Head	Date	Lion Passant
1776-7		a	
1777-8	"	b	"
1778-9	"	c	"
1779-80	"	d	"
1780-1	"	e	"
1781-2	"	f	"
1782-3	"	g	"
1783-4	"	h	"
1784-5	"	i	"
1785-6	"	k	"
1786-7	"	l	"
1787-8	"	m	"
1788-9	"	n	"
1789-90	"	o	"
1790-1	"	p	"
1791-2	"	q	"
1792-3	"	r	"
1793-4	"	s	"
1794-5	"	t	"
1795-6	"	u	"

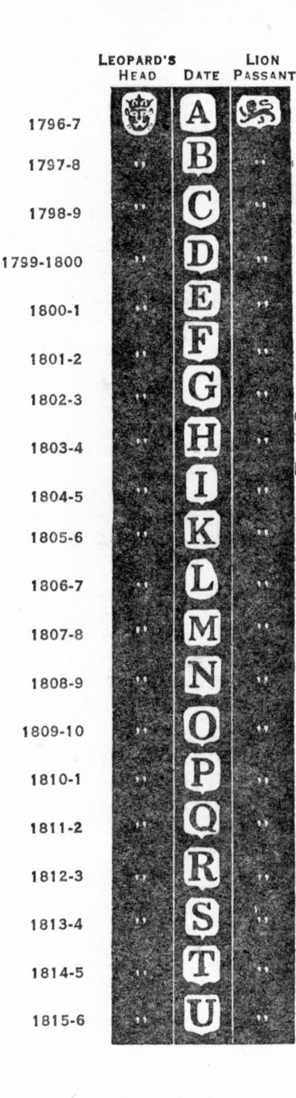

	Leopard's Head	Date	Lion Passant
1796-7		A	
1797-8	"	B	"
1798-9	"	C	"
1799-1800	"	D	"
1800-1	"	E	"
1801-2	"	F	"
1802-3	"	G	"
1803-4	"	H	"
1804-5	"	I	"
1805-6	"	K	"
1806-7	"	L	"
1807-8	"	M	"
1808-9	"	N	"
1809-10	"	O	"
1810-1	"	P	"
1811-2	"	Q	"
1812-3	"	R	"
1813-4	"	S	"
1814-5	"	T	"
1815-6	"	U	"

The Year's Best Books on Collecting

ANNUALLY A SURVEY IS MADE HEREIN OF THE BEST BOOKS ON VARIOUS DEPARTMENTS OF THE COLLECTING OF ANTIQUES, EACH CHECKED BY AUTHORITIES ON THE SUBJECT.

ALAS that we cannot say too much—for the general reader—about the really outstanding collector's book of the year. But Messrs. Country Life's *Catalogue of Sassoon Chinese Ivories*, compiled in three giant volumes by S. E. Lucas, is issued only in a limited, signed edition of 250 copies at one hundred guineas. However, we cannot start this section without saying that this work is perhaps the finest modern piece of bookmaking we have seen, bound beautifully, printed perfectly in two colours on hand-made paper, and superbly illustrated. Never were such ivories so finely depicted. Caviare for the general, no doubt—but probably a first-rate investment all the same.

Next in importance we assess the new edition from Messrs. Benn's of Oliver Brackett's already-classic *English Furniture Illustrated*, a fine large volume replete with plates at four guineas, revised and edited by H. Clifford Smith. Collectors and dealers know the value of the original volume as published in 1927, also its steady growth in value. The new edition, brought up-to-date especially in its attention to Regency, is an essential reference book for the serious collector.

Messrs. Benn have also issued yet another of Arthur Hayden's " Chats " series, the basic and still delightful *Chats on Old Furniture*, which at 12s. 6d. provides a useful handbook for the beginner. Saleroom prices at the ends of chapters have been brought up to date usefully—though their chief use, it must be insisted, is to saleroom habitués, as ordinary collectors have naturally to pay dealer's commissions and costs of restoring, carriage, etc.

While on the subject of furniture, moreover, we must mention with pleasure a new edition received of John Gloag's *Time, Taste and Furniture*, at 15s. from The Richards Press. Mr. Gloag brings a breezy note into the discussion of our subject which is healthful if sometimes provocative. The work is definitely made for the knowledge-thirsty beginner.

Which is not exactly the case with J. B. Morrell's *Woodwork in York*, from Messrs. Batsford at 30s. This is a book peculiarly valuable to the advanced student of furniture and decoration, limited in scope but nevertheless applicable in what it teaches to all oak furniture and many aspects of design. The book has a great many valuable illustrations. By minutely examining the wood carvings, structures and furniture of York's unique assemblage of old buildings, Mr. Morrell evokes knowledge of wider application.

DECORATION—AND THE COUNTRY HOUSE

Yet another sumptuous and definitive work of the year is Miss Margaret Jourdain's *English Interior Decoration* 1500–1830, from Messrs. Batsford at three guineas. This would be a still more astonishing work of scholarship if only Miss Jourdain had been able to escape from her facts for a while. All the facts are there, and the work will be most useful to those who take their interior decoration seriously. We must have this book on the reference shelf, though not necessarily on the bedside table.

We turn with relief indeed to Miss Dorothy Stroud's *Capability Brown*, from Messrs. Country Life at two guineas. Here is a better example of how to make the dull readable. Miss Stroud invests her treatment with a certain amount of humanity, and the strange personality of Lancelot Brown himself sometimes enters her pages. We cannot collect landscapes or grottoes or ha-has anymore, but an appreciation of the great architectural gardener's work is essential background knowledge to those who do collect furniture and *objets d'art* of the 18th century.

And we congratulate Messrs. Country Life still further on the publication of a handbook *Country*

Houses, only 5s. and consisting of a concise guide to all those houses of historic or architectural interest in England which are open to the general public, with details of times of opening, prices of admission, special features. Most useful.

ASSORTED CERAMICS

We have ourselves found the best book on ceramics of the year to be Sydney B. Williams' *Antique Blue and White Spode*, from Messrs. Batsford at two guineas. Possibly it is not the most scholarly, but we can have too much of pedants. Possibly the attraction is just Spode itself, a subtle attraction compounded of homeliness, and cleanliness, and Englishness, and maybe also some memories of early collecting days in country shop and saleroom.

Still, Mr. Williams writes easily and keeps you awake. The reader will *enjoy* his book.

The reader will not necessarily enjoy W. B. Honey's latest work in the Faber series of Monographs on Pottery and Porcelain, namely *French Porcelain of the 18th Century*, 25s. He will *admire* the careful and erudite if somewhat brief treatment of the subject, and will be delighted with the copious illustrations. This is in fact the first English book for forty-five years on the subject, so it is recommended as an essential addition to the library.

We have also received Griselda Lewis's *Introduction to English Pottery*, from Messrs. Art and Technics at 10s. 6d., a handy elementary review of the subject, suitably illustrated.

AND SILVER

Two useful works on silver can be recommended. *Old Silver for Modern Settings*, by Edward Wenham (former Editor of *The Connoisseur*) is published by Messrs. Bell at one guinea, and is just what the beginner and the " ordinary " collector wants both as a handbook and as an interesting work to read. Mr. Wenham is a writer as well as an expert. He covers the entire field, illustrating with photographs, drawings and marks. We feel that this is likely to be a lasting book.

Then we have read with pleasure Peter Wilding's *Introduction to English Silver*, from Messrs. Art and Technics at 10s. 6d. This is an amusing if slight book with some excellent photographs at the end (why are publishers sticking all the illustrations at the end nowadays ? They should illustrate the text in the right place). Mr. Wilding's intention is to provide an inquiring friend with information about silver. He succeeds, and is entertaining by the way.

CLOCKS—GLASS—ENAMELS

There have been few works on antique clocks. That is why we particularly welcome a new edition of G. F. C. Gordon's *Clockmaking Past and Present*, revised by A. V. May, and coming from the Technical Press, Ltd., at 17s. 6d. Here for once is a thorough manual from which an apprentice could very nearly learn his trade. Yet we could read it even ourselves with intense interest. Every collector interested in clocks and every dealer should have this book for sure, especially as its like may not appear again for a long while to come.

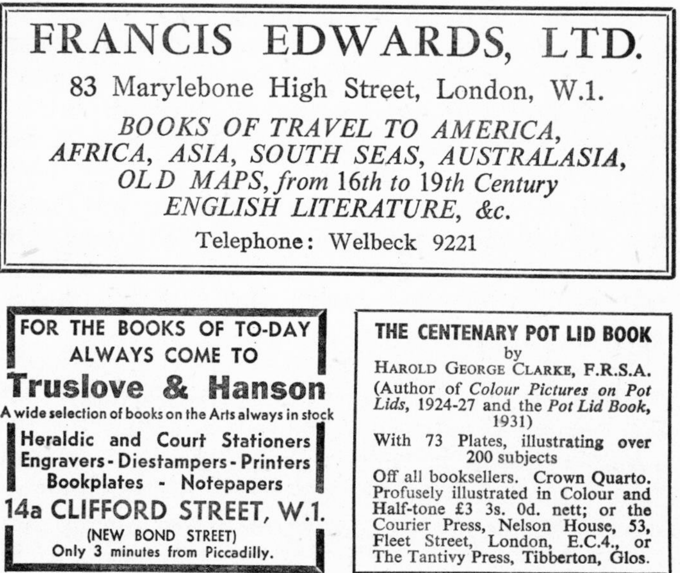

And as a companion piece buy H. Alan Lloyd's *Chats on Old Clocks*, in the famous Benn series at 12s. 6d. This book, to be released in the summer of 1951, provides a sound but not over technical conspectus of the subject illustrated by seventy-four photographs of cases and movements specially collected by the author.

Then in glass we have at last a thoroughly useful work for the average collector in E. M. Elville's *English Tableglass*, beautifully produced by Messrs. Country Life at two guineas. The author addresses the reader of our *Yearbook* who collects or aims to collect English glass. He devotes successive sections to Glass the Material, Early History, Drinking Glasses, Form and Decoration, Development of Cut Glass, even Chandeliers. An excellent work.

Messrs. Country Life are indeed doing us proud in these days. Their production of books on collecting subjects in the last year or two places them at the head of their class of publishers in the world and will always be remembered as a vintage period. There is, for example, *English Painted Enamels*, by Therle and Bernard Hughes, from Country Life at two guineas again, a charming book, produced like a jewel, and providing at last the compact information we needed on the subject, illustrated nobly from the collections of Her Majesty Queen Mary and the Hon. Mrs. Ionides.

HAMMOND ON CHESSMEN

And now for a pleasant aside. Mr. Alex Hammond, the well-known collector of Burlington Arcade, has at last put his great knowledge at our permanent service in *The Book of Chessmen*, from

Messrs. Arthur Barker at 21s. He has created a permanent work which will long be definitive in its class, but this is no dry-as-dust fact-grinder's pot-boiling. It is a live book, with the personality of the author in every line, often wise and very frequently witty, covering the whole subject of chessmen, and providing the collector with his vade-mecum. Illustrations are most carefully chosen. Buy this book for sure and turn again to the dusty chess pieces seen by chance in the corner of the antique shop. You might be surprised.

But of course another Country Life book crops up. This is *Chinese Export Art in the 18th Century*, a most unusual work compiled by Margaret Jourdain and R. Soame Jenyns at two guineas. The accent is not on porcelain and jade so much as on

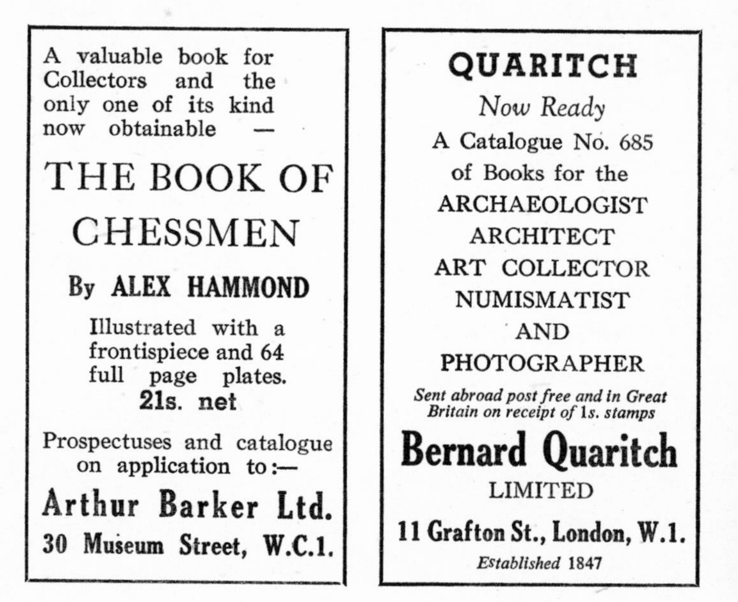

Chinese products such as lacquered furniture, paper hangings, glass paintings, ivories, tortoiseshell and mother-of-pearl, also silk textiles. The information will be most valuable not only to those who collect Oriental but also to dealers who seek to thread the narrow path between Chinese and European work in the Oriental manner of the 18th century.

PICTURES—MAINLY WATER COLOUR

Books on pictures have been mainly concerned with water-colours this year, an interesting fact which points to the growing popularity of the class. It is certain that never again can the collector complain of not having sufficient good books on water-colours.

Magnificent and leading all is Adrian Bury's *Two Centuries of British Water-Colour Painting*, from George Newnes at three guineas, a cheap book at the price considering its size, bulk and most comprehensive gallery of finely-screened plates, including many in colour. Mr. Bury not only tells us all we wish to know about the subject in excellent language, but writes opposite each plate a brief conspectus of the painter's life which is most helpful and revealing. With this book Messrs. Newnes enter the ranks of the publishers of really fine books.

But Messrs. Country Life are as usual to the forefront, and give us in Graham Reynolds' *An Introduction to English Water-Colour Painting* at only 25s. what is an equally interesting though of course not so comprehensive a book.

Then Messrs. Benn have issued a new, revised edition of what has for many years been the stan-

dard work on *Early English Water Colour*, by C. E. Hughes, 15s. This is not a large picture book, but it is still as sound as ever and as essential.

With the above three books the collector will have the beginning of a useful library on the subject, to which he might well add—a revision from Messrs. Newnes of Sir William Orpen's *Outline of Art*, extraordinarily good value, a veritable bible of the subject and nearly as heavy, at the absurdly low price of 30s. This is a gift—while it lasts. You can read Orpen right through, with pleasure, and still have the one and only reference work of its kind.

Among other art books of the year we were taken most ourselves with Frederick B. Deknatel's *Edvard Munch*, from Messrs. Max Parrish at one guinea. Munch is by no means antique and canonised as yet, but may well be. It is a fascinating study of the man and his work and may lead to some appreciation in prices.

ON THE SIDE TABLE

We find outside the normal categories but worth noting one or two books and publications, such as issues of Messrs. Seaby's *Coin and Medal Bulletin*, each number of which contains sufficient information for a book (from the publishers at 5s. per annum or 10s. clothbound whole year), and *Store Annual*, from Newman Books Ltd., (a Directory of Department Stores of great value to those interested in antique furniture departments, names of buyers and the like), also a work *Contemporary Jewellery and Silver Design*, which from Messrs. Heywood and Company at 30s., by E. D. S. Bradford, will be of interest to those who handle antique silver and jewellery as well as to tradesmen in the department.

And we have a new printing of H. G. Clarke's famous *Under-Glaze Colour Picture Prints on Staffordshire Pottery*—the POT LID BOOK—which at three guineas plus post, tenpence, was one of the principal collector's book successes of 1949–50, and is available still from The Tantivy Press, Tibberton, Glos., together with the free booklet of Pot Lid Prices.

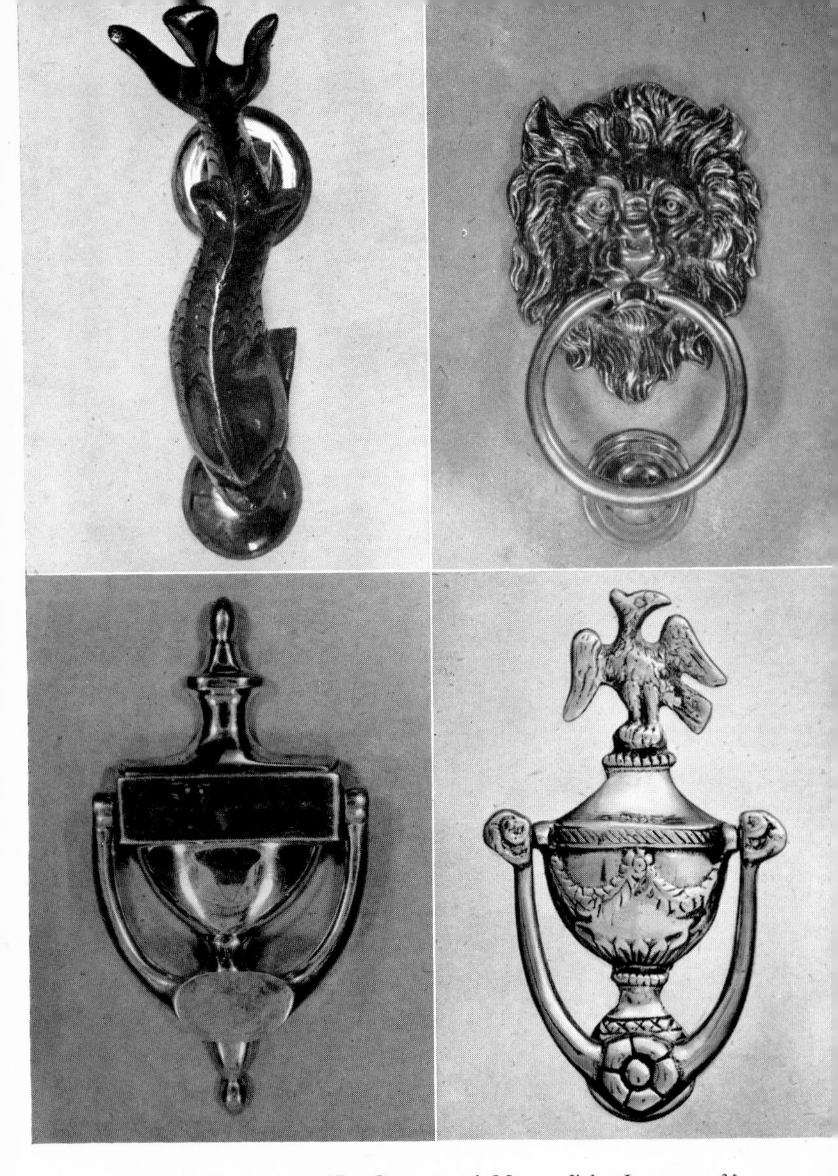

(By Courtesy of Messrs. John Lawrence & Co., Handle and Knocker Experts, Dover.)

ANTIQUE DOOR KNOCKERS

Top Left. 18*th Century Dolphin Knocker*. Top Right. *Typical* 18*th Century Lion Mask Knocker*. Bottom Left. *Severely Classical Adam Knocker*. Bottom Right. *Early Regency Knocker*.

(Courtesy of Messrs. Charles E. Thornton, York.)

(*By Courtesy of Messrs. Alfred Bullard, 12, North Row, Park Lane, London.*)

Lovely 18*th Century Serpentine Front Mahogany Sideboard.*

H

Members of the British Antique Dealers' Association

STRATFORD GALLERIES,
59/61 WIGMORE STREET,
LONDON, W.I

Est. 1889 *Tel.:* Welbeck 8664

Woolletts of Wigmore Street have a very interesting Stock of Antiques, and a visit from you will find Furniture, Silver, China, Miniatures, Jewellery, etc., at reasonable prices backed by a personal guarantee and courtesy to all who visit these Galleries.

Exquisite Antique "Hochst" Group of Children by famous modeller, J. P. Melchior. Date 1775. 7" high.

NYMAN of NORTH LONDON

230 CAMDEN HIGH ST., LONDON, NWI
(Gulliver 1907)

ANTIQUES &
DECORATIVE FURNISHINGS
HOME & OVERSEAS TRADE
INQUIRIES INVITED

178 HIGH ST., EPPING
(Epping 2093)

HIGHEST PRICES PAID FOR WEBB CAMEO GLASS

A Directory of London Dealers

(Revised 1951)

ACTON SURGEY, LTD., The Albemarle Galleries, 6 Albemarle St., W.1.

ADAMS, NORMAN, LTD., 8–10 Hans Rd., S.W.3.

AGNEW, THOS. & SONS, LTD., 43, Old Bond St., and 3, Albemarle St., W.1.

AMOR, ALBERT, LTD., 37, Bury St., St. James's, S.W.1.

APPLEBY BROS., 27 William IV St., W.C.2.

ARCHER, 34, Harrington Road, S.W.7.

ARMSTRONG, HARRY & SONS, LTD., 277, Fulham Road, Chelsea, S.W.3.

ARTHUR & PURKIS, LTD., 23, Motcomb St., S.W.1.

ASHTON, C., 171, Piccadilly, W.1.

ASPREY & CO., LTD., 165–169, New Bond St., W.1.

BALDWIN, A. H. & SONS, LTD., 3, Robert St., Adelphi, W.C.2.

BARNETT, B. 26 Lancaster Court, Newman St., Oxford St., W.1.

BARTLETT, A. & G., 20, Beauchamp Place, S.W.3.

BAXTER, H.C. & SONS, 191–3, Fulham Rd., S.W.3.

BEARE, JOHN & ARTHUR 179, Wardour St., W.1.

BEAUCHAMP GALLERIES, 8 Beauchamp Place, S.W.3.

BERENDT (ANTIQUES), LTD., 34, Fitzroy Square, W.1.

BERNARD, M., 21, Ryder St., S.W.1.

BERRY, FREDERICK, LTD., 64, New Bond St., W.1.

BIER, HERBERT N., 13B, Cunningham Place, N.W.8.

BIRCH & GAYDON, LTD., 153 Fenchurch St., E.C.3.

BIRD, VERA, 174A, Kensington Church St., W.8.

BIRKS, HENRY & SONS, LTD., 19–21, Hatton Garden, E.C.1.

BLACK, DAVID & SONS, 1, Burlington Gardens, New Bond St., W.1.

BLACK, HENRY, LTD., 10, St. Albans St., Haymarket, S.W.1. (and New York).

BLACK & SWONNELL, 10, St. Albans St., S.W.1.

BLAIRMAN, H. & SONS, LTD., 23, Grafton St., New Bond St., W.1.

BLOOM, N. & SON, LTD., 15, Norton Folgate, E.C.2.

BLUETT & SONS, 48, Davies St., Brook St., W.1.

BOSWELL & WARD, 30, Dover St., W.1.

BOTIBOL, J. M., 28–30, Hanway St., W.1.

BRADBURY, THOS. (AN-

TIQUES), LTD., 11, Charterhouse St., E.C.1.

BULLARD, ALFRED, 12, North Row, Park Lane, W.1.

BURFITT, LTD., 1B, Albemarle St., W.1.

BURNE, W. G. T., 27, Davies St., Berkeley Square, W.1.

CAMEO CORNER, 26, Museum St., W.C.1.

CAMERONS, 67, Duke St., Grosvenor Square, W.1.

CANTERBURY'S (ANTIQUES), LTD., 17, King St., St. James's, S.W.1.

CARRINGTON & CO. LTD. 130, Regent St., W.1.

CATCHPOLE & WILLIAMS, LTD., 14, Grafton St., Bond St., W.1.

CHALMERS, E. W., 177A, Brompton Rd. and 19 Cheval Place, S.W.3.

CHAMPNESS, LTD., 3, George St., Baker St., W.1.

CHRISTY'S OF KENT, LTD., 104 Mount St., W.1.

CHURCHILL, ARTHUR LTD., 34, Marylebone High St., W.1.

COHEN, A. J. & SON, 93, King's Rd. (op. Markham St.), Chelsea, S.W.3.

COMYNS, WILLIAM & SONS (ANTIQUE DEALERS) LTD., 47, Beak St., Regent St., W.1.

COOK, A., 13–16, St. Christopher's Place, Wigmore St., W.1.

COPPER & ADAMS, 41, James St., W.1.

CRADDOCK & BARNARD, 32, Museum St., W.C.1.

CRICHTON BROS., 96, Jermyn St., S.W.1.

CRICK, MRS. M. E., 106, Kensington Church St., W.8.

CROWTHER, T. & SON, LTD., 282, North End Rd., Fulham, S.W.6.

DANIELL, FREDERICK B. & SON, 32, Cranbourn St., Leicester Square, W.C.2.

DAVIDSON, B. & CO., LTD., Pall Mall Safe Deposit, 10, St. Alban's St., Haymarket, S.W.1.

DAVIS, CECIL, 3, Grosvenor St., New Bond St., W.1.

DAVIS, HAROLD, 39, King St., St. James's, S.W.1.

DELOMOSNE & SON, LTD., 4, Campden Hill Road, Kensington, W.8.

DODD, P. G. & SON, LTD., 42, Cornhill, E.C.3.

DONALD (MRS.), E. A. E., 12, Queen St., Mayfair, W.1.

DREY, F. A., 32, St. James's St., S.W.1.

DROWN, WILLIAM, 110, New Bond St., W.1.

DRUKKER, J. J., 17, George St., Baker St., W.1.

DRURY & DRURY, 40, Eaton Terrace, Sloane

Square, S.W.3.

DUITS, W. E., 6 Duke St., St. James's, S.W.1.

ELLIS & SMITH, 16b, Grafton St., New Bond St., W.1.

EMIL (Alex Hammond), 16, Burlington Arcade, W.1.

EYRES, DEREK, 65, King's Rd., S.W.3.

FALCKE, JAMES, 43, Davies St., W.1.

FERGUSON, ELLIOTT & WALKER, LTD., 191, Sloane St., S.W.1.

FICK, BEN, LTD., Melton Court, 5–7 Old Brompton Rd., S.W.7.

FILKINS & CO., 9A, Thurloe Place, S.W.7.

FINE ART SOCIETY, The, Ltd., 148, New Bond St., W.1.

FITZROY, L., 11, Norris St., Haymarket, S.W.1.

FLEURONT, 5, Cheval Place, S.W.3.

FOWLER, C. T., 72, Comeragh Rd., Baron's Court, W.14.

FOWLER, E. L. W., 1A, Duke St., Manchester Square, W.1.

FRANK ROBERT, 4, St. James's St., S.W.1.

FRANKLIN, 20, Brompton Rd., S.W.1.

FRANKLIN, L., 39, Duke St., St. James's, S.W.1.

FREDERICKS, ALFRED, 265–7, Fulham Rd., S.W.3.

FREDERICKS, C. & SON, 76, Old Brompton Rd., S.W.7.

FREEMAN, HARRY, Pall Mall Safe Deposit, 10, St. Alban's St., S.W.1.

FRODSHAM, CHAS. & CO., LTD., 173, Brompton Rd., S.W.3.

FROST & REED, LTD., 41, New Bond St., W.1.

GADBURY, E., 265, Balham High Rd., S.W.17.

GALITZINE, PRINCE VLADIMIR, 20A, Berkeley St., W.1.

GARRARD & CO., LTD., 24, Albemarle St., Piccadilly, W.1.

GARRICK, 154, King's Rd., S.W.3.

GENERAL TRADING CO., THE (MAYFAIR), LTD. 1, 3, & 5, Grantham Place, Park Lane, W.1.

GERED (ANTIQUES) LTD., 10, Piccadilly Arcade, W.1.

GILBERT, ALFRED, Pall Mall Safe Deposit, 10, St. Alban's St., Haymarket, S.W.1.

GILLINGHAM, J. H., 1 and 5, Harrington Rd., South Kensington, S.W.7.

GILLINGHAM, W. Brooks, 345, Fulham Rd., Chelsea, S.W.10.

GLORIA ANTICA (prop : C-L de Beaumont, M.A., Cantab.), 170, Brompton Rd., S.W.3.

GLOYN, W. J., 125, Mount St., W.1.

GOLDSMITHS & SILVERSMITHS CO., LTD., 112, Regent St., W.1.
GOODALL & CO., LTD., 24, High Road, W.4.
GOODE, THOMAS & CO. (LONDON), LTD., 19, South Audley St., W.1.
GRAHAME-BALLIN, J., 37, Beauchamp Place, S.W.3.
GREGORY & CO. (Bruton St.) LTD., 27, Bruton St., Berkeley Square, W.1.
GROSE, RICHARD H., 8, Exhibition Rd., S.W.7.
GUERAULT, DANTON, 13, Park Place, St. James's, S.W.1.
HAKIM, M., 33, Cranbourn St., W.C.1.
HAMMOND, CHARLES, LTD., 64–9, Sloane St., S.W.1.
HAMPTON & SONS, LTD., 8 Pall Mall East, S.W.1.
HANCOCKS & CO. (Jewellers), LTD., 25, Sackville St., W.1.
HANCOCK, H. R. & SONS, 37, Bury St., S.W.1.
HARDY, JAMES & CO., 235, Brompton Rd., S.W.3.
HARMAN & CO., LTD., 177, New Bond St., W.1.
HARMAN, LOUIS P., 47, Beulah Hill, S.E. 19.
HARRIS, M. & SONS, 44–52, New Oxford St., W.C.1.
HARRIS, SAMUEL H & SON, 5, Hatton Garden, E.C.1.
HARRIS, T. W., 13 Brook St., W.1.
HARRODS, LTD., Brompton Rd., Knightsbridge, S.W.
HARVEY & GORE, LTD., 1–3 Vigo St., W.1.
HEMING & CO., LTD., 28–9, Conduit St., W.1.
HESTERS, LTD., 163, Victoria St., S.W.1.
HICKLENTON & PHILLIPS, 83, Cheapside, E.C.2.
HILFORD, 14, Marylebone High St., W.1.
HILL, WILLIAM E. & Sons, 140, New Bond St., W.1.
HOLLIDAY, A. W., Pall Mall Safe Deposit, 10, St. Alban's St., S.W.1.
HOLMES & CO., 24, Burlington Arcade, W.1.
HOLMES (Jewellers), LTD., 29, Old Bond St., W.1.
HOW (of Edinburgh) LTD., 2–3, Pickering Place, St. James's St., S.W.1.
HOWE, DEREK & CO., LTD., 23, Motcomb St., S.W.3.
HURST, FRED, 321, Fulham Rd., S.W.10.
HUTCHINS, H. A. & SON, 350B, King's Rd., S.W.3.
JEREMY, LTD., 255 King's Rd., S.W.3.
JESSOP, H. R. LTD., 3, Motcomb St., Belgrave Square, S.W.1.

JETLEY, G., 24, Bruton St., Berkeley Square, W.1.

JEWELL, S. & H., 131–2, High Holborn, W.C.1.

JONES & SON (Long Acre), LTD., 229 Brompton Rd., S.W.3.

KAUFFMANN, A. I., 21, Grafton St., Bond St., W.1.

KEEBLE, LTD., 4, Audley Square, South Audley St., W.1.

KERIN, GERALD, 15, Davies St., W.1.

KING SMITH, U. H. & CO., LTD., 133, Sloane St., S.W.1.

KNIGHT, LEONARD, LTD., 89, Park Lane, W.1.

KNOEDLER, M. & CO., LTD., 14 Old Bond St., W.1.

KUTIAK, P., LTD., 7, West Halkin St., S.W.1.

LANSBOROUGH, LTD., 32, Park Lane, W.1.

LARSEN, PAUL, 43, Duke St., St. James's, S.W.1.

LEE, MISS EDITH, 28, Charlotte St., Rathbone Place, W.1.

LEE, H. MORTON, 9, Buckingham Place, S.W.1.

LEGER, J. & SON, 13, Old Bond St., W.1.

LEGGATT BROS., 30, St. James's St., S.W.1.

LENYGON & MORANT, LTD., 31, Old Burlington St., W.1.

LEVENE, M. P., LTD., Empire House, Thurloe Place, S.W.7.

LEWIS & KAYE, LTD., 13, Norris St., Haymarket, S.W.1.

LEWIS, JAS. A. & SON, 136, Brompton Rd., S.W.3.

LEYTON, H. LAW, 19A, Arundel Gardens, Kensington, W.11.

LIBERTY & CO., LTD., 210–20, Regent St., W.1.

LLOYD, FRANCIS K., 19, George St., W.1.

LOCK, R. F., 152, Brompton Rd., S.W.3.

LOEWENTHAL, L., 4, St. James's St., S.W.1.

LONGDEN, R. H. T., 2, Brunswick Gardens, W.8.

LORIES, LTD., 89B, Wigmore St., W.1.

LUMLEY, THOMAS, LTD., 3, Bury St., St. James's, S.W.1.

MAGGS BROS., LTD., 50, Berkeley Square, W.1.

MALLETT & SON (ANTIQUES), LTD., 40 New Bond St., W.1.

MANHEIM, D. M. & P., 7, Manchester St., W.1.

MANN, D. S., LTD., 120B, Mount St., W.1.

MAPLE & CO., LTD., Antiques Dept., 149, Tottenham Court Rd., W.1.

MARCHANT, S. & SON, 15 Bryan Avenue, Willesden Green, N.W.10.

MATTHIESEN, LTD., 142, New Bond St., W.1.

MEUBLES FRANCAIS, 44,

Sloane St., S.W.1.

MILLAR, CECIL, 30, Newman St., W.1.

MOSS, SYDNEY L., 81, Davies St., W.1.

MUNDEY, RICHARD, 19, Chiltern St., W.1.

NACHEMSOHN, JACOB, 130, Mount St., W.1.

NEPHEWS, 4, Hertford St., and 34, Curzon St., Mayfair, W.1.

NEWMAN, M., LTD., 43A, Duke St., St. James's, S.W.1.

NOONAN'S CORNER, 36, Old Brompton Rd., S.W.3.

NORTON, H. R. N., 46, Museum St., W. C. 1.

NOTT, CHARLES, 38, Bury St., St. James's, S.W.1.

NYMAN, CHAS. L. & CO., 230 Camden High St., N.W.1.

OAKES, JAMES, 6 Duke St., S.W.1

OGDEN, JAMES R. & SONS, LTD., 42, Duke St., St. James's, S.W.1.

OGDEN, RICHARD, 4, Princes Arcade, S.W.1.

OLD & NEW, 26, Bury St., St. James's, S.W.1.

OLD METALCRAFT SHOP, THE (Harold Casimir), 194, Brompton Rd., S.W.3.

OLIVER, HENRY, 11, Charterhouse St., E.C.1.

PAGE, F., 7 North End Parade, W.14.

PARKER GALLERIES, 2, Albemarle St., W.1.

PARKER, PHILIP & RICHARD, 98, Fulham Rd., S.W.3.

PARKES, J., 1, Burlington Gardens, W.1.

PARTRIDGE, FRANK & SONS, LTD., 144–6 New Bond St., W.1.

PARTRIDGE, GORDON C., 10, Davies St., Mayfair, W.1.

PAWSEY & PAYNE, 1, Bury St., St. James's, S.W.1.

PAYTON, Ltd., 32–4 Liverpool St., E.C.2.

PELHAM GALLERIES, 155 and 157, Fulham Rd., S.W.3.

PEREZ (LONDON), LTD., 168, Brompton Rd., S.W.3.

PHILLIPS, H., 68, Marylebone Lane, W.1.

PHILLIPS, S. J., 113, New Bond St., W.1.

PINDOCK GALLERIES, 9 Pindock Mews, W.9.

PRATT, CHARLES JAMES, 186 Brompton Rd., S.W.3.

PRATT & SONS, LTD., 158–60, Brompton Rd., S.W.3.

RAYMAN, JACK, 10, St. Alban's St., S.W.1.

READER, ARTHUR, 71, Charing Cross Rd., W.C.2.

REFFOLD, A. J. & PARTNERS, LTD., 1, Pont St., Belgravia, S.W.1.

RICHARDS, 140, Brompton Rd., S.W.3.

ROBINSON, W. H. Ltd., 16 Pall Mall, S.W.1.
ROBINSON & CANNON, 10A, Thurloe Place, S.W.7.
ROE, J. OWEN, National Provincial Bank Buildings, Southgate, N.14.
ROBINSON & WILLIAMS, 12, Baskerville Rd., S.W.18.
ROLAND, BLOWSE & DELBANCO, 19, Cork St., Old Bond St., W.1.
ROSENBERG, S. & R. LTD., 32, St. James's St., S.W.1.
ROYER-COLLARD, F. B., 124, Cromwell Rd., S.W.7.
RUDKIN BROS., 4 Paddington St., W.1.
SABIN, FRANK T., Park House, Rutland Gate, S.W.7.
SAINT, Sloane St., S.W.1.
SALE, CHARLES, LTD., 50–60 Kensington Church St., W.8.
SANDOR, A., 144, Brompton Rd., S.W.3.
SEABY, B. A. LTD., 65 Great Portland St., W.1.
SHAPLAND, 207, High Holborn, W.C.1.
SHEPPARD, SYLVIA, 71, Kensington Church St., W.8.
SHRUBSOLE, S. J., 61, Eagle St., W.C.2.
SLATTER, EUGENE, 30, Old Bond St., W.1.
SOUTH AUDLEY ART GALLERIES, LTD., 36, South Audley St., W.1.
SPANISH ART GALLERY, THE, LTD., Garden Lodge Studios, Logan Place, Kensington, W.8.
SPARKS, JOHN LTD., 128, Mount St., W.1.
SPILLER, H. J., 37, Beak St., Regent St., W.1.
SPINK & SON, LTD., 5–6–7, King St., St. James's, S.W.1.
STAAL, CHARLES, 154 Brompton Rd., S.W.3.
STAAL, I. & SONS, 138, Brompton Rd., S.W.3.
STAFFORD'S, 13A, New Bond St., W.1.
STONER, MALCOLM, LTD., 10, Davies St., Mayfair, W.1.
SUTCH, HENRY A., 11, Bury St., St. James's, S.W.1.
TESSIERS, LTD., 26, New Bond St., W.1.
THOMAS, J. Rochelle, 14, King St., St. James's, S.W.1.
THOMSON, LOCKETT, 1D, King St., St. James's Square, S.W.1.
TILLEY & CO. (Antiques), LTD., 2, Symons St., Sloane Square, S.W.3.
TITE, ARTHUR G., 30, St. George St., Hanover Square, W.1.
TROLLOPE & SONS (LONDON), LTD., 11A, West Halkin St., S.W.1.
TURNER, MAURICE H. LTD., 245, Brompton Rd.,

S.W.3.

TURNER, LORD W. & CO., 20, Mount St., W.1.

TYLER, LEITH, Pall Mall Safe Deposit, 10 St. Alban's St., Haymarket, S.W.1.

VAN, GEOFFREY, LTD., 10, Beauchamp Place, S.W.3.

VANDEKAR, E. & A., 84, Charlotte St., W.1.

VANDER, C. J. (Antiques), LTD., 58–61 Fetter Lane, E.C.4.

VICARS BROTHERS, LTD., 12, Old Bond St., W.1.

WALTER, WILLIAM, Chancery Lane Safe Deposit, W.C.2.

WALTER, GILBERT, 9, Henrietta Place, Vere St., Oxford St., W.1.

WATKINS, E. A. LTD., 51, Carey St., W.C.2.

WEBBER, F. H., 185–7, Fulham Rd., S.W.3.

WEBSTER, PERCY, 17, Queen St., Mayfair, W.1.

WELLBY, D. & J., LTD., 18 and 20, Garrick St., Covent Garden, W.C.2.

WELLS, R. G. A., 56 Beauchamp Place, S.W.3.

WHEELER, W. & SON, LTD., 23, Ryder St., St. James's, S.W.1.

WILLETT, WM. LTD., Antiques Dept., Sloane Square, S.W.1.

WILLIAMS & SON, 2, Grafton St., Bond St., W.1.

WILLIAMS, T. M., 65, Frith St., Soho Square, W.1.

WILLIAMS, Wm. (Kensington) LTD., The Doll's House, 27A Kensington Church St., Kensington, W.8.

WILLSON, WALTER H. LTD., 1D, King St., St. James's, S.W.1.

WINE, FRANK & SON, Pall Mall Safe Deposit, 10, St. Alban's St., Haymarket, S.W.1.

WINSTON, G. LTD., 272, Brompton Rd., S.W.3.

WOLFF, J. J. (Antiques) LTD., 29–30, Dering St., New Bond St., W.1.

WOOD, J., 163, King's Rd., S.W.3.

WOLSEY, S. W., 71 and 72 Buckingham Gate, S.W.1.

WOODHOUSE, A. & SON, LTD., The Silver Mouse Trap, 56, Carey St., Lincoln's Inn, W.C.2.

WOOLLETT, CHAS & SON, 59–61, Wigmore St., W.1.

WREY, DENYS, LTD., 26, Gloucester Rd., S.W.7.

WRIGHT, W., 1, Edge St., W.8.

WYBURD, LEONARD, LTD., 73, Sloane Avenue, S.W.3.

The George III Twopenny Piece

IT was owing no doubt to the inferior quality and manufacture of our coinage towards the end of the 18th century, and the large quantity of spurious copper money then to be found in the country that Matthew Bolton, manufacturer of Soho, submitted designs of coins to King George III's Government, that would make it impossible to counterfeit profitably. These designs were accepted in 1797 and the twopenny piece came into being.

Its perfection in die sinking, nicety of proportion, beauty of design, and uniformity of weight has given it an artistic position amongst our coins that has never been excelled, but its size, weight and unwieldiness, condemned it as current coinage and was only manufactured for the one year 1797.

Good specimens are yearly becoming rarer and consequently much sought after.

Weighing exactly 2 ounces, these coins were used for years afterwards as weights by small shopkeepers, innkeepers and traders.

—MESSRS. EVERSHED & SONS,
121 CHURCH ROAD, HOVE

Collecting Caucasians: A Dictionary for Reference

By R. E. G. MACEY

of PEREZ (London) Ltd.

INTRODUCTION

NOW wholly Russian, Caucasia and Transcaucasia were at one time parts of the Russian, Ottoman and Persian Empires, the old boundaries meeting at Mount Ararat, traditional resting place of Noah's Ark. Close to the cradle of civilisation, this mountainous isthmus has bred sturdy independent stock compounded of the elements of countless invasions from every direction, and this independence of outlook is expressed in their rugs by the weavers.

Being predominantly Mahommedan, prayer rugs are fairly common, but the majority follow the same pattern with a simple geometrical arch, though Kazaks may be found with an additional square set in the base of the field, and Shirvans occur with an octagonal arch attached by a short narrow neck to an oblong field. Karabaghs with a stepped arch rising at an angle of 45 degrees may occasionally be seen. All Caucasian rugs are woven with the Ghiordiz knot.

DICTIONARY

BAKU (HELA, KHILA, HYLA): From area surrounding the port of Baku on the Caspian Sea. Field usually bears a central medallion of diamond shape with heavily stepped sides, with the corners of the field stepped to match, the remainder of the field bearing a number of highly stylised decorative pear motifs. Medallion and corners usually covered with a large number of small geometric forms. Three to five stripe border; main stripe usually geometric or of barber pole type. Colours include black, brown, tan, yellow ochre, and blue, all rather dull and lustreless. Forty to a hundred knots per square inch, rather firm texture and weave inclined to be coarse. Woollen warp on one level, two shoots of cotton weft (occasionally wool) between every two rows of knots. Usually a weft selvage, but occasionally weft overcast sides.

CHICHI (TZITZI, TCHETCHEN) : From the Terek Valley, north of the main East-West range. Narrow field usually covered with a mosaic of eight-pointed stars, diamonds, or rosettes ; occasionally with pear motifs, or with two or more large geometrical figures surrounded by smaller devices, in blue, red, yellow, ivory and green on a ground usually of pale blue. Three to five stripe border ; main stripe is very characteristic and consists of stylised rosettes alternating with broad diagonal bands. Fifty-six to a hundred knots per square inch, giving a firm texture with a medium weave. Woollen warp on one level. Two shoots of woollen weft between every two rows of knots. Usually double overcast sides.

DAGHESTAN : From the Daghestan district lying to the north and east of the main east-west mountain range. One of the finest of the Caucasian group. Field covered with a mosaic pattern consisting of geometric figures or very stylised pear or floral motifs bounded by a trellis pattern. Rich colours with strong contrasts which, with the short clipped pile, gives a very clean cut effect ; colours are light and dark blue, red, yellow, ivory and green. Fifty-six to 180 knots to the square inch, giving a firm texture and fairly fine weave. Woollen warp on one level ; two shoots of woollen weft between every two rows of knots. Three to five stripe border ; main stripe either barber pole, running triangular latch hook or diamond shaped rosettes. End webs and warp fringe. Two to four cord *added* selvage at sides (see Kabistan).

DERBEND : City on the Caspian Sea half-way up the coast of Daghestan. Designs are mostly rather crude, loosely woven copies of Daghestans with a generally bolder effect, carried out in red, blue, ivory and yellow with some brown and green. A few fine old pieces exist with diamond lattice pattern containing geometrical or stylised floral forms. Forty-five to sixty knots per square inch, giving a rather coarse weave with a loose texture. Warp of wool or cotton (occasionally goat's hair) on one level ; two or three shoots of woollen or cotton weft between every two rows of knots. Pile is longer and more lustrous than that of Daghestans. Border invariably of three stripes. Usually a two or three cord double selvage at sides, though sometimes a double overcasting. Mainly a knotted selvage at ends, but quite often a broad end web.

KARABAGH : From southernmost district of Caucasia, adjacent to the Karadagh district of Persia. Oldest pieces show strong Persian influence, particularly in the borders. Patterns of fields very varied, carried out mainly in red, blue, yellow and white, though other colours may be introduced. Borders usually have a Persian type stripe flanked by Caucasian stripes. Earlier pieces have richer and less crude colouring than later examples, which are poor. Forty to a hundred knots per square inch, with a coarse weave and loose texture. Brown or white woollen warp on two levels ; usually two shoots of coarse red woollen weft between every two rows of knots. Mostly a vari-coloured two to three cord selvage at sides, though later pieces are overcast. Variable finish to ends.

KAZAK : Woven by the Kazak or Cossack tribes living in the northernmost area of Caucasia. Patterns of field are very varied and of a bold and primitive character. Many pieces have no formal design, the field bearing a heterogeneous collection of typical nomadic devices such as S-forms, eight-pointed stars and octagonal forms ; in other pieces the field may be occupied by one or more large octagons bearing smaller devices. Borders vary, but the most popular is the "tarantula" pattern—a series of eight-pointed stars with elongated interconnected arms. Colours include red, yellow, white, brown, blue, and a considerable amount of green. Forty to ninety knots per square inch, giving a coarse weave but a stout texture. The long nap (not noticeable on very old pieces) is characteristic. Woollen warp on one level ; coarse red or brown woollen weft, with from two to four shoots between every two rows of knots. Three to five stripe border, with only one of the stripes of any consequence. Double overcast sides or a three to five cord selvage. Narrow coloured end webs.

LESGHIAN : Rather rare. From the mountainous region to the north of the main east-west range in the area of the Dariel Pass. Field covered with detached geometrical designs such as eight-pointed stars, octagonal discs, and S-forms. Blue and yellow are the dominant tones, with the addition of red, brown and ivory. Two or three stripe geometrical border. Forty to ninety knots per square inch, giving a rather coarse weave of firm texture. Brown woollen warp on two levels ; single shoot of woollen weft between every two rows of knots. Two to four cord *added* selvage at sides ; end webs, finished with knots and fringes.

KABISTAN : From the south-eastern area of the province of Daghestan. Very similar to Daghestans, but with greater variety of designs. Colours are blue, red, ivory, brown, and green, but the hues are not so brilliant as those of Daghestans. Most frequent border design is a bracket motif, usually in ivory on a dark ground. Fifty-six to 192 knots per square inch, giving a moderately firm texture and a fairly fine weave. Woollen warp on one level ; two shoots (occasionally three) of woollen or cotton weft between every two rows of knots. Three to five stripe border. Warp loops at top, and warp fringe at base. One of the main distinctions from Daghestans is the weft overcast sides or, alternatively, the two cord weft selvage.

KUBA : From the town of Kuba in the south-east corner of Daghestan, once an outpost of the old Persian Empire. Rugs, more especially the very old pieces, show pronounced Persian influence in their designs which, although stiff and formal, are nevertheless definitely floral. In later pieces local influence appears, and the field is often covered with large stars or octagonal figures with serrated edges. Borders of older pieces are usually running vines with or without rosettes. Colours are blue, red, brown and green, with the addition of fawn and golden yellow in very old examples. Forty to a hundred knots to the square inch, well pressed down, giving a medium weave but a rather loose texture. Fine woollen warp on one level; two shoots of woollen weft between every two rows of knots. One to three stripe border. Sides are finished with a two to three cord double selvage of blue, while both ends have a narrow blue end web.

SHIRVAN: From the eastern part of Caucasia immediately below Daghestan, and separated from it by the main east-west range. Very old pieces now getting rare. Field usually bears several large figures joined to form a pole medallion which occupies most of the field, the remaining space being covered with small geometric devices in blue, red, green, ivory and a brown containing a suggestion of purple. Most common border is the wine glass and serrated leaf pattern, though others common to Daghestans and Kabistans may be found. In very old pieces borders may contain floral forms. Fifty-six to 140 knots to the square inch, giving a coarse to medium weave with texture rather on the loose side. Woollen warp on one level; two shoots of woollen weft (sometimes cotton) between every two rows of knots. Usually a two or three cord weft selvage, though the sides sometimes have a double overcast.

SOUMAK (SUMAK, SHEMAKHA): From the hill districts surrounding Shemakha, the capital of the Shirvan district. Pile-less rugs woven with a flat stitch, with all loose ends left hanging at the back. Fields mostly composed of three or more large diamond shaped medallions with flattened corners and incised sides. Centres of medallions and triangles left by sides of medallions carry flattened octagons with small adventitious designs. Border designs vary widely, but the outer stripe almost invariably consists of running latch-hooks. Colours mostly red and blue, with brown, white and yellow, and occasionally a rich green. Two to five stripe border; double selvage at sides, and narrow end webs.

TCHERKESS: From Circassia, the north-west province of Caucasia. Rather rare. Field displays large "sunburst" patterns in blue outlined in white on a field of reddish brown or tawny yellow, with small adventitious geometrical figures dropped willy-nilly into any blank space. Three stripe border; main stripe of "tarantula" pattern, with a narrow guard stripe on either side bearing a reciprocal saw-tooth motif. Forty to ninety knots to the square inch, giving a coarse to medium weave with a firm texture. Woollen warp generally on one level: usually two shoots (sometimes more) of woollen weft between every two rows of knots. End webs and warp fringes, with a two cord selvage at sides.

Dates of Antique Weapons

TOUCH-HOLE: Ghent, Belgium, 1247–1364.

First Hand Gun in England, 1386.

MATCHLOCK, 1509–47.

WHEELLOCK: Invented by Johann Kiefuss, Nuremburg, 1515–17.

First Rifled Barrel by Augustin Kutter, Nuremburg, 1520.

First used in England, 1635.

FLINTLOCK: 1600–1810.

Massachusetts records importation of Snaphance Weapons from Holland in 1628–29.

John Kim of Boston was making Pistols in 1720.

MIQUELET LOCK (i.e., lock showing action outside lock plate) taken from Raiders called Miqueletos of 17th and 18th century.

PERCUSSION LOCK: 1807–45.

PIN FIRE: By Lefauchaux of Paris, 1845.

RIM FIRE: By Frobert of Paris, 1847.

RIM FIRE: By Smith and Wesson, made the first .22 in 1855.

CENTRAL FIRE: 1855.

John Wigington.

TYPICAL EXAMPLES OF CAUCASIAN RUGS

Kazak

Daghestan Prayer Rug

Chichi

Shirvan

ILLUSTRATIONS BY COURTESY OF PEREZ (LONDON) LTD.

TYPICAL EXAMPLES OF CAUCASIAN RUGS

Baku or Hela — *Kazak runner* — *Kabistan*

Soumak — *Kouba*

ILLUSTRATIONS BY COURTESY OF PEREZ (LONDON) LTD.

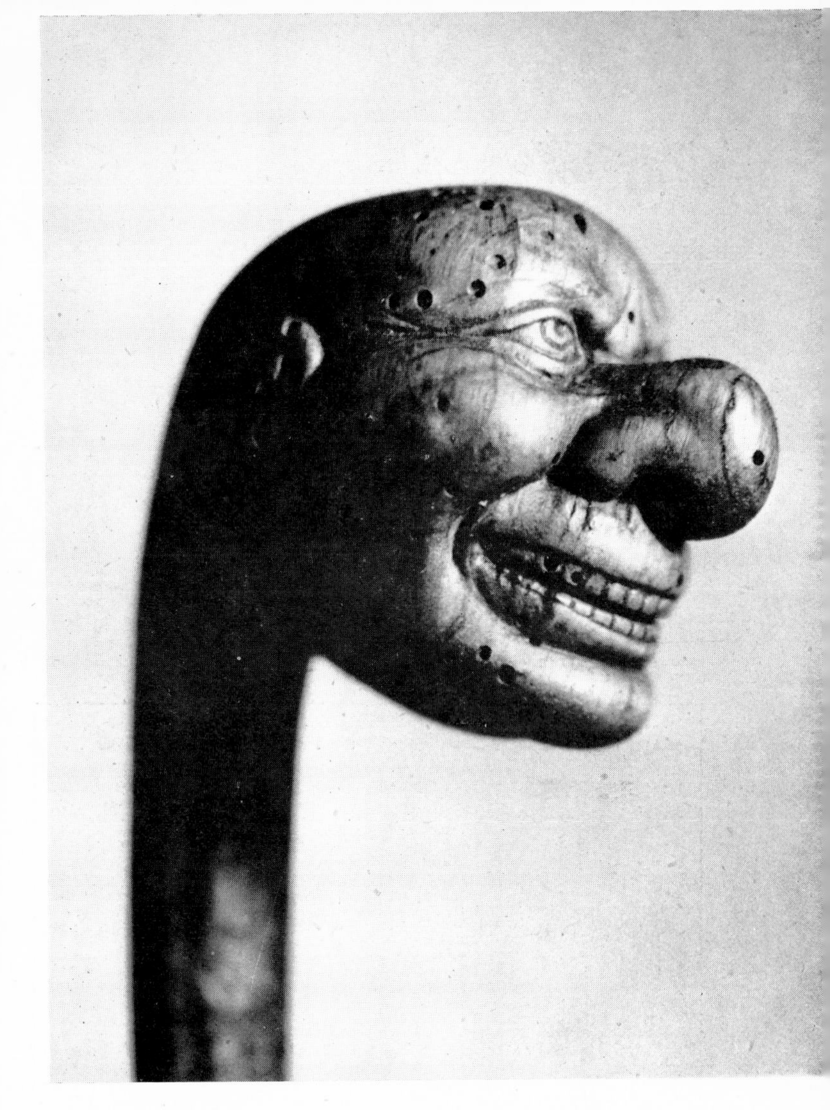

(By Courtesy of Messrs. Wykamol, Winchester.)

Our Problem Picture of the Year: Head of Walking Stick Attacked by Woodworm.

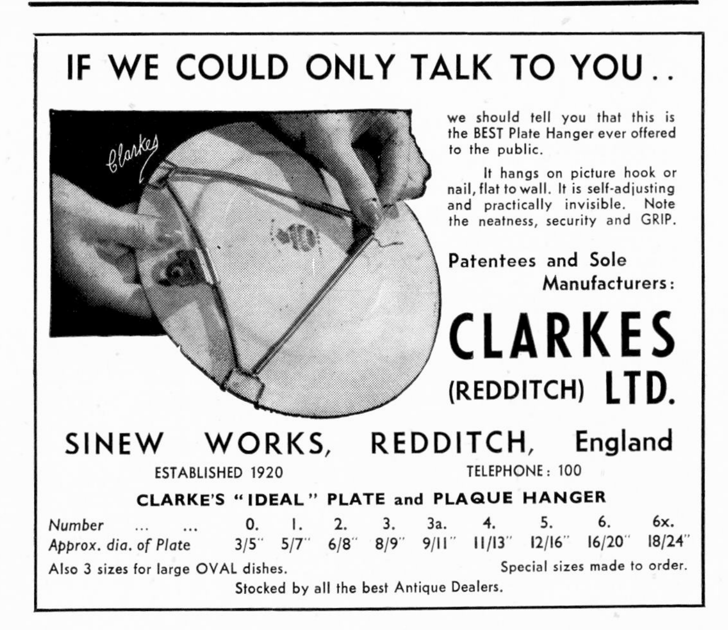
IF WE COULD ONLY TALK TO YOU . .
Clarkes
we should tell you that this is the BEST Plate Hanger ever offered to the public.
It hangs on picture hook or nail, flat to wall. It is self-adjusting and practically invisible. Note the neatness, security and GRIP.
Patentees and Sole Manufacturers:
CLARKES
(REDDITCH) LTD.
SINEW WORKS, REDDITCH, England
ESTABLISHED 1920
TELEPHONE: 100
CLARKE'S "IDEAL" PLATE and PLAQUE HANGER
Number ... ... 0. 1. 2. 3. 3a. 4. 5. 6. 6x.
Approx. dia. of Plate 3/5" 5/7" 6/8" 8/9" 9/11" 11/13" 12/16" 16/20" 18/24"
Also 3 sizes for large OVAL dishes.
Special sizes made to order.
Stocked by all the best Antique Dealers.

Ye Olde Georgian Wax

For many years we have been manufacturing polishes solely for use in the Trade. We have now perfected a Wax Polish which we feel sure will be of great interest to you, both for your own use and for re-sale. This product can be used in perfect safety on all

ANTIQUE AND PERIOD FURNITURE

As a matter of interest a tin was sent to a London Art Gallery and the following is an extract from the letter received from them : " We have tried your Wax on Old Oak Pieces as well as on Antique Walnut and Mahogany and the results have altogether surpassed our expectations. An old Table top, for example, appeared dull and lifeless at first, but after it had been polished in the prescribed manner, the surface looked really splendid."

Also 5XP French Polish Reviver and Super Chilled Wax Car Polish.

SOLE MANUFACTURERS :

J. Nicholson and Sons

LONGLANDS WORKS, WINDERMERE

The Care of Antiques

AN ANNUAL SECTION OF ADVICE ASSEMBLED FROM NEW MATERIAL PROVIDED BY AUTHORITIES ON THE VARIOUS DEPARTMENTS.

FRENCH POLISHING

Old furniture was french polished and we should like to give you some idea as to how this was, and still is, done. It has often been said that the french polishing trade holds the most carefully guarded secrets. This, we can assure you, is not true. Most polishers can, and will, tell you what to use and how to use it and it may be of interest to many if we give some idea as to the processes involved.

French polish is composed of shellac, gums and spirit. The surfaces of the work are carefully prepared, the grain being filled and the whole stained, if required. In the periods when inlays became fashionable, white polish was used, as this did not colour them, but later a stain was discovered which would darken the mahogany but not the inlays. Many of the mahoganies, such as Spanish, did not require a stain. Many believe that in those days a grain-filler was not used but that a wonderful finish was obtained by constant polishing and rubbing down, thereby filling the grain with french polish, which is applied with a cotton-wool pad after the work has been lightly rubbed over with linseed oil. Steady rubbing only is now required and this is where the so called secret of polishing comes in.

The clever french polisher can tell you what he is using and you can carefully watch him, but it is only by years of experience that the expert touch can be achieved. When the surface is fully coated, there is still surplus oil in the work and if left a few hours, the bright surface becomes dull. Now, more than ever, the expert touch is required in the process of " spiriting off." This means, taking out the oil. Apart from that applied in the first place, a few drops have been used on the rubber to prevent sticking. Methylated spirits are now used on the rubber. This softens the whole body of the polish and allows the oil to come away, leaving a skin of hard shellac. Many differing preparations can now be used to burnish but we will not weary our readers further on this subject. Many " finishes " are now used but none can compare with the old french polished surface and time only will prove how long they will last.

WAX POLISH

There are many who say, " Never use wax polish but keep the surface clean with vinegar and water." We quite agree this will keep a clean surface, but at what a cost! We have had many pieces of furniture in our workshops in the past which had been treated in this manner, and to put the matter briefly—they all needed re-french polishing. NEED WE SAY MORE ?

Any highly polished surface must be protected, and the only known protective material is wax-polish. The ideal way, of course, would be to apply raw wax but this being impossible, the waxes are mixed with spirit to allow for their application. Here again, it is surprising how few people know how to wax-polish.

The average person applies the polish, then polishes at once ; this means that practically the whole of the wax-polish is rubbed off. Wax polish should be applied and time given for the spirit to evaporate. This leaves the thin film of wax to polish, and finally a thin shell of hard wax, which keeps out the damp, protects the surface and prevents bloom.

Another great mistake is to use TOO MUCH wax-polish ; the smaller the amount you can use the better, as this avoids finger-marking later.

Many fine pieces have passed through our workshops, the surfaces of which were dull and lifeless, due to an accumulation of polish and grime, collected throughout the years. There again, in some cases, vinegar and water would have cleaned off the accumulation, but some were so deep-seated that a polish reviver had to be used.

This reviver is a combined cleaner and burnisher and is known to the trade as 5XP. It is quite a safe and simple product to use, and cannot possibly do any harm to the most delicate surface. The cleaning agent takes off the grime and the jeweller's rouge burnishes, and removes the bloom. It can also be used when carrying out the " spiriting off " process in french polishing, thereby obtaining what is known as a " piano finish." These measures are not needed in most cases.

OAK

We should now like to touch on the earlier period furniture, chiefly oak. The treatment of this is rather difficult as practically the whole of it was wax polished. Beeswax and turpentine was used and the brilliant shine obtained came only after years of rubbing—" elbow grease " they called it.

Many are under the mistaken impression that old oak must be almost black to be genuine. This is wrong, as you will quickly find if you wash off the accumulated grime and wax. Under this you will find the mellow colour so loved by experts. The late Major Birkett, for whom we had the pleasure and privilege of restoring and maintaining his wonderful collection of antiques, in his country house at Winster, always gave us the following orders when he had purchased any oak antiques—" Wash it off! "—that was all.

The procedure was then as follows ; Caustic Soda and warm water was used. This cleaned off all polish and the accumulated dirt of years. The work was then thoroughly washed down and allowed to dry out. When dry, a coat of vinegar was applied and when this had dried, the whole of the work had to be sand-papered, as the water raised the grain. This rubbing down was the most particular part of the whole proceedings. If the surfaces for waxing were not smooth, the high polish aimed at was difficult to obtain. Chilled Wax No. 1 was used. This was applied and allowed to stand 12 to 24 hours. It was then polished off and a second coat applied. The finished result, in a few hours, was equal to that obtained by years of tedious rubbing by the old method and even experts could not distinguish it from the old polish.

Should anyone wish to carry out the above method, the greatest care must be taken when using caustic soda ; rubber gloves must be worn, and splashes, especially on the face, must be avoided. This method applies only to antique oak and must not be carried out on french polished furniture.

VICTORIAN PERIOD FURNITURE

Victorian period furniture, most of which is of mahogany or faced with mahogany veneers, needs much the same treatment as that given to antiques. A good wax polish is most essential as this keeps out the damp. The glue used in those days was not waterproof; damp softens it and the veneers leave their base. Once this happens, they are most difficult to re-glue. Many have the mistaken idea that polishing is necessarily a daily or weekly job. This is not so, for furniture polished in the correct manner will retain its glossy surface for months. A clean duster is all that is required. A good test after polishing, is to see if it will finger-mark. If it does, too much wax has been used. Allow to stand for some time and then re-polish.

Before leaving the subject of " cleaning off," we should like to deal briefly with the " cleaning off," of mahogany and walnut pieces. We advocate the use of the scraper as little as possible. Use a good class stripper such as Cromit Varnish and Polish Remover. This is applied to the work with a brush, allowed to stand for a time, then the polish can be wiped off with cloths. This does not destroy the surface or raise the grain. Care must be taken however to apply turps, to counteract the stripper.

It may be a point of interest to be familiar with the recipe of the stain for mahogany, mentioned on a previous page. This stains mahogany only and will not affect lighter coloured woods. Take two ounces of bichromate of potash, one ounce of Glauber's salts, one ounce of Epsom salts and add a pint of boiling water; apply to the work with a cloth or brush and allow to dry. This will raise the grain of the wood a little and the work must be well sandpapered down. At this stage, no apparent effect will be noticed, but the application of linseed oil, and later, french polish, will bring up the old shade so admired in Spanish mahogany. This method produces very successful results on even the cheapest mahogany.

A very difficult subject to advise upon is that of scratches on furniture and in many cases, their removal is a job for the expert. 5XP Polish Reviver will not entirely remove the scratches, but it will definitely be found to be a great help. We appreciate that there are many and varied tips given for the treatment of scratches; some of which the trade read with horror and in some cases, with a smile, knowing full well there is another polishing job in the offing.

The delicate finish of either french polished or lacquered furniture will not stand up to rough usage and expert advice should always be sought before any treatment is undertaken. To fully appreciate the position, is to understand that the thickness of the polish is, in most cases, thinner than the finest paper and is, consequently, easily damaged.

Wax-polishing, correctly done; gradually, coat by coat, covers the whole surface, protecting it from damp, chemicals in the air, and bloom.

J. B. NICHOLSON.
(Authority on Furniture Polish, Windermere.)

THE PROTECTION OF FURNITURE FROM WOOD WORM ATTACK

EVERY now and then some species of animal or plant life will suddenly increase in numbers. The exact cause of such an expansion in number is seldom discovered—but there appears to be some surge of extra vitality which leads to greater prolificacy and survival. Empires rise and fall in the world of plants and animals as they do with us.

Such a development has happened of recent years with that widespread pest the "Woodworm"—the Furniture Beetle (Anobium punctatum), and all owners of antique furniture or panelling and timbering in old houses must be on their guard against an increased danger of attack.

The names of the pest—"wood worm" and furniture beetle are liable to lead to confusion, and before going further it is necessary to explain them. The "wood worm" is not a "worm" in the strict scientific meaning of the word. It is a grub or caterpillar. Let us start with the egg. This is laid by the female beetle in a crack or joint in the wood. A very small grub hatches out which at once tunnels its way into the wood and continues to do this—usually for two years—eating the wood as it goes. This is the "wood worm" stage when the damage is done. Then in the spring of its second year the grub comes up near the surface—changes first into a pupa or chrysalis and then into a beetle. During the summer months, the beetles bite their way out of the wood, mate and lay, and so another generation comes into being.

In short, the "wood worms" or grubs do the damage, the adult beetles carry on the race.

Of course there is nothing new about the furniture beetle. It is a native of this country and lives in the dead branches of trees. Any inspection of the timbers of old houses will reveal exit holes of this insect which were made possibly some hundreds of years ago. Dean Swift in the 17th century advised the use of boiling water—poured into the holes—as one means of dealing with wood worm, though it is hard to see what useful effect this could have had. It shows, however, that the insect was well known as a pest in those days.

It has been said already that the beetles are " wild animals " living in the dead wood that may be found in any garden. Hence it is always liable to attack fence posts and outbuildings made of wood. From here a short flight—for the beetles can fly—will bring them into a house. Once there the woodwork or furniture which, after all, are made of the same dead wood to which they are accustomed, affords congenial laying ground.

In the past this invasion of houses and attacks upon structural timber and furniture has been on a relatively small scale and was largely confined to furniture—that of course is how the beetle got the name. This was apt enough in the past, but is misleading to-day, since house-owners, witnessing the wholesale destruction of floorboards and joists, cannot see where the connection with furniture comes in.

Whatever is the cause of the present increase in the beetle population, the fact remains that all over the country, houses in increasing numbers are found to be seriously attacked. The timbers of lofts and cellars will often be found to have many thousands of exit holes in them. Recently in the cellar of a small terrace house the writer calculated that there must have been 20,000 exit holes in the floor boards and joists. Where such infestations are in progress, outlying colonies will be found in skirting boards, door frames and furniture in all parts of the house.

How does this affect those who collect or deal in antique furniture or who are owners of houses containing valuable timbering and panelling ? It means that there is to-day a vastly increased beetle population and in consequence that more furniture is attacked and more possible sources of infection are in circulation. The only way to overcome the danger lies in constant vigilance. The most careful search should be made for the exit holes of the insects. But remember one thing—a piece may have been infected this year and no sign of the presence of the pest will be seen until two years later, when the adults emerge. The grubs burrowing in the wood cannot be detected.

As to general precautions—if a piece of furniture has been exposed to infection, if it has been stored with pieces known to have the " worm " in them, it should be treated with a reliable insecticide. It is of course no use treating flat polished surfaces since no liquid would penetrate them, but all joints, cracks or unpolished undersides of furniture surfaces should be treated as a precaution. It is in cracks and crevices that the beetle lays her eggs. Such a treatment will prevent the grubs from burrowing into the wood and may be the means of preventing an attack. The summer months from June to August is the time when the adult beetles emerge, and if any obviously new holes or piles of powdered wood are seen they must at once be treated with an insecticide.

CLAUDE SISLEY, *Cuprinol Department, Messrs. Jenson & Nicholson, Ltd.*

A NEW PLATE HANGER

The problem with plates—that fine piece of blue and white Spode, that invaluable Worcester oddment—is how to display and at the same time keep them out of harm's way, whether in home or shop. They have a nasty way of slipping off mantelpieces, sliding off tables ; and the ingenuity of amateur, atomic man may be defied to the uttermost if he attempts to affix his treasure to the wall with string or wire, or nails or plain brute force.

Consequently all true lovers of their antique porcelain and pottery (and of their bank balance) will welcome the introduction of Clarke's Patent " Ideal " Plate and Plaque Hanger, and we describe the device here not just to gain advertising revenue, but because we feel that we are doing a real service to our readers. The " Ideal " Hanger is made of tough spring wiring, in triangular shape, with hooks at each end of the triangle, and attaches a plate to the wall in a jiffy—and almost invisibly. It is rustless, absolutely reliable, and very cheap, ranging from a few pence for the small size to under two shillings for the largest, plus, of course, the inevitable and accursed purchase tax. *Recommended.*

THE DEATH WATCH BEETLE

THE death watch beetle (*Xstobium rufovillosum*) is that ominous uninvited guest who slowly and insidiously gnaws his way through the hardest wood, assimilating its substance and destroying its strength. Many fabulous legends and ghost stories have been created as a result of this creature's habit of calling to its mate by tapping. Even now, this tapping is regarded by many as a certain indication that Death will soon cross the threshold.

Although this insect and its tapping was described so long ago as 1698, little was known of its life history and habits until recent times. Death watch beetles live their lives in four definite stages—the egg, from which emerges the larva, which in turn changes to the pupa (chrysalis) from which comes the adult beetle. The eggs are deposited in cracks and joints as with the smaller furniture beetle. They are flattened and lemon-shaped, and hatch in from two to eight weeks. The minute larva may then wander over the wood until it finds a suitable spot in which to bore. The insect remains in the larval stage of the cycle much longer than the other three stages ; in fact, the period may be prolonged to ten years where the wood is dry and hard and the atmospheric conditions fresh and cool. Where the wood has been softened by fungal attack, usually caused by damp conditions, the larvæ gnaw through more easily, and more rapidly reach the pupal stage. This is generally reached in August, and after a period of two or three weeks the adult beetle emerges to remain dormant beneath the surface of the wood until the following spring, when it gnaws its way to the surface.

Death watch beetles can fly, and their dead bodies can frequently be found in spiders' webs in windows and ventilators. The power of flight enables them to travel from their natural source, possibly a dead oak or willow tree in the garden, into a house or church, and so establish themselves in the structural timbers, furnishings, or decorations of old oak, chestnut, or other indigenous hardwood. They rarely attack softwoods, and then only when adjacent to the hardwood in which they had first established themselves.

TREATMENT

Treatment is somewhat slow and tedious, and must be carried out by workers who appreciate the significance of the work and are prepared, conscientiously and systematically, to cover every inch of the wood with a protective coating of insecticide, as well as impregnate all the timber in which the activity of the insects has been manifested by the appearance of flight holes and the little heaps of granular wood powder. The holes of the death watch are about $\frac{1}{8}$ inch in diameter, and the powder is quite characteristic, being composed of coarse bun-shaped pellets, quite easy to recognise when magnified by a powerful lens.

Impregnation is carried out by means of a pneumatic apparatus that can work at a pressure of, roughly, 50 lb. to the square inch. The injecting nozzle is tapered to fit into the flight holes, and the flow of the insecticide is controlled by a trigger-operated valve. It is not necessary to inject into every hole, as so many lead to the general ramification below the surface. In some cases a gallon or more of insecticide will be forced into one small hole, when suddenly it will squirt out ten feet or so from the point of injection. The worker will then test a number of holes until he finds one into which the fluid flows without resistance. He will then continue to force the fluid in until the space is saturated. A certain amount of experience is required to judge just when to cease injecting. With little chance of evaporating, the penetrating fluid will slowly percolate through the cellular structure of the wood, which generally is very dry and absorbent. When satisfied that there is sufficient insecticide in the wood to saturate the affected parts, the worker turns his attention to spraying the surface and into the shakes and joints. It is sometimes necessary to drill the wood to reach tenons in which activity is suspected. In fact, the worker must use his imagination quite freely when carrying out his task. It is imperative that no part of the surface, no crack, joint, or hole be left untreated if future immunity is to be assured.

The greatest activity is often found in the wall plates, studding and ends of tie beams, joists, and rafters where they make contact with the outside walls. This may be attributed to damp in the walls themselves, giving rise to fungal activity, which often precedes, and certainly encourages, insect attack.

Good ventilation has been advocated as a cure for the death watch activity, but this is not so ; it may retard the activity, but it certainly does not eradicate it. Bad ventilation encourages activity because of the damp atmosphere, which it usually creates, giving rise to fungal growth. The fact that the insects can emerge and mate without being disturbed or conveyed by air currents to the outside of the building, where no doubt many enemies await, may also account for the greater activity invariably found in unventilated corners.

S. A. Richardson, M.P.S., A.M.I.B.E.
(of Richardson & Starling Ltd., Winchester.)

A Directory of Provincial Antique Dealers

THE FOLLOWING DIRECTORY, NEW EACH YEAR, IS ALWAYS IN PROCESS OF REVISION, AND SUGGESTIONS FOR ALTERATIONS AND ADDITIONS WILL BE GRATEFULLY RECEIVED. MEMBERS OF THE BRITISH ANTIQUE DEALER'S ASSOCIATION ARE INDICATED BY ASTERISKS.

ABERDEEN, Scotland
*__Bell, John,__ 56 Bridge St.
Edwards, E. C., 16 Holburn St.
*__Young, Wm.,__ 1 Belmont St.

ABERGAVENNY, Mon.
Fine, Leo, Frogmore St.

ALTRINCHAM, Cheshire
Gilliard, L. H., 64, Manchester Rd.

AMBLESIDE, Westmorland
*Todd, Fred, The Studio, Lake Rd.
Tyson, E., Busk House.

AMERSHAM, Bucks.
Bailey, R. M., 79, High St.
*__Millard, Vyse,__ The Mill Stream.
Templeman, Constance, Old Forge.
Toovey, F. S., High St.

ASCOT, Berks.
Ascot Galleries, High St.

ASHFORD, Kent
Harper's, 1 High St.

ASHTON-UNDER-LYNE, Lancs.
*__Kenworthys, S., Ltd.,__ 226, Stamford St. (**Silver**).

AYLESBURY, Bucks.
Aylesbury Antique & Furnishing Co., 15 Temple St.
Ritchie, Rene, 16 Silver St.

BAKEWELL, Derbyshire
Broomhead, J. H., Bath St.

BALDOCK, Herts.
*Randolph, 41 High St.

BARNSTAPLE, Devon
Aze, H., 24 Litchdon St.
Aze, W., Church Lane.
Denny, M. & Son, Parish Churchyard.
Hunt, B. G., 45 High St.

BASINGSTOKE, Hants.
*Dellafera, A., New St. House (**Trade**).

BATH, Somerset
Angell, A., Pickwick Stores, Broad St.
*Angell, C., 34 Milsom St.
Ayer & Co., Quiet St.

Blackburne, M., 15 Bladud Bldgs., Broad St.
Chatelaine, The, 11, St. John's Place.
Christie, Francis, Abbey Green.
Dando, Andrew, 13, Old Bond St.
*Dickinson, D. & B., 22, New Bond St. **(Silver).**
*Dickinson, W. G. & Sons, 19 New Bond St. **(Silver)**
Georgian, Antiques, 21 Broad St.
***Gilmer, Charles T., Ltd.,** 16, Old Bond St. (**Silver**).
Lake, Charles, 31 Broad St.
Number One, Beaufort Square.
Pardon Bros., Gay St.
Savery, P., 2, Abbey St.
Smith, H. P., 36 Gay St.
Symes, F. J., 1 Barton St.

BATTLE, Sussex.
Barrow, J. W., Market Green.
McLeod, H., & Bridges, S., Old Church House, High St.

BAWTRY, Yorks.
Davison, L., Market Place.

BEACONSFIELD, Bucks.
***Brown, H. L.,** 26, High St.
Tilbury, W. E., Marlborough House, Wycombe End.
***Wood, Florence, H.,** 43–5 London End.

BEDFORD
Gedge, S. N., 19, St. Peter's St.

BEEDING, Sussex
Gray, John, " Antiques."

BELSTONE, nr. Okehampton, Devon
Moody, W. G., Brenamoor House.

BERKHAMSTED, Herts.
Norwood, F. E., Ltd., 146 High St.

BETCHWORTH, Surrey
Woodroffe, E., Ltd., Old House.

BEVERLEY, Yorks.
Tudor House.

BEXHILL, Sussex
Anderson, Malcolm, 13, St. Leonard's Rd.
Courtenay, Stanley, 9, St. Leonard's Rd.
Forge House, Old Town.
Mayfair Antiques, 37 Sackville Rd.
Thorpe, Bradley, St. Leonard's Rd.

BEXLEY, Kent
Christy's of Kent, Ltd., 52 High St.

BIDEFORD, Devon
Bishops, Ltd., 18, Market Place.
Stuart, R. A., 52 Mill St.

BILLINGHURST, Sussex
Thurlow-Smith, T., Jengers Mead, High St.

BIRKENHEAD, Cheshire
Heath, E. G. & Co., 121, Oxton Rd.
Wolfe, H., 24 Hamilton St.

BIRMINGHAM
Abbot & Attwood Antiques, 152 Alcester Rd., Moseley.

Allen, A., 12 Hill St.
*Brooks, J., 11 Woodbourne Rd., Edgbaston (**Private**).
*Davis, D. & M., 3, Livery St.
Hayes, F., 129, Broad St.
*Howell, D. R. L., 112 Alcester Rd.
Luton, C. E., 214 Broad St.
Reeve, J., Ltd., 13 Cumberland St.
*Richards, F. C., 67 Temple Row (**Silver**).
*Silvester, A. T. & Sons, Ltd., 666, Warwick Rd., Solihull.

BLACKBURN, Lancs.
Marshall, J., 1, Bolton Court.
Tierney, 13c, Astley Gate.
Tinker, F. E., 14, Mincing Lane.

BLACKHEATH, Kent
Parker, 23 Tranquil Vale.

BLACKPOOL, Lancs.
Curio Shop, 1, Queen's Square & 130, Promenade.
Speak, J., 9 Queen's Square.

BLANDFORD, Dorset
Croom, E. L., 10 Market Place.

BLEWBURY, Berks.
Warne-Browne, E., "Antiques."

BOGNOR REGIS, Sussex
Sichel, Ursula, 2, Goodwood Place, West St.

BOURNEMOUTH, Hants.
Allen, J. J., Ltd., The Quadrant.
Arts & Crafts, Fir Vale Rd.
Castle, B., 71, Poole Rd.
Fox, Chas. (Jewellers) Ltd., 21, The Arcade (**Silver**).
Geneen, Lionel, Ltd., 210, Old Christchurch Rd.
Hayes, Betty, 27, Holdenhurst Rd.
King & Hayman, 202, Old Christchurch Rd.
***Needham, Victor, Ltd.,** 8, Lansdowne Rd.
Porter, R. E., 2, Post Office Rd.
Shaw, Herbert S., 3, Yelverton Rd.
Wheatley, J. H., 844, Christchurch Rd., Boscombe.

BOURTON-ON-THE-WATER, Glos.
Dawkes, D. J., Portland House.

BOWNESS, Westmorland.
***Telford, Mr. and Mrs. T. H.,** Lake Rd.
Winder, T. H. & Co., Lake Rd.

BRACKLEY, Northants.
Chester House, 28, High St.
***Clare, John,** 28, Market Place.

BRACKNELL, Berks.
White, A. C., Priestwood House, London Rd.

BRADFORD, Yorks.
Bethell, A. E., 142, Manningham Lane.
***Croft, J. H.,** 34, Keighley Rd.
Sutcliffe, G., 372, Leeds Rd.

Thompson, R., 332, Leeds Rd.
*Tweed, J. & W., 408 Leeds Rd.
Wriglesworth, J. L., 128, Manningham Lane.

BRADFORD - ON - AVON, Wilts.
Eden, Robin, 5, Woolley St.
Pitt, David, 27 and 28, Market St.
Teed, John, 17, Silver St.

BRAEMAR, Aberdeenshire
***Bell, John,** " Antiques."

BRAMHALL, Cheshire
Burton, W., 10, Woodford Rd.
Crosdale, C., 1 Birch Rd.

BRAMLEY, Hants.
Cotter, R., " Antiques."

BRECON, Wales
Hutchinson, W. F., Llanfaes Bridge.
Odwyn-Jones, E. and I. G., 6, Ship St.

BRENTWOOD, Essex.
Miller, W. J., 49 Hart St.

BRIDGWATER, Som.
Camp, J. Blake, 67, High St.
Harding, F., 28, High St.

BRIDPORT, Dorset.
Gillham, Ernest L., 36, South St., and 42, Gundry Lane.

BRIERFIELD, Lancs.
Blakey, J. H., 5 Colne Rd.

BRIGHTON AND HOVE, Sussex

THE LANES

Chalcraft, S. H., 22, Meeting House Lane.
Coulson, E., 30, Meeting House Lane.
Coulson, M., 7, Brighton Place.
Dennett, A. T., The Lanes.
De Witt, J. W. H., 38, The Lanes.
Doyle, J. & Son, The Lanes.
Fewell, Leonard, 45, The Lanes.
Hanningtons, Ltd., Meeting House Lane.
Holgate, F., 46–50, The Lanes.
Minivers, 23, Meeting House Lane.
Otter & Moore, 6 Brighton Place.
Trevor, Margaret, (Antiques), 52, The Lanes and 15A Ship St. Gardens.
Van, Geoffrey, 47, The Lanes.
Vann, Rex, 49, The Lanes.

SHIP STREET, ETC.

*Acton, S. & Sons, Ltd., 12, Prince Albert St.
Cadman, Margaret, 25, Ship St. and 12, Marine Square.
Carmichael, Peter, 14, Ship St. Gardens.
*Davis, H. A., 10, Duke St. **(Silver).**
Dragonwyck, 59B, Ship St.
Goodleys, 24, Market St.
Ross, Samuel, 9, Union St.
Russell, Mary, 15C, Prince Albert St.
***Shann's (of Harrogate) Ltd.,** 73, East St. and 83, Marine Square.
Style, J. & D. H., 5, Duke St.
Telfer, A., 4 Prince Albert St.
Ward of Brighton, 5, Prince Albert St. **(Silver).**
Weller, J., 10, Duke St.

NORTH STREET

*Davis, W. & Sons, 26 and 56 North St. **(Silver).**
Fileman, John, 4, Upper North St.

NEW ROAD

Asquith, Cynthia, Ltd., 25 New Rd.
*Biddle Geo. & Sons Ltd., 22, New Rd. **(Pictures).**
Friar Tuck, 26 New Rd.
*Sussex Goldsmiths and Silversmiths Co., Ltd., 13, Pavilion Buildings, **(Silver).**

KENSINGTON GARDENS

Coleman, E. A., 35 Kensington Gardens.

EDWARD STREET

Arnold, C. & Son, 62–4, Edward St.
White, Anne, 179, Edward St.

KING'S ROAD

Curio Corner, 20–1, King's Rd.

Chessmen in Piccadilly: Mr. Alex Hammond with Part of his Unique Collection at 16 Burlington Arcade.

Romantic Cotswold Architecture at its Best, where Messrs. H. W. Keil Display their Fine Antiques at Broadway, Worcestershire.

Beautiful and Historic Bassetsbury Lane Mill, High Wycombe, where Mr. G. A. Turner Displays his Antiques to the Public.

" Over the Way," Lovely Guest House Associated with Mr. J. B. Wilson's Antique Business at Westerham, Kent.

Corner of one of the Showrooms in the premises of Mr. Courtney Beer, Brixham.

Kisch, A. Herbert, 34, Regency Square. (**Private**).

HOVE

Ashleys (L. Strawbaum, Ltd.), 42, Lansdowne Place.

Buckler, H., 51, Palmeira Avenue (**Silver : Private**).

Cabinet, The, 156 Portland Rd.

Choretz, H., 65, Langdale Gardens (**Silver : Private**).

*__Evershed & Sons,__ 121, Church Rd. (**Silver : porcelain**).

Moore, Phillip, 1, Victoria Terrace, Kingsway.

Treasure Chest, The, 146, Church Rd. (**Silver : porcelain**).

Ward, D. F., 90, Furze Croft, Furzehill (**Private**).

Wilkinson, W. C., 23, St. Aubyns (**Private**).

TELSCOMBE

Grey, Ernest A., Telscombe Antique Shop South Coast Rd.

BRISTOL

*Adams C. W., Denmark Avenue, Unity St.

Coopper, D., 76, Alma Rd.

Elson, W. S. Fred., Christmas Steps.

Dembo, 6, Park St. (**Silver**).

Frederick, Gordon, 42, Park St.

*Frost & Reed, Ltd., 10, Clare St. (**Pictures**).

Hall & Rohan, The Mall, Clifton.

Higgins, R., 269, Gloucester Rd. and 376 Cotham Hill.

Smith, Herbert W., 7, Christmas Steps.

Taylor, J. F. & Son, Ltd., 45, Queen's Rd.

Wheeler, O. M., 88, Queen's Rd.

BRIXHAM, Devon

*__Beer, W. J. Courtney,__ 48, Fore St.

BROADWAY, Worcs.

*__Bailey, R. Halford,__ Grey Gables.

*__Christie's,__ Yew Tree House.

*__Keil, H. W.,__ Tudor House.

BROCKENHURST, Hants.

*Blanchard, J. A. & Son, Greatham House.

BROMSGROVE, Worcs.

Townsend, W. A. & Son, 105 High St.

BUCKINGHAM

*__Trolly Hall,__ Castle St.

BUDE, Cornwall

Thorn, Spencer, 21, The Strand (**Silver**).

BUDLEIGH SALTERTON, Devon

Bavington, Guy, 30, Fore St.

*__Bennett, G. M.,__ 14, High St.

Quinneys, High St.

BUILTH WELLS, Breconshire

Knowles, Leslie, 6, Castle St.

BURFORD, Oxon.
Bowermans, High St.
***Warner, Roger,** High St.
Williams, F. A., High St.

BURY, nr. Pulborough, Sussex
Barton, The, " Antiques."
Old Forge, The, Bury Gate.

BURY ST. EDMUNDS, Suffolk
Dutton Bros., Arlington House.
Forster, John, Norman Tower House (**Prints : maps**).

BUSHEY HEATH, Herts.
Green, A. F., 193, Sparrows Herne.

BUXTON, Derbyshire
***Hockenhull, A.,** 6, Cavendish Circus.
Plant & Sons, 6, Hall Bank.
***Salt, Walter,** 42, High St.
Wooliscroft, R., 9, Hall Bank.

CAMBERLEY, Surrey.
Byrne, M. H. & E. M., 206, London Rd.
Collins, L. H., 141, London Rd.
*Weare, R., Highway Cottage, London Rd.

CAMBRIDGE
*Beazor, J. M., 80, Regent St.
Clark, M. G., 9A, Guildhall St.
*Collins & Clark, 81, Regent St.
Essex, P. W., 27, Bridge St.
*Gardner, John, 30, Trinity St. (**Prints**).
Gotobed, T. C., 12 and 18, Lensfield Rd.
Roe, G. F., 70, St. Andrew's St.
Roe, Hedworth L., 31, Trinity St.
*Stockbridge, C. H. & Son, 7-8, King's Parade.
*Stockbridge, W. & Sons, Ltd., 49, Sidney St.
Woolston, Stanley, 67, St. Andrew's St.

CANNINGTON, Som.
Harding, F., " Antiques."

CANTERBURY, Kent
Andrew, Douglas, Summerhill, Harbledon (**Spinning wheels**).
Bennett, J. & Sons, 60, Palace St.
Dawson, R. W., Tudor House, Palace St.
Elms, L. & A., 70, Broad St.
*Matthews, F. A., 25, St. Margaret's St.
McCormick, H. B., 4, Palace St.
Powell & Sons, Conquest House, Palace St.
***Stringer, W. H.,** 45-6, Palace St.

Vidler, E. M., Thanet House, Broad St.

Wheeler, 40, Burgate St.

CARDIFF

***Bents, G. E. H.,** 131B, 131C, Albany Rd.

Bond, H. J., 207, City Rd.

Jolly & Son, Ltd., 5A, High St.

Kingston Bros., 33, St. Mary St. (**Silver : porcelain**).

Philp, Alfred T. & Son, 36, Royal Arcade.

Wharton Galleries, Ltd., Morgan Arcade.

Ye Olde Curiosity Shoppe, 2, Albany Rd.

CARLISLE, Cumberland.

Clements, James W., 56, Castle St.

Rickerby, B. R., 14–16, St. Cuthbert's Lane.

Thompson, E., 15, Castle St.

CARMARTHEN

Williams, D., 19-20, King St.

CASTLE COMBE, Wilts.

Watson, Mrs. J. M.

CASTLE DONINGTON, Leics.

Astle, A., Barroon St.

CASTLE DOUGLAS, Scotland

Stuart, Miss, 234, King St.

CHALFONT ST. PETER, Bucks.

Bates, Sidney.

CHEADLE, Cheshire

Salt, Vauncey, Depleach Hall.

CHEAM, Surrey

Tracy, J. A., 37, Station Way.

CHEDWORTH, Glos.

Golding-Barrett, A., Peach Tree Cottage.

CHELMSFORD, Essex

Ratcliffe, G. T., Ltd., 24, Duke St.

CHELTENHAM, Glos.

Ashwell, Georgina, 22, Montpellier Walk.

***Asprey, Ltd.,** The Promenade (**Silver**).

Bowles, H. Carter, 6, Queen's Circus. (**Clocks**).

Bull, Audrey, 7, Royal Well Place.

***Cooper, Scott, Ltd.,** 52, The Promenade.

Dobson, R., Ormond Place.

Harding, G., 3, Suffolk Rd.

Hayman, A. & Co., 5, Queen's Circus.

Higgins, P. & Son, Oxford Buildings.

*Isher, A. H. & Son, 19, Bennington St.

Martin & Co., Ltd., The Promenade.

*Oliver, A. H., Lansdown Rd. (**Private**).

CHESTER

Catherall, A. P., 45, Watergate Row.
Clark, T. H., 15, Watergate St.
Cousens, 29, Watergate Row.
*Crawford, H. L., 49, Watergate Row.
*Kenyon, H., 21, Watergate Row.
*Lowe & Sons, 11, Bridge St. Row. (**Silver**).
Nicholas, J. P., 24, Watergate St.
*Quinneys, Ltd., 61, Bridge St. Row.
Wilman, A., 7, St. Michael's Row.
*Wilson, Wellesley, 43, Bridge St. Row.

CHESTERFIELD, Derbyshire

Hall, E. J., 11, Beetwell St.

CHICHESTER, Sussex

Batty, W., Orchard St.
Farr's Depositories, Ltd., St. John's St.
Leng, J. & Sons, East Gate.
Shackleton, G. M., The Crypt, South St.
West, 30, North St.

CHIPPING CAMPDEN, Glos.

***Woolstaplers' Hall**

CHORLTON-CUM-HARDY

Crosdale, C., 477, Barlow Moor Rd.

CHRISTCHURCH, Hants.

Arts & Crafts, 16, Church St.
Oldwoods, Ltd.
Treasure Chest, 11, Church St.

CIRENCESTER, Glos.

Blowing, F. E., 120, Gloucester St.
***Legg, E. C. & Son,** 29, Castle St.

CLACTON ON SEA, Essex

*Partridge, E. C., 80A, Station Rd.

COBHAM, Surrey

*Lock, A. W., Vine House.

COGGLESHALL, Essex

Barnes, E. A. & Son, Corner Shop, Market Hill.
Beckwith, E. W.
*Gardner, John, Bridge House.

COLCHESTER, Essex

Bond, S. & Son, 14, North Hill.
Simkins, W. R., Ltd., North Hill.

COLNBROOK, Bucks.

***Piner, Richard J.,** High St.

COLWYN BAY, N. Wales

Needham's, "Antiques."
Royle, Rhos Promenade.

CONWAY, N. Wales

"Antiques," 22, Rosehill St.
Beswick's, Rosehill St.
Dean, Aberconwy, High St.

CRANLEIGH, Surrey

*Mann, David & Sons, Ltd., High St.

CREDITON, Devon

Hall, Jocelyn, 105, High St.
Hayward, 14, The Green.

CRIEFF, Scotland

*Trotter, John, 44 Comrie St.

CROMER, Norfolk
*Antique Galleries, The, Church St.
*Levine, H., Church St. (**Silver**).
Learner, T. R., 28, Louden Rd.

CROWBOROUGH, Sussex
Cluny Gallery, 4, High St.

CULLOMPTON, Devon
Neatby, Nigel, The Walronds, Main Rd.

CULTER, Aberdeenshire
Edwards, E. C., 22, Church Terrace.

DARLINGTON, Co. Durham
Corlett, Mrs., Grange Rd.
Laybourn, M. & W., Jnr., 31, Skinnergate.
*Richardson, R., Post House Wynd.

DARTMOUTH, Devon
Richard (R. E. Martin), Hauley Rd.

DAWLISH, Devon
West, Arthur, The Strand.

DENHAM, Bucks.
Charles, P., 5, Station Parade.

DENMEAD, Hants.
Radford, P. J., Robin Hood Cottage, Furzeley Corner (**Maps**).

DONCASTER, Yorks.
Forster, Mrs. J. L., 37, Silver St.
***Peerage Antiques** (L. Spero), 36, Bennetthorpe.
Ye Olde Curio Shoppe (J. Green), 110, St. Sepulchre Gate (**Antiques, Porcelain, Pottery, Glass, Pictures, Prints, Engravings**).

DORCHESTER, Dorset
Barrett, Gordon, 18A, South St.
*Legg, E. W. J., Regency House.
Pitman, J. T., 7, Icen Way and 20, High St.
West, Lorna, 62, High West St.
*Willats, A. M., "Judge Jeffreys' Lodgings."

DORCHESTER-ON-THAMES, Oxon.
Greenwood & Clark, "Antiques."

DORKING, Surrey
*Colvin, C. E., Grange Cottage, Horsham Rd.
Jefferson, J., 18c, Horsham Rd.
Treasure Chest, The, 180, High St.

DULVERTON, Som.
Court, A. J., High St.

DUMFRIES, Scotland
Ferrow, Ross, "Antiques."

DUNDEE, Scotland
***Beaton, W. S.,** 37, Albert Square.

DUNMOW, Essex
Pole, J., 7, High St.

DUNSTABLE, Beds.
***Podd, A. L.,** 57, High St. South.

***Preston, Blaise, Ltd.**, 152, High St. North.
***Rixson, Harry, Ltd.**, Ye Olde Retreate, High St. South.
Rixson, Wm., Ltd., 26, Church St.
Wallis, P. E., 51, High St. South.

DUNSTER, Som.
Hole, A. L., " Antiques."

DURHAM
Appleton, Michael, 55, Saddler St.
Edwards, H. B., 58, Saddler St.
Walton, V., 1, Queen St.

EAGLESCLIFFE, Co. Durham.
Bouch, J. H. D., Bank Top.

EASTBOURNE, Sussex
Bonfiglioli, M., 3, Carlisle Rd.
*Bruford, Wm. & Son, Ltd., 132, Terminus Rd. (**Silver**).
Byrne, M. H. & E. M., 11, Cornfield Rd.
Corrys, 19, Cornfield Rd.
*Dew, Lilian M., 18, South St.
Goddard, 1, Cornfield Terrace.
Pickering, E., 44, South St.
Quaint Conceit, 1, Carlisle Buildings, Carlisle Rd.
Quality Corner, 55, Gildredge Rd.
Seldon's Ltd., 40, Grove Rd.
*Williams, W., 36, South St.
Wright, A. & Sons, 102, South St.

EAST GRINSTEAD, Sussex
*Streeter, R. D., 193, London Rd.

EAST MOLESEY, Surrey
*Andrade, J. F. da Costa, 26, Bridge Rd.
Smelt, A. W., 52, Bridge Rd.

EDINBURGH
Adamson, Alex., 12, Randolph Place.
Alouf, V., Bros., 39, Frederick St. (**Carpets**).
***Brown, Lea**, 290, Lawnmarket and 539 Castle Hill.
***Chernack, Harry**, 12, Rose St. (**Silver**).
***Cockburn, George**, 20, Shandwick Place (**Silver**).
Fairley & Co., 57, Frederick St.
*Hamilton, T. B., 27, Frederick St.
Henry, J., High St.
Henry, Louis, 54, Hanover St.
Herrald, F. E., 38, Queen St.
Lumsden, J. G., 4, Drumsheugh Place.
***McIntosh, J.**, 52-60, Grassmarket (**Clocks**).
Mackay & Chisholm, Ltd., 59, Princes St. (**Silver**).
McNair, Geo., 503, Lawnmarket.
McNair, R., 82, Lady Lawson St.
Miller, P. & Sons, 38, Haymarket Terrace.

An Open Letter to the Reader from THE TANTIVY PRESS.

March 1st, 1951.

Dear Reader,

You would scarcely be holding this book if you were not interested in the beautiful, good and rare. Consequently we feel that you should be apprised of certain volumes we have in stock by our leading literary author which you might care to read. The author, of course, is DONALD COWIE, poet and satirist, whose bitter-sweet, traditional poetry has earned as much appreciation from lovers of fine things as his wildly humorous novels have gained popular readers.

We have in stock, then, Cowie's *Collected Poetical Works*, Vols. I and II, 256 pp. each finely produced, both in the general edition at 10s. 6d. per volume, and in the signed and limited edition (originally 100 copies only) at One Guinea per volume.

Next we have Cowie's *Rape of Man: or The Zoo Let Loose*, the remarkable prose fantasy of which L. P. Hartley in *Time & Tide* said: " Learned, witty, light in hand, beautifully written," both in a general edition at 12s. 6d. and in a limited edition (50 only originally) at 25s.

After which there are *The Indiscretions of an Infant: or The Baby's Revenge*, 9s. 6d., and towards the end of this year, a new extravaganza of almost surrealist proportions entitled provisionally *Spinifex: or The Adventures of a Young Devil from Down-Under*, provisionally 12s. 6d.

Very sincerely yours,
THE TANTIVY PRESS.

from Tantivy House,
Tibberton, Glos.

***Neilson, George,** Holyrood Square.

Norman, R., 118, Canongate.

Small, Gordon, 90, Princes St.

White, W. T., Ltd., 36–52, Lady Lawson St.

Whytock & Reid, 7, Charlotte Square.

Wildman, Bros., 80, Princes St.

***Wilson & Sharp, Ltd.,** 139, Princes St. (**Silver**).

EGHAM, Surrey

Head, P. & Sons, 80, High St.

ELGIN, Scotland

Anderson & England, 48 and 50, Lossie Wynd.

EPPING, Essex

Nyman, Chas. L. & Co., 178, High St.

ESHER, Surrey

Lock, A. G., Esher Galleries.

*March, H. E., 91, High St.

ETON, Bucks.

*Pearson, J. A., 52B, High St.

Rye Galleries, 60, High St.

Shefford, D., 106, High St.

Taffler, M., 17, High St.

EXETER

Brock, W. & Co., Ltd., Fore St.

*Bruford, Wm. & Son, Ltd., 5, Station Buildings (**Silver**).

Gee's of Topsham, 5, Fore St., Topsham.

Mansfield, F. G. & Sons, Ltd., North St.

Murray's Antiques, Cathedral Close.

Sellicks of Exeter, 22, Cathedral Close.

Smith, R. Bradshaw, 82, Holloway St. (**Silver**).

EXMOUTH, Devon

Curtis, A. & Co., 15, Albion St.

Smith, D. & G., Market St.

FALMOUTH, Cornwall

Bailey & Co., " Antiques."

Maggs, John, 54, Church St.

FARNHAM, Surrey

*Antique Shop, Lion & Lamb Courtyard.

***Gosling, W. A.,** The Spinning Wheel.

FARNINGHAM, Kent

Chivers, Mrs. P. C., The Antique Shop.

Greenfield, E., " Antiques."

FELIXSTOWE, Suffolk

Clarke, E., 5, Orwell Rd.

Downing, S., 3, Hamilton Mansions, Hamilton Rd.

Young, P. A., 5, Crescent Rd.

FFYNNONGROEW, N. Wales

***Morris, Gilbert,** North Wales Antique Galleries.

FLIMWELL, Kent

Post Boy Antique Galleries, Hastings Rd.

FOLKESTONE, Kent
*Boughton, T. H., 22, Bouverie Rd. West.
McCausland-White, R., 41, Sandgate High St.
Michael, 130, Sandgate Rd.
Nordens, 43, Sandgate High St.

FORDINGBRIDGE, Hants.
Scamell, S. C., Avon House.

FRAMLINGHAM, Suffolk
Lanman, H. H. & Son, Castle St.

FRINTON-ON-SEA, Essex
Pickwick's Antiques, 89, Connaught Avenue.

FROME, Som.
Rawlings, Laeta, 33, Vallis Way.
Smart, F. & Co., Vallis Way.
Smart, G. F., 21, Fromefield.
Sutton & Sons, 15, Vicarage St.

GALASHIELS, Selkirk
Foley, L. D., Market St.

GARVAGH, Co. Derry, N. Ireland
Kerr, D. Glynn, "Antiques."

GERRARDS CROSS, Bucks.
Bates, Sidney, "Antiques."

GLASGOW
Alexander, B., 134, W. Nile St.
***Alexander, Ernest,** 5-9 Dundas Place.
***Bell, John,** 398 Sauchiehall St.
Bercot, Saul, Argyle Arcade, Buchanan St. (**Silver**).
Chisholm-Hunters, 27-9, Trongate.
***Kirkhope, J. L.,** 59, Cambridge St.
***Macdonald, A.,** 188, Woodlands Rd.
Megahy, Jean, 481, Great Western Rd.
***Moffat, Muirhead & Co.,** 132–6, Blythswood St.
Rushmer, J. E., 220–8 Woodlands Rd.
*Winestone, S. & Son, Ltd., 14, Newton St.

GLASTONBURY, Som.
Blackburn, N., Street Rd., and Magdalene St.
Pattemore, E. G., Somerton.

GLOUCESTER
Frith, G. C. & I., 5, 7 & 11, College St.
*Pennington, W. A., 82, Westgate St.

GODALMING, Surrey
***Brooker, A. J.,** 8 Meadrow.

GOOLE, Yorks.
Wale, Allan, 62–4 Pasture Rd. (**Trade**).

GORDON, Berwickshire
*Antiquary, The, Spottiswoode.

GRANTHAM, Lincs.
Hopkin, H., 19, Westgate.
Redmile, "Antiques."

GRASMERE, Westmorland
***Telford, Mr. & Mrs. T. H.,** How Toe.

GREAT BOOKHAM, Surrey.
Bumley, J. A., "Antiques."

GREAT MISSENDEN, Bucks.
Webb, I. F., High St.

GRIMSBY, Lincs.
Leigh, P. K. & R. H., Granby Mews, Bull Ring.

GUILDFORD, Surrey
*Gillingham, P. H., 3, Chertsey St. and Lyndhurst, London Rd.
Cranshaw & Co., Shalford Rd.
Methley, H., 18, Friary St.
*Old Metalcraft Shop, 16, Tunsgate.
*Oliver, G. & Sons, 98, High St.
Purser, H. B. & Son, Bury Fields.
Trower, Mrs. V. G., 5, Friary St.
Wells, R. G. A., Ltd., St. Catherine's House, Godalming Rd. (**Clocks**).
***Williamson, W. & Sons,** 49, Quarry St.

HAILSHAM, Sussex
Kerridge's, High St.

HAMBLE, Hants.
Channing, E., 24, Crowsfoot.

HAMPSTEAD, London, N.W.3.
Adair, Mary, Ltd., 3, Heath St.
Heath Galleries, Ltd., 89, Heath St.

HANLEY, Staffs.
Antique Box, The, 49, Piccadilly.
Steadman, J., Piccadilly.

HARROGATE, Yorks.
***Barnard, E. G.,** 1, Crown Place (**Prints**).
Beevers, A. M., 1, Montpellier Gardens.
***Blairman, H. & Sons, Ltd.,** 12, Montpellier Parade.
Bolam, G. Shaw, 29A, Parliament St.
***Cooksley, D. A.,** 6, Montpellier Gardens.
***Edwards, Thomas,** 35, Swan Rd.
*Greenwood, W. F. & Sons, Ltd., 3, Crown Place (**Silver**).
***Hardcastle, H., Ltd.,** 15, Princes St. (**Silver**).
*Hardy, E. M., 16, Montpellier Parade.
*Lumb, C. & Sons, Ltd., 34, Montpellier Parade.
*MacConnal, R., Grosvenor Galleries (**Pictures**).
*Ogden, J. R. & Sons, Ltd., 38, James St. (**Silver**).
***Old Pewter Shop, The,** 10, Royal Parade.
*Priestley, H., 99, Hookstone Drive (**Private**).
*Sanderson, F., 4, Montpellier Gardens.
Shaftoe, F. R., 15, Regent Parade.
Shutt, D. V., 17, Commercial St.
***Waddingham, W.,** 39, Swan Rd.
*Wilson, Miss N., 19, Cold Bath Rd.

HARROW, Mddlx.
Brown, Maurice, 13, West St.
Farrow, D. H., 4, Fairholme, Marlborough Hill.

HASLEMERE, Surrey
*Glover, T., Town House
***Green Frog, The,** Petworth Rd.

HASLINGDEN, Lancs.
Holt-Haworth, J., 18, Maple Avenue (**Clocks**).

HASTINGS, Sussex
*Cracknell, A. H., 39, High St.
Fine Arts (Hastings) Ltd., 78, High St.
James, 73, High St.
Palser, J. & Sons, 35, High St.
Richardson, 78A, High St.

HAWORTH, Yorks.
Hodgson, Lawson, 1, Main St.

HEACHAM, Norfolk
*Robinson, G. & Son, Pear Tree House.

HENDON, London, N.W.4.
Ingram, Richard, 48, Downage.

HENLEY - ON - THAMES, Oxon.
Clark, Douglas W., Adam House, 71, Bell St.
Giles, E., 6, Hart St.
Smith, Gregory, Maltster's House, Bell St.
Treble, H. S., Elizabethan House.

HEREFORD
Beer, H. T., 29, Church St.
*Stephens, J. W. & Sons, 26, Church St.

HERTFORD
Beckwith & Son, Old Cross.

HIGH WYCOMBE, Bucks.
Turner, G. A., Bassetsbury Lane Mill, Bassetsbury Lane, London Rd.

HIGHGATE, London, N.6.
Johnson, 68, High St.
Nicholas, 76, High St.

HITCHIN, Herts.
***Phillips of Hitchin, Ltd.,** The Manor House.
Rodwell, P. A., 7–8, Sun St.

HONITON, Devon
Adams, "East-Wing," Wilmington.
Bryant, J., 8, High St.
*Butler, G. N., Marwood House.

HOOK, Hants
Weston Galleries, Ltd., Crossways Manor

HORSHAM, Sussex
Lampard, L. E. & Sons, 23, Springfield Rd.

HULL, Yorks.
*Best, J. W., 4, Kingston Square.
***Carmichael, R. P. & Co., Ltd.,** 53–63 George St.
*Rapstone, L., 11, Savile St.

HUNGERFORD, Berks.
*Bagshaw, M. H., Friar's Pardon, Charnham St.
***Bellis, Mary,** Charnham Close.
Butters, W., Charnham St.

HUNSTANTON, Norfolk
Winlove, High St.

HYTHE, Kent
Ninnes, High St.
*Porter, C. A., 14A, High St.
ILCHESTER, Som.
*Vaux, S. & Son, "Antiques."
ILFRACOMBE, Devon
Bridgewater, G., 5, The Promenade.
Old Curiosity Shop, 6, Station Rd.
ILKLEY, Yorks.
Antiques & Arts, Brook St.
"Century Antiques, Ltd., The," 35, The Grove.
Cooper, J. H. & Sons, 33–5, Church St.
"Minton," Box Tree Cottage, 39, Church St.
Skillington, F., South Bridge Rd.
ILMINSTER, Som.
Hedgecoe, F., 7, West St.
INGATESTONE, Essex
Tunbridge, C. J., High St.
INKBERROW, Worcs.
Alldridge, N. C., Thorn Cottage.
INVERNESS, Scotland
*Fraser, A., Ltd., 7-9 Union St.
IPSWICH, Suffolk
Aprile, 1, St. Stephen's Lane.
Buck, F. M., 13, St. Stephen's Lane.
Frasers (Ipswich), Ltd., Princes St. (**Silver**).
*Green & Hatfield, Old Curiosity Shop, Northgate St.
*Silburn, C. & Son, 17, St. Stephen's Lane.
KELVEDON, Essex
Radcliffe, G. T., Ltd., Antique Shop, and "Old Queen's Head," also Durward's Hall, Rivenhall.
KENDAL, Westmorland
*Cookson, J. R., Ltd., 99, Highgate.
Gateway, The, Kirkland.
*Graves, 85, Highgate.
Raffles, Old Farm House, Wildman St.
KESWICK, Cumberland
Telford, Jas. & Son, Court Buildings (**Silver**).
Young, J. & Son, 16, Main St.
KETTERING, Northants.
*Ward, C. W., 40, Lower St. (**Trade**).
KILLIN, Scotland
Wallace, E. Stuart, "Antiques."
KINGSBRIDGE, Devon
Halsey, A. K., Boffins Boft, New Bridge.
KING'S LYNN, Norfolk
Lincoln's, 2, Saturday Market Place.
Page, G. B., 2, New Conduit St.
KINGSTON-ON-THAMES, Surrey
Smelt, A., 27, High St.
KINGSWINFORD, Staffs.
Woodall, G., Market St.
KINGSWOOD, Surrey
*Dade, C. J., Kingswood Cottage, Brighton Rd.
KINGSWORTHY, Hants.
King, Mr. & Mrs. M., London Rd.

KNARESBOROUGH, Yorks.
Driver, Ann, 48, High St.
Morrisons, Market Place.
Token House, High St. (**Horse brasses**).
KNUTSFORD, Cheshire
***Curbishley, John O.,** 72, King St.
Lee, Arthur, Hollingford House.
Shaw, J. & Sons, "Antiques."
LANCASTER
*Ordish, W. A., China St.
Wiggans, W., 31, China St.
LANGPORT, Som.
Hedgecoe, F., Picts Hill.
LAVENHAM, Suffolk
McCausland-White, R., 4, High St.
LEAMINGTON SPA, Warwicks.
Clarke, H. R., 14, Clarendon Avenue.
Eborall, 75, Clarendon St.
Greenley, A., 86, Warwick St.
Rowberry, R. E. & Son, 36, Warwick St.
LEEDS
Bulmer, G. H., 75, Raglan Rd.
Cook, A., 28, Meanwood Rd.
Cryer, P., Stocks Hill, Seacroft.
***Dimery, G. C.,** 145, Shadwell Lane, Moortown.
Hutchinson, G. F. H., Windy Lea, Lee Lane, Horsforth (**Clocks**).
***Slee, W. W., Ltd.,** 30 Duncan St.
LEICESTER
Abbey Galleries, 172, Belgrave Gate.
Bentley, Oliver, 33, Church Gate.
Jean's, 6, Rutland St.
*Law, T. E. & Son, Leicester Rd., Oadby.
Moores, W. & Son, 89, Wellington St.
Stevenson, Frank, Ltd., 8, Wharf St.
***Withers (of Leicester),** St. Martin's Galleries, Loseby Lane.
LEIGHTON BUZZARD, Beds.
*Lucking, J., 33, High St.
LEWES, Sussex
Geering, E., Cliffe Corner.
*Moore, S., 103, High St.,
Webber, A., 24, Station St.
LICHFIELD, Staffs.
Capper, C. T., 13, St. John St.
Lowrence J. A., 27, Bird St.
LINCOLN
*Cottam, C. & Son, Jews House, 15, Strait.
Morris, F. B., 5, Strait.
*Usher, J. & Son, Ltd., 14, Newland (**Silver**).
LINDFIELD, Sussex
Masters & Son, High St

LIVERPOOL
Hanover Fine Art Galleries, 37, Hanover St.
Leonard, 26, Tarleton St.,
***Maggs, J.,** 114, Bold St.
Owens, E. & Son, 5, Exchange St. East (**Chinese ceramics**).

LLANDUDNO, N. Wales
Morgan, 16, Mostyn St.
Wartski's, Mostyn St. (**Silver**).

LOOE, Cornwall
Dowland&Bray, 1666House, Fore St.

LONDON
(See Separate Directory.)

LOUGHBOROUGH, Leics.
Briggs, C. W., 10, Leicester Rd.
Lantern Galleries, Leicester Rd.
Lowe, Charles& Sons, 37–8, Church Gate.

LOUTH, Lincs.
Fytche, E. & Son, James St.
Horsewood, A., Vicker Lane.

LUDLOW, Salop.
Foxall, F. H., 17, Bull Ring, and Reader's House.
Maxwell, R., 22-3, Bull Ring.

LYME REGIS, Dorset
Antique Shop, The, 4, Broad St.
Lyme Bridge Antique Shop.

LYMINGTON, Hants.
Ford, C. & Co., Ltd., 60–2, High St.
*West, A., 38, Southampton Rd.

LYNDHURST, Hants.
Quantrell, W. S., High St.

MALDON, Essex
Morrison, C. & M., 5, Silver St. (**Clocks**).

MAIDENHEAD, Berks.
*Biggs, E. T. & Sons, Ltd., 30, High St.
Lewis, F., 49, King St.

MAIDSTONE, Kent
Draycon, W., 52, King St.
Old Malt Shovel, Broadway.
Style & Kirby, 63, King St.

MALMESBURY, Wilts.
Grabham, E. B., 32, Gloucester St.
*Hatchwell, D. I. H., 52, Gloucester St.

MALVERN, Worcs.
***Price, Miss M. W.,** Holland Cottage, Church St.

MANCHESTER
Antique Shop, The, 158, Wilmslow Rd., Didsbury.
Clark, Chas. (Antiques) Ltd., 25, Market Place.
Gilbert, Harold, 9, South King St., Ridgefield (**Silver**).
*Glass, G., Ltd., St. Ann's Churchyard (**Silver**).
Hall, J. & Co., Ltd., 56, King St.
*Henderson-White, Ltd., 95, Bridge St.
Jackson, Charles A., 12, St. Ann's Square. (**Pictures and Oriental ceramics**).
Johnson, W. E., 112, Washway Rd., Sale.

Milner, J., 63, Oxford Rd.
Neal, H. J., The Curio Shop, Cathedral Yard.
Needham, J. W. (1915) Ltd., Deansgate Arcade.
Ollivant & Botsford, Ltd., 12, St. Ann St. (**Silver**).
Treasure Chest, The, 118, Wilmslow Rd., Didsbury Village.
*Wine, F. & Son, 18, Barton Arcade, Deansgate (**Silver**).
Wolff & O'Meara, Ltd., 16, John Dalton St.

MARKET HARBOROUGH, Leics.
Burgess, Geo., Church Square.

MARLBOROUGH, Wilts.
Leadley, H. A., 100 High St.

MARLOW, Bucks.
Bishop, 8–10, West St.
Kendall & Price, High St.
*Toller, C. H. N., The Old Vicarage.

MELROSE, Roxburgh
Purves, J. & Son, Abbey St.

MIDDLESBROUGH
*Richardson, R. S., 84, Linthorpe Rd. (**Silver**).
Thorniley-Walker, Ltd., 40, Wilson St.

MIDHURST, Sussex
Payne, C. T., Knockhundred House.

MILFORD, Staffs.
Phillips, " Antiques."

MILFORD, Surrey.
*Drake, A., Portsmouth Rd.

MILFORD-ON-SEA, Hants.
Whistance, Cecil, The Old Smithy, High St.

MINEHEAD, Som.
Bullivant, J. E., 11, Park St.
Cracknell & Roberts, 19, Friday St.
White, John T., 6A, The Parade.

NANTWICH, Cheshire.
Clarke, Griffiths, 8, Dysart Buildings.
Neal, W. S., 59, Pillory St.
Myott, R. V., Churche's Mansion.
Pearson, A. H., 20, Beam St.
Smith, Paul, 12, Welsh Row.

NEWARK, Notts.
***Ford, G. W. & Son (Newark), Ltd.,** 6, Market Place (**Carpets**).
***McCarthy, F. J.,** 14, Castle Gate.

NEWBURY, Berks.
***Dower House, The, Ltd.,** London Rd.
***Jarvis, M.,** 69, Northbrook St.
***Stuart & Turner, Ltd.,** Clarendon House, London, Rd.

NEW CROSS, Kent
Lane, J. M., 147, Lewisham Way.

NEWCASTLE-ON-TYNE
Agnew, J. J. Russell, 3 & 34, St. Mary's Place.
Bell, T., 12, Saville Row.

Hill, Harold & Sons, Ltd., 12c, Saville Row.
*Reid & Sons, Ltd., 23, Blackett St. (**Silver**).

NEWCASTLE, Staffs.
Chadwick, J., 11–13, Merrial St.
Chadwick, R. A., 4, Merrial St.
Gordon, Mrs. Jane, Church Lane.
Little, H. E., Brunswick St.

NEWNHAM, Glos.
Luddington, J. B., Mount Severn (**Silver**).

NEWPORT, Isle of Wight
Nobbs & Scott, 97A, Upper Pyle St.

NEWPORT, Mon.
*Fletcher, J. Kyrle, Ltd., 79, High St.

NEW ROMNEY, Sussex.
Matthews, L. W., St. John's Priory.

NEWTON STEWART, Wigtownshire.
Stuart, Miss, 8, Arthur St.

NEWTON ABBOT, Devon
Oliver, P., 11, Market St.
Sellick, Mrs. M., Forde House, Torquay Rd.
Waite, C. & M., 3, Wolborough St.

NITON, Isle of Wight
Bright & Sons, " Antiques."

NORTHAMPTON
Baldwin, L. A., 158 Kettering Rd.
Baldwin, R. A., 182, Kettering Rd. (**Clocks**).
***Cave, F. & C. H., Ltd.,** 111, Kettering Rd.
Roberts, John, 28, Newland.

NORTHLEACH, Glos.
Brackenbury, Margaret, King's Head House.

NORTHWOOD, Middlx.
Block, S. J., 16, Wolsey Rd., Moor Park.

NORWICH
Boswell, W. & Son, Tombland. (**Pictures**).
*Brett, A. & Sons, Ltd., 42, St. Giles.
Eastoe, E., 82, St. Giles St.
Field, J. G., 3, Palace St.
Mace, M., 101A, Prince of Wales Rd.
Plowright, E. B., 14A, Princes St.
*Plowright, W. C., 1 & 29, Tombland.
Ransom, W., 18, Wensom St.
Townshend, R., 29, Elm Hill.
Watling, R., 40, St. Giles St.
*Wordingham, J. L., Hope House, Crown Rd. and Augustine Steward's House, Tombland.

NOTTINGHAM
Cameron, Malcolm, 185, Mansfield Rd.
Lee, Albert & Burton, Ltd., 88 Friar Lane & 29 Rutland St.
***Lewitt, W. A.,** 100 Friar Lane.
***Pease, W. & Son,** 86, Friar Lane.
*Turner, J. T. B., 265 Mansfield Rd.

" At number 3, Wolborough Street. Newton Abbot, in a fine Black and White building scheduled as an Ancient Monument will be found the Really Attractive Antique Shop of Mr. and Mrs. C. Waite."

Very Famous Old Antique Business—that of Messrs. Harry Rixson, Ltd., at Dunstable.

"Now on the way into Exeter enjoy an interlude in charming Topsham . . . an Excellent Antique Shop known as Gee's."

(By Courtesy of Messrs. Vesey Manor, Sutton Coldfield.)

Rare Chelsea-Derby Group, "Sacrament of Penance."

(By Courtesy of Messrs. Hallidays, 86–87 High St., Oxford.)

Fine Small Hepplewhite Mahogany Escritoire in Untouched Condition, formerly at Blenheim Palace, Oxfordshire. Circa 1780. *Height* 4 *ft.* 11 *in. Width* 2 *ft.* 6 *in.*

ODIHAM, Hants.
***Phillips, G.W.,** "Antiques"
OLD SHOREHAM, Sussex
Georgian Cottages (A. G. and E. M. Winter).
OTLEY, Yorks.
Bowes Antiques
OXFORD
*Davis, R., 34, High St. (**Silver**).
***Goodban, A. H.,** "Hallidays," 86–7, High St. and "The Antiquary," 50, St. Giles St.
Hopkins, F. A., 71, High St.
*John, C., 36, High St. (**Carpets**).
***Jones, H. W. & Son,** 1, 2 and 7, Little Clarendon St.
Oxford Gift Shop, 5, Ship St.
PAIGNTON, Devon
Manning, Commercial Rd.
Rosen, A., 1, Totnes Rd.
PATCHING, Sussex
Christopher's, Selden Manor, Arundel Rd.
PENRITH, Cumberland
Jordan, Mrs. L., Duke St.
PENZANCE, Cornwall
Ameye, H. M. & Sons, Trelawney Works, New St.
Jackson, Chas., "Antiques."
PERRANPORTH, Cornwall
Booker, Mrs. Lee, White Walls.
PERSHORE, Worcs.
Perrott House, Bridge St.
PERTH, Scotland
Deuchar, South St.
***Fettes, Wm. & Son,** 15, Atholl St.
Henderson, W. T. Graham, 5, Murray St.
***Love, Thos. & Sons,** St John's Place.
***McLeish, M. A.,** John Ruskin House, 10, Rose Terrace.
PETERBOROUGH
Potter, 293, Lincoln Rd.
***Skevington, Frank,** Stibbington Manor, Wansford.
Smith, G. & Son, Ltd., 21, Queen St.
PETERSFIELD, Hants.
Durston's Antiques, 4, College St.
PETTS WOOD, Kent
Christy's of Kent, Ltd., 181, Petts Wood Rd.
PETWORTH, Sussex.
***Denman, C. & Son,** East St.
***Streeter, Ernest & Daughter,** The Clock House, Church St.
PEVENSEY, Sussex
Mint House, The Old.
PLYMOUTH
Alvin, 51, Union St., Stonehouse, and 24, New St., Barbican.
*Andrade, R. C. da C., 7, Boringdon Villas, Plympton (**Private**).
Benton & Coleman, 30, Southside St., Barbican.
Mauretania, 43, Southside St.
Mayflower Antiques, 6, The Barbican.
Lethbridge, Island House, Barbican (**Nautical**).

Milman, S. C. L., 54, Southside St. (**Silver**).
Stevens, E. W. R., Ridgeway, Plympton.

PORLOCK, Som.
Neatby, Nigel, High St.

PORTSMOUTH, Hants.
Fairhurst, J. M., 243, London Rd.

PRESTATYN, Flint.
Owen & Hindley, Tudor House, High St. (**Furniture, glass, silver, pottery, Liverpool jugs, etc.**).
Williams, M. E., Priory House.

PRESTEIGNE, Radnorshire
Knowles, L., Belmont House.

PRESTON, Lancs.
Miller, W., 50A, Fishergate.
***Nield, E.,** 223 Corporation St.
Parkers, 91, Park Rd., & 8–10 North Rd.
Potts, M. E. & A. J., 13, Corporation St.
***Treasure, Frederick, Ltd.,** Pitt St. Galleries, Pitt St.

PURLEY, Surrey
*Fisher, H. V., 60, Russell Hill.

QUORN, Leics.
Jeboult, Mercy, 5, 7 & 9, High St.

RAMSBURY, Wilts.
Pullen, Thos., " Antiques."

READING, Berks.
Antiques, 49, London St.
*Bracher & Sydenham, 26, Queen Victoria St. (**Silver**).
Coleman, A. J., 3, Harris Arcade, Friar St.
Gemmel, F., 157, Oxford Rd.
Silver, Duke St.

REDCAR, Yorks.
*Richardson, R., Central Hall (**Silver**).

REIGATE, Surrey
Spooner, 9, West St.
*Worley & Son, 59, High St.

RHYL, N. Wales
Williams, T. C. & M., 127, High St.

RICHMOND, Surrey
Ellis, S. O. S., 1, The Green.
Duckett, L. D., Richmond Hill.
*Hotspur, Ltd., Streatham Lodge, Sheen Rd.
*Lee, R. A., 1, The Terrace, Richmond Hill (**Private**).
Lethbridge, D. J. L., 9–11, Richmond Hill.

RICKMANSWORTH, Herts.
Bruton, W. & D., 125, High St.

RIPLEY, Surrey.
*Lee H. M. & Sons Ryde House. (**Private**).
*Old Metalcraft Shop, Green Cottage.

RIPON, Yorks.
Hemsworth, " Antiques."

RIVERHEAD, Kent
*Warn, E., 50, Bullfinch Lane.

ROCHESTER, Kent
***Woollett, Chas. & Sons,** 12, 18 and 19, High St.

ROTHERHAM, Yorks.
Mason, John, Ltd., 36, High St. (**Clocks, silver, Oriental ceramics**).
ROTTINGDEAN, Sussex
Grey, E. A., Antique Shop, Telscombe.
Upward, Kittie, Lavender Cottage, Dean Court Rd.
ROYSTON, Herts.
Hardiman, P. N., Old Brewery House, Baldock St.
RUGELEY, Staffs.
Mellows, " Antiques."
RUNCORN, Cheshire.
Braverman, B., 58, High St.
RYE, Sussex
Bragge & Son, " Antiques."
Delves, W. H., Lion St.
*Gasson, H. G., Lion Galleries, Lion St.
Hargreaves, R. T., Dolphin House, High St.
Mermaid Inn.
ST. ALBANS, Herts.
*Crowhurst, W. H., 17, Holywell Hill.
Dunnings Antiques, 58, Holywell Hill.
***Lomas, W. J.,** 9, Holywell Hill, and 26, George St.
Mayles, Mayles Corner.
Norwood, F. E., Ltd., 23, Holywell Hill.
ST. AUSTELL, Cornwall
***Coon, J. Morland,** 4, Market St.
ST. IVES, Hunts.
*Smith, C. S., 9, Broadway.
ST. LEONARDS-ON-SEA, Sussex
Beeson, Rimington, 13, Marine Court.
Hartleys, 89, London Rd.
SALISBURY
***Bates, Percy H.,** 23, High St.
Denholm Drew, Ltd., 13, St. John's St.
***Hibberd & Sons,** 60, St. Ann St.
Scammel, S. C., 46, Fisherton St.
Sparks, M. T., 19, Castle St.
SCARBOROUGH, Yorks.
***Boothman & Smith, Ltd.,** 14, York Place.
Brigham, D., 9, St. Martin's Place, South Cliff.
Cranston, 14, Queen St.
Edward, Helen, Treasure House, Valley Bridge Parade.
Graham, Angus, 7, Marine Parade.
King Richard III House, Harbour Side.
*Linn, J. & Sons, Ramshill Rd.
Mann, M., 179, Columbus Ravine.
Period Antiques Ltd., 20, South St.
SEAFORD, Sussex
Old House, The, 15-17, High St.
SEDBERGH, Yorks.
*Jackson & Son, Main St.
SELSEY, Sussex
St. George's House, High St.
SETTLE, Yorks.
Robertson, Elizabeth, Bishop Court House.
SEVENOAKS, Kent
Harrison, O., 120, Tubs

Hill.
*Martin, J. & Sons, Tubs Hill
Martin & Dolton, White House.

SCOLE, Norfolk
Mallows, Jessie, "Antiques."

SHANKLIN, Isle of Wight
Gibbs, F. J. R., 76A, High St.

SHEFFIELD
Connelly, Glossop Rd.
***Ford, G. W. & Son (Newark) Ltd.,** 288-290, Glossop Rd.
Jameson, A. E. & Co., 257, Glossop Rd.
Olivant & Son, 277-99, Eccleshall Rd.

SHERBORNE, Dorest
Durrant, H., Long St.
Elliott, J. H. & G., Newland.

SHERE, Surrey
*Askew, A. G. & Son.

SHERINGHAM, Norfolk
Anderson, Topler, Station Rd.
Harrold, J. J. & Sons, Station Approach.
Harrold, W. R., High St.
Silburn, A. & E., Station Rd.

SHREWSBURY, Salop.
***Dugdale, W. G.,** 1–3, School Gardens.
Garcia, J. & F., 20, St. Mary's St.
Heywood, F. & Sons, 33, Abbey Foregate.
Lewis, G. M., 182, Abbey Foregate.
Reynolds, George L., Ltd., 4 and 5, Dogpole.
***Robinson & Co., Ltd.,** 9–10, The Square.
Ward, George, Milk St.
Wycherley, G. R. & Sons, 42, High St.
Wynn, E., 83, Wyle Cop.

SIDMOUTH, Devon
Allan, Harold, Fore St.
Huggett, C. E., Church St.
Hyatt, E. R., Old Fore St.
Winckworth, N., Church St.

SKIPTON, Yorks.
*Laycock, F., Water St.
Myers, R. N. & Son, Coach St.

SOUTHAMPTON
Leslie, C., 8A, Commercial Rd.
Prentice & Sinclair, Addis Square, Portswood.
Swaythling Antique Galleries, Mansbridge Rd., Swaythling.
Veal, A. H., 27, St. Aubins Avenue, Sholing (**Private**)

SOUTHSEA, Hants.
Beer, P., 29, Osborne Rd.
Challis, A. R., 95–7, Palmerston Rd.
Clarence, 67, Castle Rd.
*Fleming, A., Ltd., 49–57, Castle Rd.
***Moreton, C. S.,** 43, Castle Rd.
Wheeler, Edmund, 67–9, Clarendon Rd.

SOUTHWICK, Sussex
Rolan, 205, Albion St.

STAMFORD, Lincs.
*Edinborough, B., 4, St. Mary's St.
*Oates & Musson, High St.

***Scotney & Son,** The Old Crypt, 13 and 15, St. Mary's Hill.
Smith, A. F. & Son, 35, St. Martin's.

STANMORE, Middlx.
Abercorn Bookshop, 8, Stanmore Hill.

STANWAY, Essex
Partner, S. H., Wisemans, London Rd.

STEYNING, Sussex
Williams, H., 29, High St.

STIRLING, Scotland
McIntosh, I., Corn Exchange Rd.
***Yates, John & Son,** 56, Spittal St.

STOCKBRIDGE, Hants.
Scamell, T., " Sarum."

STOCKPORT, Cheshire
Milner, J., 292, London Rd.

STOGUMBER, Som.
Mullins, W., " Antiques."

STONY STRATFORD, Bucks.
***Brett, Michael,** 1, Market Square.

STOW-ON-THE-WOLD, Glos.
Pritchard, T., Cotswold House.

STRATFORD-ON-AVON, Warks.
Baker, Oliver, 40, Sheep St.
***Grainger-Brown, C.,** opp. Shakespeare's Birthplace.
Whately, J., 39, Henley St.
Wigington, C., 15, Guild St.
***Wigington, J.,** 31, Henley St.

SUNNINGDALE, Berks.
Antiques, 6, Broomfield Hall Buildings, Chobham Rd.

SUTTON COLDFIELD, Staffs.
Vesey Manor, 64, Birmingham Rd.

SWINDON, Wilts.
Cleverley, 34, High St.

TADWORTH, Surrey
Clarke, A., Burgh Heath Corner.

TAUNTON, Som.
Brunt, C. H., 66, East St.
*Franklin & Hare, Ltd., 28, Parade (**Silver**).
Halliday, F. G., Billet St.
Hughes, H., 35, Paul St.
Langford, F. J., Billet St.
*Morgan, W., East Cottage, East Reach.
*Webber, W., 12, Fore St.

TAVISTOCK, Devon
Dann, 5 King St.

TEIGNMOUTH, Devon
Extence, Thomas, 2, Wellington St.
Williams, F., Teign St.

TENTERDEN, Kent
*Boughton, T., 38, High St.

TEWKESBURY, Glos.
Abbey Antique Shop, (Capt. Sandford Shone), 62, Church St. (Main Rd. opposite the Abbey).
***Crow, T. Leonard,** Old English Ceramic Galleries, 10, Church St.

THAME, Oxon.
Arts Ltd., High St.
Beresfords, High St.
Newitt, George (Peter

Newitt), High St.
Witch Ball, The (T. Evelyn Swain), 2, Cornmarket.

THAMES DITTON, Surrey
Burge, C. P., The White Shop, Portsmouth Rd.

THAXTED, Essex.
Armigers, 4 Park St.

THORNHAM, Norfolk
Greef, A. E., High St.

TIDESWELL, Derbyshire
Lomas, Ben, " Antiques."

TITCHFIELD, Hants.
Campbell-Howes, Ltd., St. Margaret's Priory.
Collis, R. & L., 31 The Square.
Wimbush, C., 35, The Square.

TIVERTON, Devon
Stoyell, W. H. & Co., " Antiques."

TONBRIDGE, Kent
Crutch Bros., Ltd., High St.
Lawson, G. E., 165, High St.

TORQUAY, Devon
Braham, F., 4, Torwood St.
Chamberlin Galleries, St. James, Victoria Parade.
Lovegrove, F. E., 40, Tor Hill Rd.
*O'Donoghue, C. & D., 12, Victoria Parade.
Russells, 13, Fleet St.
Simpson, H. W., & Porter, D. A., 15, Torwood St.

TOTNES, Devon
Budd, 29, Fore St.
Ramsay, 49, Fore St.

TREDINGTON, Warks.
***Brown, Shirley,** The Green.
Jameson, M., The Little Shop.

TRING, Herts.
***Bly, F. S.,** 2–4, Brook St.
***Bly, John,** 50, High St.

TROWBRIDGE, Wilts.
Drinkwater, Geo., Mortimer St.
Pitt, H. B., 7, Silver St.

TRURO, Cornwall
Antique Galleries, (M. Chesterman), 20 Lemon St.

TUNBRIDGE WELLS, Kent
Ceci, J., 42, The Pantiles.
Crutch Bros., Ltd., 11, High St.
Gardner, S. A., Ltd., 18B, The Pantiles.
*Hillarys, The Pantiles.
Kent, D., 35, Crescent Rd.
Littleton Antiques, Ltd., Culverden St.
Sampson, T. G., Ltd., 103, Mt. Pleasant Rd.
Strawson, L., The Pantiles.
Wright, Whittier, 67, Grosvenor Rd.
Young, G. J. F., 78 High St.

TWICKENHAM, Middlx.
*Hoad, C. V., 2, Cypress Avenue.

UCKFIELD, Sussex.
Barton, J. H. & N., 206, High St.

ULVERSTON, Lancs.
Williams, C., 25, King St.

UPPINGHAM, Rutlandshire
*Thorpe, C. H., High St.

UXBRIDGE, Middlx.
***Turner, H. R. S.,** 2, Cross St.

VENTNOR, Isle of Wight
Antique Box, The, 76,

High St.

WAKEFIELD, Yorks.

Cooper & Launder, 11–13, Warrengate, The Springs.

WALLINGFORD, Berks.

***Summers, Davis & Son, Ltd.,** Calleva House.

WALTHAM CROSS, Herts.

***De Haan, J. & Son, Ltd.,** 73, High St. (**Trade**).

WANSTEAD, Essex

The Old Cottage, 8, High St.

WARWICK

***Grainger-Brown, C.,** 2, High St., and Oken's House.

***Quinneys of Warwick,** 9, Church St. and 7 High St.

WATFORD, Herts.

*Perry, A. E., 237, High St.

WEDNESBURY, Staffs.

*Glaze, J., High Bullen.

WELLINGBOROUGH, Northants.

Blake, Palace Buildings.

Dykes, L. T. R., Market Place.

Olde Shoppe, Sheep St.

WELSHPOOL, Mont.

*Anderson, F. E. & Son, 5–6, High St.

WEMBLEY, Middlx.

*Vanderkar, D., 31, Crawford Avenue.

WESTERHAM, Kent

Hook, John C., The Green.

Wilson, J. B., Antiques Shop, Verrals Corner, and Pitt Cottage.

WESTON-SUPER-MARE Som.

Browning, W., 12, Baker St.

Denner, E. W., 73, Orchard St.

WEST WYCOMBE, Bucks.

***Donald, Miss Irene,** Apple Orchard.

WEYBRIDGE, Surrey

Lewis, Lewis C., 17, Baker St.

*Saunders, R. 71 Queens Rd.

WHALLEY, Lancs.

Hebden M., 45, King St.

WHEATHAMPSTEAD, Herts.

Collins, " Antiques."

WHITCHURCH, Hants.

***Alliston, A. W.,** 11, London St.

*Pembery, A. C., Ltd., Dorset Square Gallery, Kingsclere Rd.

WHITCHURCH, Salop.

Hancock, F. W., 2A, Watergate St.

Wood, A. L., Ye Olde Shoppe, High St.

WIGAN, Lancs.

Sheargold, F. A., 45, Standishgate.

WIMBLEDON, Surrey

Lyons, J. H., 57, High St.

Ward, M. A., 56, Hill Rd.

WIMBORNE MINSTER, Dorset

Quarter Jack Antiques, The, 6, Cook Row.

WINCANTON, Som.

*Sainsbury, D.T., 14, High St.

WINCHESTER, Hants.

***Bell, G. H.,** 32A, The Square (**Clocks**).

Bernfeld Bros., Ltd., 101, High St. (**Silver**).
***Blanchard, J. W.,** Goodworth House, St. Cross and 48, Jewry St.
Brooks, 46, Jewry St.
Cooper Bros., 10, High St.
Heather, F. J. & Co., Ltd., 1 and 2, The Square (**Silver**).
King, Philip, 23, Southgate St.
***Spicer, Ivy,** The Casket, 2, Market St. and " Redruth," 96, St. Cross.
***Viney, H. J.,** Chesil St.
Welford, R. A. Ettrick, 22, The Square.
Winkworth, A. J., 4, Upper High St.

WINDSOR, Berks.
*Barber & Son, 3, High St.
Creak, W. Ltd., 37, Thames St.
Sheldon, 38, Thames St.
Thorne, A., Ltd., 11, Peascod St.

WITHAM, Essex
Redman, F. & Sons, 37, High St.

WITNEY, Oxon.
Castle, L. O., 108, Newland.
Granny, High St.

WOLVERHAMPTON, Staffs.
Davis, Chas., Newbridge Crescent.
Little Gallery, The, 62, Chapel Ash.
***Morris, E. J.,** 26, Chapel Ash.
Pearson's English Furniture Galleries, Chapel Ash.

WOMBOURNE, Staffs.
Battlefield Antique Shop, Stourbridge Rd.

WOODHALL SPA, Lincs.
*Best, J. F., The Broadway.

WORCESTER
***Philpott, A. J.,** 34, Sidbury.
Tolley, T., 46, Sidbury.
***Wyatt, Thomas,** The Barn, Hawford.

WORKSOP, Notts.
Bric-a-Brac, 103–5, Bridge St.

WORTHING, Sussex
Christopher's, 28, Goring Rd.
Cottage Furnishing, 43, Market St.
***Godden of Worthing,** 17, Crescent Rd.
Lines, C., 30A, High St.
Old Craft Shop, 8, Liverpool Rd.
Waldron, L., 103, Rowlands Rd.
Williams, Hugh, 126, Montague St.
Wilson, Harold, 28, High St.

WREXHAM, Denbighshire
*Goddard, Percy, 35, King's Mill Rd.

YEOVIL, Som.
Clarke, O. A., Westminster St.
***Vincent, Edgar & Son,** The Casket, 48–50, Middle St.

YORK
*Greenwood, W. F. & Sons, Ltd., 24, Stonegate.
***Hardcastle, H., Ltd.,** 31, Stonegate (**Silver**).

***Hope, Ron,** 3, Minster Gate.

***Lee, William,** 39, Stonegate.

Morrison, R., 70, Petergate.

Stonegate Furnishing Co., 41, Stonegate.

Thornton, Charles E., Adams House, Petergate and Georgian House, Blossom St.

Restorers, Cabinet Makers and Repairers

BARNSTAPLE, N. Devon
Denny, M. & Son, Parish Churchyard.

BERKHAMSTED, Herts.
Norwood, F. E., Ltd., 146, High St.

BIRMINGHAM
Nightingale, W., 154, Alcester Rd.

BRENTFORD, Middlx.
Lippiatt, J. C. (Veneers), 2, Avenue Rd.

BRISTOL
Hall & Rowan, The Mall, Clifton.

BURY ST. EDMUNDS, Suffolk
Dutton Bros., Arlington House.

CANTERBURY
Andrew, D., Summerhill, Harbledown. (**Spinning Wheels and Looms**).

CIRENCESTER, Glos.
Blowing, F. E., Corinium Cabinet Shoppe.

DOVER, Kent
Lawrence, John & Co., (Dover) Ltd., (Antique Handles).

DORCHESTER
Barrett, G., 18A, South St.

EDINBURGH
Whytock & Reid, 7, Charlotte Square.

EXETER
Mansfield, F. G. & Sons Ltd., North St.

FROME, Som.
Sutton & Sons, 15, Vicarage St.

GLASGOW
Moffat, Muirhead & Co., 132–6, Blythswood St.

GUILDFORD, Surrey
Oliver, G. & Sons, 98, 98A, 99 & 100 High St.

HARROGATE, Yorks.
Marsh, G. H., 4, Wheatlands Rd.

HASLINGDEN, Lancs.
Holt-Howarth, J., 18, Maple Avenue (**Clocks**).

ILKLEY, Yorks.
Cooper, J. H. & Sons, 33–5 Church St.

LIGHTWATER, Surrey
Noakes, W. H. W., The Folly (**China**).

LINGFIELD, Surrey
Hancock Industries, Ltd., 15, The Old Barn. Metalwork.

LITTLE WENLOCK, Salop
Shaw, H. Lloyd, The Heights (**Brass and Copper**).

LOUGHBOROUGH, Leics.
Lantern Galleries, 37, Leicester Rd.

MAIDENHEAD, Berks.
Lewis, F., 49, King St.

MINEHEAD, Som.
Cracknell & Roberts, 19, Friday St.

NORTHAMPTON
Baldwin, R. A., 182, Kettering Rd. (**Clocks**).

PENZANCE, Cornwall
Ameye, H. M. & Sons, Trelawney Works, New St.

PERTH, Scotland
Love, Thomas & Sons, Kirkside.

PORTSMOUTH, Hants.
Fairhurst, J. M., 243, London Rd.

REDRUTH, Cornwall
Andrew, M. & Co., 57, West End.

RHYL, N. Wales
Charlesworth, S. & Son, 48, Abbey St.

SHERBORNE, Dorset
Elliott, J. H. & G., Newland.

SOUTHSEA, Hants.
Ventham, J. & Son, 5, Chester Place.

STAMFORD, Lincs.
Bliss, W. H., Easton-on-the Hill.

STRATFORD-ON-AVON Warks.
Wigington, C., 15, Guild St.

STREATHAM, London, S.W.16
Walker, Jas., Ltd., Century House, Streatham High Rd. (**Silver**).

TAUNTON, Som.
Hughes, H., 35, Paul St.
Langford, F. J., Billet St.

TEIGNMOUTH, Devon
Extence, Thomas, 2, Wellington St.

THAME, Oxon.
Arts, Ltd., 23A, High St.

TITCHFIELD, Hants.
Collis, R. & L., 31, The Square.

TONBRIDGE, Kent
Crutch Bros., Ltd., 198, High St. and 11, High St., Tunbridge Wells.

WHEATHAMSTEAD, Herts.
Collins.

WHITCHURCH, Salop.
Hancock, F. W., 2A, Watergate St.

WINCHESTER, Hants.
Bell, G. H., 32A, The Square (**Clocks**).
Sayers, P. F., Volunteer Inn, Twyford (**French Polisher**).
Viney, H. J., Chesil St.

Directory of Specialists

CARPETS

Alouf, V., Bros., 39, Frederick St., Edinburgh

Arditti & Mayorcas, 22–22A, Princes Arcade, London, W.1.

Connoisseur's Corner, 17, St. Martin's and 12, Loseby Lane, Leicester.

Ford, G. W. & Son (Newark), Ltd., 288, Glossop Rd., Sheffield and 6, Market Place, Newark.

John, C., 36, High St., Oxford.

Perez (London) Ltd., 162–8, Brompton Rd., London, S.W.3. and 528 and 534, Sauchiehall St., Glasgow.

Veal, A. H., 27, St. Aubins Avenue, Sholing, Southampton (**Private**).

Vigo Art Galleries, The, 6A, Vigo St., London, W.1.

COINS

Baldwin, L. A., 158, Kettering Rd., Northampton.

Brown, Lea, 290, Lawnmarket, Edinburgh.

Seaby, B. A., Ltd., 65, Great Portland St., London, W.1.

DECORATIONS

Hammond, Charles, Ltd., 164–9, Sloane St., London, S.W.3.

Stuart & Turner, Ltd., Clarendon House, London Rd., Newbury, Berks.

Turner, Maurice H., Ltd., 245, Brompton Rd., London, S.W.3.

Wyburd, Leonard, Ltd., 73, Sloane Avenue, London, S.W.3.

EXPORTERS

Alexander, E., 5–9, Dundas Place, Glasgow.

Alexander, B., 134, West Nile St., Glasgow.

Allen, J. J., Ltd., The Quadrant, Bournemouth.

Bell, John, Bridge St., Aberdeen.

Bloom, N. & Son, Ltd., 15, Norton Folgate, London, E.C.2.

Brett, Michael, 1, Market Square, Stony Stratford, Bucks.

Cadman, Margaret, 12, Marine Square, Brighton.

Curbishley, John, 72, King St., Knutsford, Cheshire.

de Haan, J. & Son, Ltd., 73, High St., Waltham Cross, Herts.

Godden of Worthing, 17, Crescent Rd., Worthing, Sussex.

McNair, Geo., 503, Lawnmarket, Edinburgh.

Sichel, Ursula, 2, Goodwood Place, Bognor, Sussex.

Spero, L., 36, Bennetthorpe, Doncaster.

Trevor, Margaret, 15A, Ship St. Gardens, Brighton.

HOROLOGISTS

Bailey, R. Halford, Grey Gables, Broadway, Worcs.

Baldwin, R. A., 182, Kettering Rd., Northampton.

Bell, G. H., 32A, The Square, Winchester, Hants.

Bowles, H. Carter, 6, Queen's Circus, Cheltenham.

Foxall, F. H., Bull Ring, Ludlow, Salop.

Frodsham, Chas. & Co., Ltd., 173, Brompton Rd., London, S.W.3.

Holt-Haworth, J., 18, Maple Avenue, Haslingden, Lancs.

McIntosh, J., 52–60, Grassmarket, Edinburgh.

Mason, John, Ltd., 36, High St., Rotherham, Yorks.

Morrison, C., 5, Silver St., Maldon, Essex.

Neal, H. J., Cathedral Yard, Manchester.

Royer-Collard, F. B., 124, Cromwell Rd., London, S.W.7.

Streeter, Ernest & Daughter, Clock House, Church St., Petworth, Sussex.

Thornton, Charles E., Adams House, Petergate, York.

Webster, Percy, 17, Queen St., London, W.1.

Wells, R. G. A., Ltd., 56, Beauchamp Place, London, S. W. 7., and St. Catherine's House, Guildford, Surrey.

MAPS

Adams, " East-Wing," Wilmington, Honiton, Devon.

Edwards, Francis, Ltd., 83, Marylebone High St., London, W.1.

Radford, P. J., Robin Hood Cottage, Furzeley Corner, Denmead, Hants.

NAUTICAL

Lethbridge, Island House, Barbican, Plymouth.

Pitt, H. J., 27, Market St., Bradford-on-Avon, Wilts.

NEEDLEWORK & LACE

Beevers, Mrs. A. M., 1, Montpellier Gardens, Harrogate.

Shann's (of Harrogate) Ltd., 73, East St., Brighton.

Warner, Roger, High St., Burford, Oxon.

PEWTER

Cameron, Malcolm, 185, Mansfield Rd., Nottingham.

Casimir, Charles, 10, Royal Parade, Harrogate.

Casimir, Harold, 194, Brompton Rd., London, S.W.3.

Mundey, Richard, 19, Chiltern St., London, W.1.

PHOTOGRAPHY OF ANTIQUES

Anning, Ilkley, Yorks.

Cooper, A. C., Ltd., 9, Lancashire Court, London, W.1.

Fortt, Raymond, 36, Linden Gardens, London, W.2.

Gibbs, E. and D., 31, Chepstow Villas, London, W.11.

Harris, John, 45, Poole Hill, Bournemouth.

Hopkins, G. Thurston, 11, Richmond St., Brighton.

Lumsden, Fraser, 5, College Place, Southampton.

Norwood Inglis, 22, Ainslie Place, Edinburgh, 3.

Pritchard, P. E., Stow-on-the Wold, Glos.

Wallace Heaton, 127, New Bond St., London, W.1.

STAMPS

Brown, Lea, 290, Lawnmarket, Edinburgh.

Henderson, W. T. Graham, 5, Murray St., Perth.

SPINNING WHEELS & LOOMS

Andrew, Douglas, Summerhill, Harbledon, Canterbury.

WEAPONS

Norwood, E. C., Ltd., 146, High St., Berkhamsted, Herts.

Lantern Galleries, Leicester Rd., Loughborough.

Wallis & Wallis, 200, High St., Lewes, Sussex.

Wigington, John, Henley St., Stratford-on-Avon.

SPECIALISTS

WEDGWOOD

Gered (Antiques) Ltd., 10, Piccadilly Arcade, London, S.W.1.

WELSH FURNITURE

Hutchinson, W. F., Llanfaes Bridge, Brecon.

Morris, Gilbert, Ffynnongroew, North Wales

Odwyn-Jones, E. & D. G., 6, Ship St., Brecon.

Wyburd, Leonard, Ltd., 73, Sloane Avenue, London, S.W.3.

Directory of Packers and Shippers

ALLEN, J. & J., LTD., The Quadrant, Bournemouth.

BOLTON & FAIRHEAD, LTD., 106, Regent St., W.1.

BROCK, Wm. & Co., 182, Fore St., Exeter.

CAMERON-SMITH AND MARRIOTT (Proprietors: Pall Mall Deposit and Forwarding Co., Ltd.), 10, St. Alban's St., Haymarket, S.W.1.

CURTISS & SONS, LTD., 13, Clarendon Rd., Southsea.

DAVIES, TURNER & CO., LTD., 4, Lower Belgrave St., Victoria, S.W.1.

FARR'S DEPOSITORIES, St. John's St., Chichester.

FENTON, C. R. & CO., LTD., Suffield House, 79, Davies St., W.1.

GANDER & WHITE, LTD., 55, Great Ormond St., W.C.1.

PACKERS & SHIPPERS

GERHARD & HEY, LTD., 1–3, Great St. Thomas Apostle, E.C.4.

HERNU PERON & STOCKWELL, LTD., 6–8, Crutched Friars, E.C.3.

HEWETT, J. D. & CO., LTD., 98, Leadenhall St., E.C.3.

LEP TRANSPORT LTD., 16–22 Shelton St., Long Acre, W.C.2.

OSBORN TRANSPORT CO., LTD., 52, Lambton Rd., N.19.

PITT & SCOTT, LTD., 1–3, St. Paul's Churchyard, E.C.4.

MANUFACTURERS OF WOODWORM SPECIFICS

LONDON

Jenson & Nicholson, Ltd., Jenson House, London, E.15.—**Cuprinol.**

Rentokil, Ltd., London, S.W.9.—Rentokil.

WINCHESTER, Hants.

Richardson & Starling, Ltd., Hyde St.—**Wykamol.**

WOTTON-UNDER-EDGE, Glos.

Extermino Chemical Co., Ltd.—Exo Wood Worm Specific.

Skilled Export Packing—in the Specially Designed Premises of Messrs. Godden of Worthing, Leading Wholesalers.

Very Charming Period Display in the Showrooms of Messrs. Peerage Antiques Doncaster

OLD MAPS

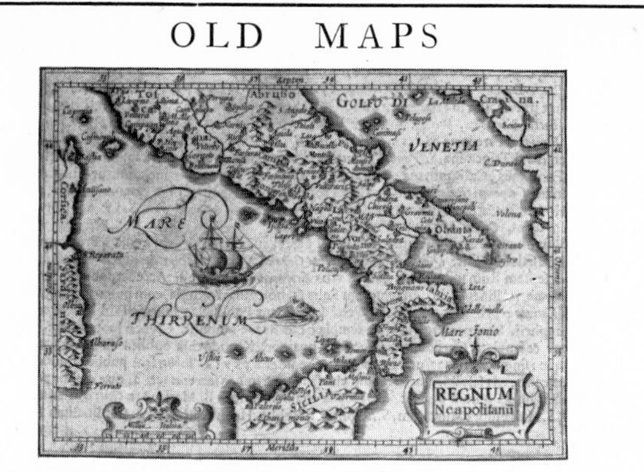

I have a large stock of early coloured maps of all counties and countries, as well as old nautical charts and road maps. Send 6d. for full lists, or call I also have coloured prints of ships, fashions, birds, flowers, and views, framed and unframed.

P. J. RADFORD

Robin Hood Cottage, Furzeley Corner, Nr. Denmead,
'Phone: Waterlooville 3063 Hants.

ALLENS

of Bournemouth

Antiques Dept.

Fine
Furniture
Porcelains
and
Objet d'Art

Illustrated

Superb Sofa Table
in faded
Rosewood

Telephone 512

J. J. ALLEN Ltd.

The Quadrant,
BOURNEMOUTH

American visitors are discovering in Britain a rich (and portable) heritage of man-made beauty.

NOTE TO AMERICAN BUYERS. To the English the past is very important and they are delighted with your appreciation of English furniture, silver, china and glass. When you have bought the antiques of your choice you will want to send them back to the United States quickly and safely, to arrive without dent, scratch or break. United States Lines have two ways of doing this. Passengers travelling in the "America" can have their purchases shipped with them, or they can make use of the special fast freight service.

Either way, U.S. Lines show by fast, careful handling their respect for precious cargo.

UNITED STATES LINES

Freight Office

38 LEADENHALL STREET, LONDON, E.C.3 · ROYAL 6677

Offices and Agents throughout Europe

Round the Antique Shops of England

THE FOLLOWING SECTIONS ARE DESIGNED TO HELP PRIVATE COLLECTORS AND TRADE BUYERS. THEY ARE RE-WRITTEN EACH YEAR AND DO NOT PROFESS TO INCLUDE ALL AREAS OR SHOPS, ONLY THOSE WHICH FIT INTO SUITABLE TOURS AND CAN OR WISH TO BE RECOMMENDED, BUT COVER THE OUTSTANDING DEALERS OF INTEREST IN A UNIQUE SURVEY WHICH IS BECOMING INCREASINGLY INFLUENTIAL EACH YEAR.

TOUR ONE

SOUTHAMPTON TO LONDON

A VISITOR arrives at Southampton, perhaps among so many others of the antiques-minded who travel on the liners *Washington* or *America* (which cater specially for buyers). He or she wants to get to work at once among the antique shops. Well, why not spend the first night in Winchester?

Few districts outside London have so many interesting antique dealers grouped together as Winchester and environs, and young Mr. J. W. Blanchard, son of a famous father in the American trade, is an acknowledged leader who will also prove a good friend. Himself an expert in Regency and Empire furniture, responsible for encouraging the present wide interest in that period, he has a very elegant black and gold shop at the centre of the town, 48 Jewry Street, and also remarkable Regency showrooms in his Georgian residence, Goodworth House, St. Cross. (To see these showrooms is, perhaps for the first time, to know Regency interiors as they originally were: a most exciting and enlarging experience.) Mr. Blanchard specialises in export and wholesale business.

The same applies to the firm of Miss Ivy Spicer, of especial interest to Americans since it was formerly established at Lexington Avenue, New York. There are a charming shop, "The Casket," in Market Street leading to the Cathedral, and a large private house at St. Cross known as "Redruth," where Miss

COOPER BROS . . .

. . . offer the largest stock of fine antiques in the district, furniture (many small pieces), porcelain, glass, etc., personally supervised by

MR. & MRS. JACK COOPER

. . . WINCHESTER

10 High Street,
('*Phone:* 4387)

Private Tel. 4736 Win.
Business 3881

Mrs. R. A. Ettrick Welford

ANTIQUES
HAND PAINTED FURNITURE
LAMP SHADES, Etc.
SOFT FURNISHINGS

ADVICE ON INTERIOR DECORATION

22, THE SQUARE
WINCHESTER

COLLECTORS' BOOKS

H. M. GILBERT

Antiquarian Bookseller, has a stock of 50,000 volumes in his 10 show-rooms at

18 and 19 THE SQUARE
WINCHESTER

Spicer sells the finest furniture, porcelain, Old Masters (particularly Dutch), silver and antique jewellery. Miss Spicer is highly recommended as a serious dealer who caters for the connoisseur.

After which visit Mr. H. J. Viney, a young dealer possessing profound knowledge particularly of fine walnut furniture: an expert who will eventually be known very widely indeed. Readers who have visited him in the past have actually written thanking us for the recommendation. The establishment is conspicuous in narrow Chesil Street, whether you enter Winchester from the Portsmouth Road, or leave the city in the direction of Petersfield, several cottages reconstructed cleverly by Mr. Viney himself into a series of intimate galleries, wherein repose such lovely and chaste examples of the finest period of English furniture as will be found in a day's march.

SUCH A RICHNESS

Or, for a general antique business of a wholly individual kind, visit Cooper Bros., at 10 High Street, at first sight a general store, but inside a labour of love where Mr. Jack Cooper and his wife have made the department their particular hobby, stocking all kinds of antiques among which you are certain to find a surprise or a bargain—perhaps the largest stock of general antiques in this area.

Such a richness Winchester contains! Now seek The Square, an ancient thoroughfare against the great cathedral, and the home of several dealers who may long be your friends. First you will see at the corner yet another fine firm of silver specialists, Messrs. F. J. Heather & Co., Ltd., whose probity and skill are the product of no fewer than one hundred consecutive years of business: a very reliable, quiet firm with the true atmosphere of the ancient guilds.

Then, nearly opposite, on no account fail to visit the unique establishment of Mr. G. H. Bell (32a The Square)—unique because it is the true clock shop of romance, yet concerned only with the very finest antique time-pieces. There are few first-class experts on antique clocks left to-day but Mr. Bell is one of them. He sells magnificent specimens, and can be entrusted with the most delicate adjustments or repairs.

Further round The Square and you come at Number 22 to the delightful shop of Mrs. Ettrick-Welford, who sells unusual little pieces of period interest, china, glass, lamps and shades, and is also—worth noting—a specialist in upholstery of antiques.

A few steps further on and the fascinating old bookshop of Messrs. Gilbert, 18 and 19 The Square, offer in ten showrooms with some 50,000 volumes a very rare collection of books not only of general antiquarian interest but also of particular interest to those who require rare works on antiques subjects.

And still Winchester is ready to delight. If the visitor now proceeds to Jewry Street and walks past Mr. Blanchard's shop to Number 46, he will find an establishment wherein the Misses Brooks conduct an extensive business in small pieces of early porcelain especially, also some fine old glass and delicate items of antique furniture—all aimed to interest genuine collectors with modest purses.

Which applies also to Mr. Philip King at 23 Southgate Street, the road leading out to St. Cross and Southampton. He sells furniture, china, glass, pictures and curios at very moderate prices indeed—so remember the Misses Brooks and Mr. Philip King if your means are straitened but you still want to buy. They really do cater for you.

STOCKBRIDGE-SALISBURY-WHITCHURCH

The time now comes to leave Winchester and explore the equally fruitful environs thereof. There is a good half-day's run of exploration, for example, to lovely Salisbury with its tallest Cathedral spire, via little, sleepy Stockbridge. In Stockbridge itself will be found at the address " Sarum " the shop of Mr. T. Scamell, who is a very real antique dealer in that he likes articles of historical and quaint interest, from weapons to musical automata, while he is always well worth contacting for his side-speciality of stone and garden ornaments.

In Salisbury there are some interesting dealers, notably Mr. Percy H. Bates, whose excellent shop will be found at Number 23 High Street in the centre of the town near the lovely cathedral. He is noted for good quality antique furniture, silver, porcelain and glass.

Equally interesting is the very old firm of Hibberd & Sons, Number 60 St. Ann's Street (the road to Southampton), not only because the fine half-timbered premises date back to 1450 (before Columbus!) but also because the proprietors are genuine tradesmen through and through, honoured by some very distinguished patrons in their time.

Then Messrs. Denholm Drew (Ralph Bull) in St. John Street specialise most usefully in several appurtenances to antiques, notably the lighting of rooms with period settings, their lamps being outstanding, while they always have antique jewellery and some pleasant French furniture.

Then return to Winchester on the Andover road, continuing from Andover to Whitchurch before turning south again. Whitchurch has at Number 11, London Street, centre of the village, the premises of Mr. A. W. Alliston, so popular and indefatigable behind the scenes of the Winchester Antique Dealers' Fair. He sells good antique furniture, china and glass.

A DAY'S DELIGHT

Or spend a day detouring as follows, first down to Southampton, which has many small dealers and at least one of importance left from the bombing—the one of importance being situated at Addis Square in the suburb of Portswood, name Prentice and Sinclair. They deal in antiques generally, porcelain and silver, with a high standard. After which continue on the Portsmouth road and do not forget to observe the hidden, charming little

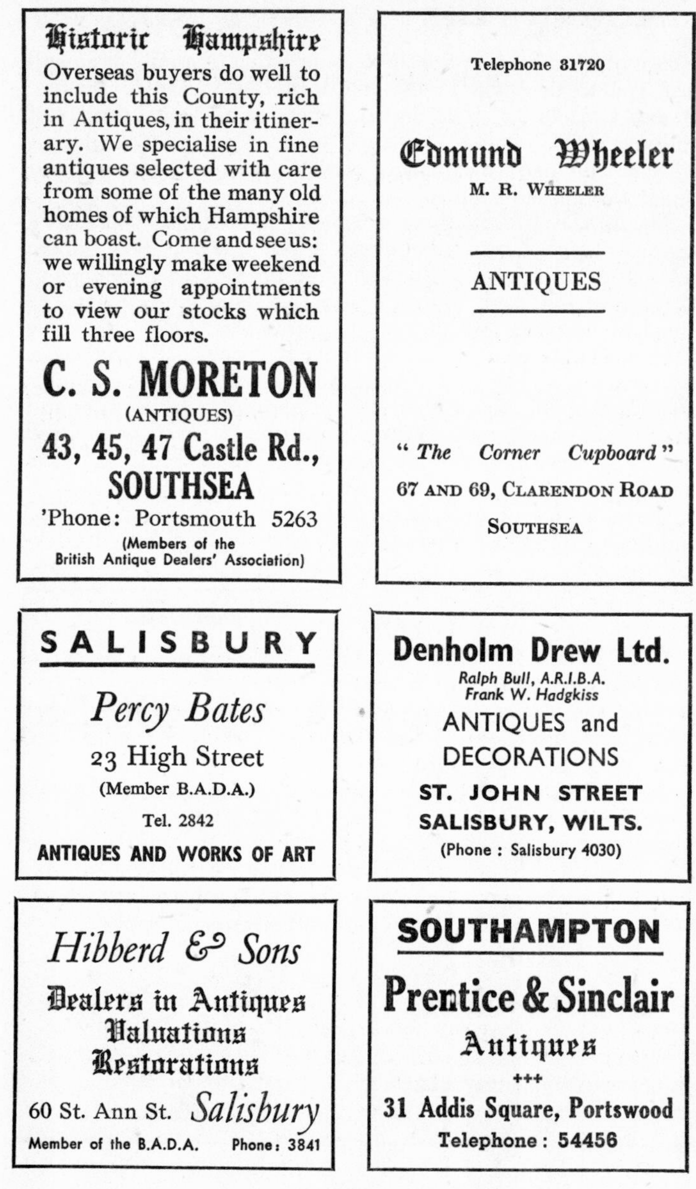
Historic Hampshire
Overseas buyers do well to include this County, rich in Antiques, in their itinerary. We specialise in fine antiques selected with care from some of the many old homes of which Hampshire can boast. Come and see us: we willingly make weekend or evening appointments to view our stocks which fill three floors.
C. S. MORETON
(ANTIQUES)
43, 45, 47 Castle Rd.,
SOUTHSEA
'Phone: Portsmouth 5263
(Members of the British Antique Dealers' Association)
Telephone 81720
Edmund Wheeler
M. R. Wheeler
ANTIQUES
" The Corner Cupboard "
67 and 69, Clarendon Road
Southsea
SALISBURY
Percy Bates
23 High Street
(Member B.A.D.A.)
Tel. 2842
ANTIQUES AND WORKS OF ART
Denholm Drew Ltd.
Ralph Bull, A.R.I.B.A.
Frank W. Hadgkiss
ANTIQUES and DECORATIONS
ST. JOHN STREET
SALISBURY, WILTS.
(Phone : Salisbury 4030)
Hibberd & Sons
Dealers in Antiques
Valuations
Restorations
60 St. Ann St. Salisbury
Member of the B.A.D.A. Phone: 3841
SOUTHAMPTON
Prentice & Sinclair
Antiques
+++
31 Addis Square, Portswood
Telephone: 54456

village of Titchfield on the right. A deviation of a mile or so will take you to the shop in the centre of this village of Messrs. R. and L. Collis, 31 The Square, where an attractive display of antiques will be found—and the craftsmen proprietors offer an efficient and most inexpensive service for the restoration and repair of antique furniture.

Thence travel to Southsea, always a good antiques centre in a region of special nautical interest. From Clarence Pier on the seafront turn into Castle Road and find the excellent premises of C. S. Moreton, Ltd., a firm which can stand with any in the kingdom as purveyors of very fine antiques. There are three floors and many pieces to see of unique importance. Then there is the fine shop of Edmund Wheeler in Clarendon Road, two minutes from South Parade Pier, a shop patronised by Royalty and particularly good for the best old furniture. It can be guaranteed that both these dealers will make the visit to Southsea really worth-while.

Hereabouts, moreover, is the headquarters of Messrs. Curtiss and Sons Ltd. (13 Clarendon Road), who are specialists in pack-

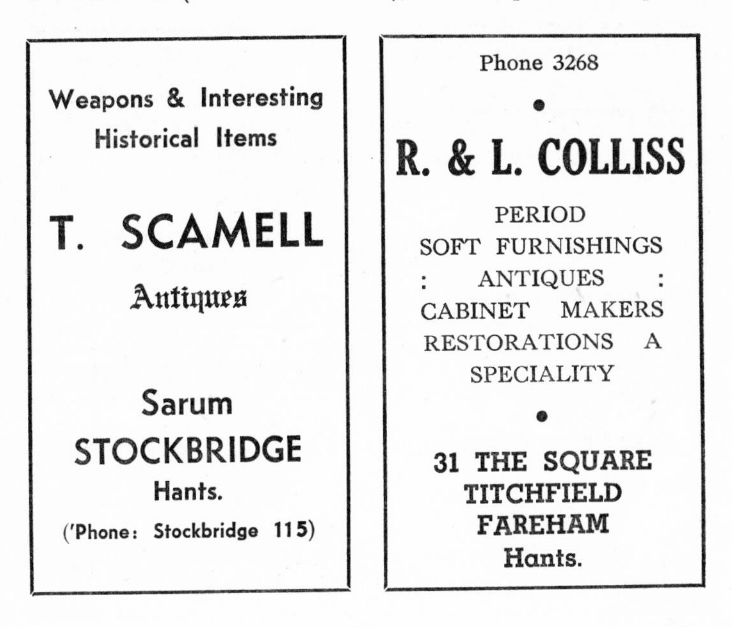

ing, forwarding and shipping antiques, with 80 years' experience, and no prejudice against accepting small jobs. They will personally attend to the packing and/or shipping of any goods you buy in Hampshire or elsewhere.

Now take the London Road from Portsmouth and climb the chalk downs to the centre of Waterlooville. Turn left where a signpost points to Denmead and Hambledon. Proceed along this very straight road for 1¾ miles, then turn left again at the first signpost. This will lead you straight to Furzeley Corner, Denmead, Hants., where at Robin Hood Cottage will be found Mr. P. J. Radford, late of Fareham, and his remarkable collection of antique maps. These are beautifully coloured across a wide range from the most valuable to those costing only a few shillings, and probably comprise one of the largest collections for sale in the country, Mr. Radford being a leading authority and foremost dealer. He sends on approval, and does a large postal business.

The main road regained, this circular tour can take you back to Winchester via Petersfield, where the shop known as Durston's Antiques, 4 College Street, sells many kinds of interesting small

antiques calculated especially to interest those who travel hopefully (an address worth noting).

And also note, while in this area, that Mr. Fraser Lumsden, of 5 College Place, London Road, Southampton, is an expert *photographer of antiques*. He did all the work for the Winchester Fair, and is most painstaking and reliable.

NEW FOREST-BOURNEMOUTH

Perhaps, however, the culminating day may be regarded as the best—a trip from Winchester to Bournemouth through the New Forest. First stop along that lovely, good road is Lyndhurst, where Mr. W. S. Quantrell has his attractive shop on the right in the High Street, a business first established in the West End of London by his grandfather a century ago. It is an important business, whose unique stock is so varied that it needs to be seen to be appreciated.

After Lyndhurst proceed through the lovely forest south to Lymington, where the old firm of Messrs. C. Ford and Co., Ltd., 60–2 High Street, have an interesting antique annexe, beautiful shopfront painted white, in which they sell pottery, porcelain, glass and small articles of the past.

Now take the Bournemouth road, and, a short distance along, turn left and travel to charming little Milford-on-Sea, where you will find the antique shop of Mr. Cecil Whistance by the village green (where he also has a cricket team!). There are two shops owned by Mr. Whistance, a famous personality hereabouts, one of them devoted to modern arts and crafts. His establishment in the narrow street by the green contains the antiques, which range over a wide field, so that there is usually something to interest collectors of all kinds.

Regain the main road after skirting the sea and gazing across to the Needles end of the Isle of Wight, then proceed the few miles to ancient Christchurch, lovely little town where the ancient priory must be visited, and just before it is reached, at 16 Church Street, a shop called " Arts and Crafts " occupying a 14th century inn, the old Eight Bells. There are modern and old sides, and the standard in the antiques department is high.

So to the main road again and onwards to Bournemouth, which is approached through the suburb of Boscombe. When Boscombe is reached look carefully on the right-hand side for the shop, 844 Christchurch Road, of Mr. J. H. Wheatley, a dealer especially in

W. S.
QUANTRELL
LYNDHURST
New Forest - Hants.
Antique Furniture
Fine Porcelain
Victorian Jewellery
Works of Art
Clocks - Copper & Brass
Main London and
Bournemouth Road
Telephones 259-148
CHARLES FOX
(JEWELLERS) LTD.
(Established 1876)
21 THE ARCADE
BOURNEMOUTH
Jewellery and
Antique Silverware
FARNHAM 6342
"The Spinning Wheel"
(WILFRED GOSLING, F.V.I., Member
British Antique Dealers' Association)
Antiques
THE BOROUGH,
FARNHAM, SURREY.

fine porcelain whose growing prosperity and reputation may be ascribed to his refusal to deceive a customer and his flair for finding old china to sell at moderate prices.

BOURNEMOUTH

Before reaching the centre of Bournemouth the Lansdowne roundabout halts traffic, and round this will be found Lansdowne Road. A few shops up on the left, Number 8, is the establishment of that fine dealer, Mr. Victor Needham, one of the best of his kind in England, whose specialities are Worcester porcelain of the Dr. Wall period, good old Staffordshire pottery, and Old Masters (though he also sells some superb 18th century furniture in several showrooms). This is a dealer who always repays visiting, good, reliable and cherished as a contact by the many readers who have got to know him through our book : heavily starred.

We have now to announce that another foremost dealer of Bournemouth, Mrs. Mary Bellis (whose shop at 3 Yelverton Road has long been famous for period furniture, particularly oak, also early fabrics, pottery, carvings, floor coverings, pictures and netsukes) has moved this year to Charnham Close, Hungerford, Berkshire. We describe this fine establishment in another section, but meanwhile would like to say that the business at Bournemouth is being carried on by Mr. Herbert S. Shaw, who is Mrs. Bellis's nephew, and who will pursue a similar policy. Good luck to your new venture, Mr. Shaw!

Bournemouth, of course, has many antique shops, but we recommend those that should be of most interest to our readers. For example, Messrs. J. J. Allen Ltd., the export packers and removal experts, exhibit a good general collection of walnut, oak and mahogany period furniture, also English and Continental porcelain, at their extensive premises, The Quadrant, Old Christchurch Road (only one minute from The Square). Keen and competitive prices are offered to the trade. Helpfulness, guidance in tasteful furnishing, and every courtesy are indeed features of this fine old firm (established 1882).

Then Mr. Whistance of Milford has a branch business known as " Arts and Crafts " in Fir Vale Road (left at Horseshoe Common after proceeding down Old Christchurch Road towards the Square from the Lansdowne). This shop, a lovely oasis amid the big-town bustle of Bournemouth, sells particularly small *objets-d'art*, with accent on the more feminine and French kind of charm.

And do not while in Bournemouth on any account fail to visit the shop in The Arcade near the Square of Messrs. Charles Fox (Number 21), which dispenses fine antique silver and jewellery, and is most enterprising in seeking to meet the requirements of collectors.

After which the short run out to Wimborne is well worth making. There, opposite the Minster at 6 Cooks Row, is an excellent business known as The Quarter Jack Antiques, offering all kinds of interesting articles gleaned from the past, good antique furniture, porcelain, pottery and glass of the kind which can be bought fruitfully by the average collector.

WINCHESTER TO LONDON

But there can be enough of everything, and the visitor will be wanting to get to London. A highly-recommended and interesting road from Winchester leads through Alton to Farnham and "The Spinning Wheel," a most beautiful half-timbered building, wherein an acknowledged expert on fine furniture, Mr. Wilfred Gosling, sells very genuine and first-rate antiques.

Now take the road out of Farnham towards Odiham, and, arrived at this pleasant village, look for the fine windows on the right of Mr. George Phillips' well-known establishment. Mr. Phillips and his wife exhibit excellent taste in the display of their fine antique furniture, porcelain and the like, but it should be expecially noted that here is an unusual sideline—in pine mantelpieces—which makes Mr. Phillips quite unique in this part of the world and well worth contacting from a distance either to buy or sell these beautiful adjuncts to the furnishing scheme.

It is a short distance only from Odiham to Hook, at crossroads on the main route to London, and a fine Georgian house to the left on the arterial highway accommodates the very large collection of antiques of Messrs. Weston Galleries, where Mr. Beardmore conducts an extensive business—in intervals of collecting old motor-cars, of which he has a large number dating back to the earliest days of motoring. (He would always like to hear from anyone who shares this interest, and please mention *The Antiques Year Book*.) Weston Galleries specialise in walnut furniture, Regency chiffoniers, bookcases, brass inlaid chairs, Knole settees, wing chairs and pillar diners.

Now take the London road through to Camberley, where there are two excellent dealers. Look for the " Three Postboys," a 17th century coaching inn (in former highwaymen's country). This is scheduled as an ancient building, and is a fitting home for the antiques of Messrs. Byrne, who sell furniture, china and glass, and cater specially for the trade.

Similarly the other Camberley dealer, Mr. Lewis H. Collins, of 141 London Road, takes the trouble to cater specially—in his case for visitors from across the Atlantic. He has himself paid no fewer than sixteen personal visits to the United States, so knows the requirements well, and his stock contains lots of the type of goods most in demand on the other side.

After Camberley proceed to Bagshot, turn right to Chobham, and thence to Weybridge, where you will find at Number 17 Baker Street, the shop of Messrs. Lewis C. Lewis, very attractive with low window giving a good view of the whole interior, which is hung throughout in grey material. This firm offers pictures, furniture (small choice pieces) and works of art generally, tastefully shown and at prices to suit all pockets.

Afterwards—to London. The suburban areas can be dealt with at another time.

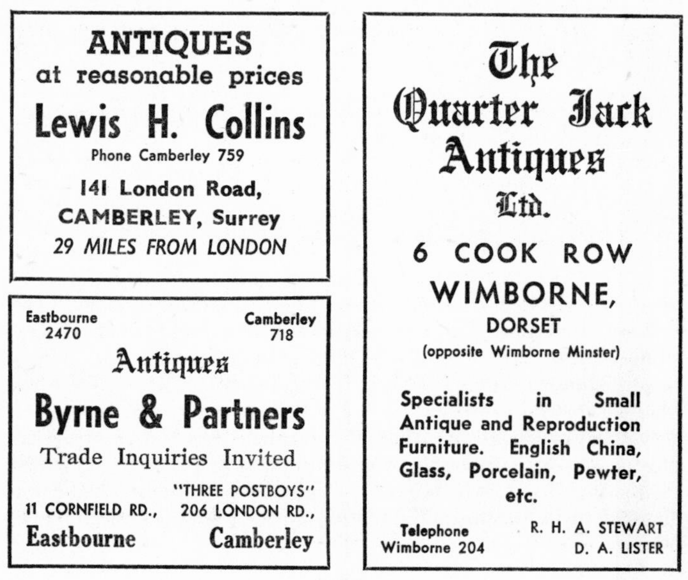

ROUND THE ANTIQUE SHOPS

TOUR TWO

WEST COUNTRY

SEVERAL tours are given in this book but none is quite so replete with antiques and pure English territorial interest as the present. It is most comprehensive, and can be taken in parts if necessary, but the reader will find that with almost transatlantic efficiency we cover everything of recommended interest in the wide, lovely area. Should the tour be too long for some, we suggest that bases be established at say, Exeter, Bath, Cheltenham.

The route Westward Ho can start via Hyde Park Corner, Brentford and Hounslow to Colnbrook—watch for a deviation sign on the left. Colnbrook, only a mile or two from London Airport, is a pleasant village, and the bright and immaculate premises at the centre thereof belong to Mr. Richard J. Piner, a young man who combines energy with a wealth of trade knowledge. He always has several of the small pieces of furniture, china and *objets d'art* which the average collector looks for nowadays : and the cars constantly calling at his premises betoken the popularity of his bargains.

After which run through Slough and Maidenhead to beautiful Henley-on-Thames. You have to turn right in the centre and proceed along Bell Street as the main Oxford Road, and will find on the left at Number 71 Bell Street the exquisitely-appointed Adam House, wherein Mr. Douglas Clark and his partner display a very sure taste in their presentation of late 18th century, Regency and early Victorian furniture, porcelain and period items. There is an export trade department which caters for American buyers of Victoriana. We understand, however, that even some good local customers have been known to buy wax fruits in addition to lovely 18th century pieces. This is a very interesting firm.

Next starred town along the road is Wallingford, where a great stone Thames bridge links Berkshire with Oxfordshire, and where the inhabitants take due pride in the fact that they possess the oldest Charter in England, date 1155. Near the bridge, on the left as you enter the town, Messrs. Summers, Davis and Son Ltd. have a well-varied display of antiques, where a motto of " lovely furnishings for lovely homes " might well be justified. This is claimed to be the most fascinating antique shop in the Thames Valley.

A few miles further on the Oxford road is Dorchester-on-Thames, one of the earliest Christian settlements in England (site of the Abbey dating back to A.D. 635). On the left as you enter the village look carefully for Messrs. Greenwood and Clark's fine antique shop, with the interesting specialities of Georgian mirrors and table silver.

NEWBURY'S FAME

Now return to Wallingford and take the road to Didcot and Harwell (atomic research centres to be passed with averted eyes), and turn left at Harwell for the main road to Newbury, which has a far more pleasant fame, being not only a charming, typically English country town, but also the home of three very well-known and trustworthy antiques establishments. Turn left as you enter the town and on the main London road at the left will be found Clarendon House, an old Georgian mansion adjoining the equally famous Dower House.

This Clarendon House is the headquarters of one of the leading firms of antique dealers in the provinces, Stuart and Turner, Ltd., of which one of the Directors, Mr. Cecil F. Turner, is Chairman of the Antique Dealers' Fair at Grosvenor House, and has been President of the British Antique Dealers' Association. There are extensive and tastefully arranged showrooms, displaying only genuine period antiques and works of art (very high standard), which are chosen for design, colour and quality.

Messrs. Stuart and Turner, specialising in oak, walnut and mahogany furniture, display Regency material also as well as porcelain, glass and silver. They carry out a very considerable amount of interior decoration, and have the highest reputation not only in this country but also in the United States. *Every antique sold by them carries a written guarantee as to its period and authenticity.*

These remarks similarly apply to the Dower House next door, Messrs. Clifford's equally well-known and fine establishment. The premises were formerly " The King's Arms," one of the most celebrated posting houses between London and Bath. The present imposing front, considered to be among the best-balanced examples of simple Georgian architecture, was added about

Within the Well-known Antique Shop of Messrs. Scotney & Son, Stamford, Lincs.

(*By Courtesy of Messrs. Roger Warner, Burford, Oxon*

Dresden Teaset in Original Case with Toilet and Writing Requisites for Taking in a Coach when Travelling, circa 1790.

Oak Snap-top Table with Quatrefoil Base.

BRADFORD-ON-AVON
NEAR BATH.
TITHE BARN ◦ ANCIENT CHAPEL ON BRIDGE ◦ SAXON CHURCH
JOHN TEED
The Pink House,
17 SILVER STREET,
BRADFORD-ON-AVON, Wilts.
Visit our seven large showrooms displaying a choice stock of Georgian, Regency and French furniture, Works of Art, English and Continental Porcelain, Pottery, Objects d'Art, Period Wallpaper
DECORATIONS
GARDEN FURNITURE
Trade Invited
'Phone : Bradford-on-Avon 3370
DAVID PITT
27 MARKET STREET
& at Town Hall Showrooms,
BRADFORD-ON-AVON,
Wilts.
ANTIQUES &
CURIOS
Trade Enquiries Invited
Telephone :
Bradford-on-Avon 2349
ROBIN EDEN
5 WOOLLEY STREET, BRADFORD-ON-AVON, Wilts.
Telephone : BRADFORD-ON-AVON 3369
OLD ENGLISH FURNITURE, CHINA, PICTURES,
GLASS, IRON & STONE WORK

1730. (Previously the inn was a simple Tudor structure, a wing of which still remains and contains a " haunted room.")

There are no fewer than thirty showrooms at the Dower House, each one furnished according to different periods and boasting innumerable examples of the most beautiful antique furniture.

Now go back into the main street of the town, Northbrook Street, and find on the right at Number 69 the very popular antique shop of Mrs. M. Jarvis, who sells good and always authentic furniture, china, glass and the like at popular prices. It is an experience to be in this shop, constantly visited by customers who rarely go away without satisfaction. The charming proprietress, so well-known and liked in the trade, has made innumerable friends thanks to her fine taste and fair business dealings. She should always be visited and can invariably produce an item of unusual interest.

MARY BELLIS—OF HUNGERFORD

As they did in the 18th century, take the old Bath Road out of Newbury to the west, and enjoy a pleasant run to Hungerford. Look for a Queen Anne house named Charnham Close facing the Bear Hotel (with a useful car park opposite).

Charnham Close is the new headquarters of Mrs. Mary Bellis of Bournemouth, leading expert on really old oak. These new premises show off to perfection her superb stock of period furniture, fabrics contemporary with that furniture, pottery, early carving, floor coverings, pictures and—a rare speciality—netsukes and jades. For a long time Mrs. Bellis has sought for a suitable place in which adequately to display these things of beauty, and at last she has found the perfect setting. We wish her every success in this excellent venture : and, by the way, if asked to recommend anyone in Britain for genuine early oak we would give Mrs. Bellis's name. She is almost unique in this respect.

A DISCOVERY: BRADFORD-ON-AVON

Continue through Marlborough and then bear left at Beckhampton along a road which proceeds to Devizes and Trowbridge. In Trowbridge turn to the right carefully to Bradford-on-Avon and one of the outstanding surprises of this trip.

Member of the British Antique Dealers' Association

RICHARD J. PINER

COLNBROOK, BUCKS.

on OLD BATH ROAD

only
2 *Miles West of London Airport*

Specialist in Old English Furniture, China and Glass of the 18th Century

Tel.: Colnbrook 243

Dorchester-on-Thames
Oxfordshire

Greenwood & Clark

Antique Furniture, Mirrors, Pictures, Silver, Decorative Accessories.

K. Greenwood J. D. Clark
Tel.: Warborough 101

CASTLE COMBE

(England's Loveliest Village, nr. Chippenham and Bath)

Antiques

(J. M. Watson)

PORCELAIN
SECOND-HAND JEWELLERY
OLD SILVER

Bradford-on-Avon is a perfect little town, sequestered, lovely and unspoilt. It has never received enough credit for its historical interest and superb 18th century buildings, an architecture coming to us as a legacy from the rich owners of mills in the ancient days of the wool trade hereabouts. There is a stone bridge with a chapel on it over the quiet Avon. Bath with its facilities is but a short distance away. And Bradford finally contains three antique shops of unusual individuality and interest.

Mr. Herbert J. Pitt, almost as organiser of antiques in Bradford—a most helpful mentor who is one of the world's leading authorities on marine art as applied to tapestries, and on old flags—is well-worth meeting in this town. The shop run by his son Mr. David Pitt at Number 27 and 28 Market Street is replete with antiques of all kinds, especially small articles, and there are extra showrooms in the Town Hall opposite.

Then Mr. John Teed at Number 17 Silver Street has a most tasteful shop for 18th and 19th century furniture and decorations both English and Continental, with china of the same periods displayed to their best advantage at prices as low as possible to cater for all pockets. There are pictures also, as Mr. Teed is

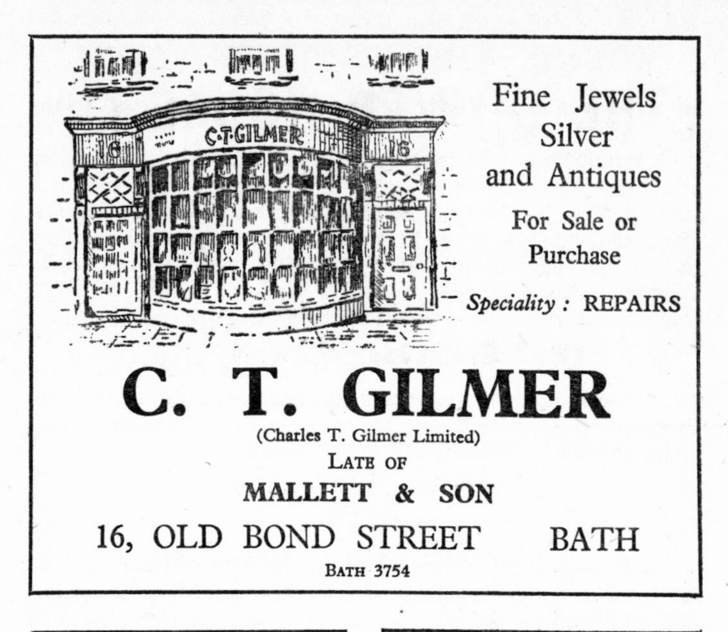
C·T·GILMER
16
16
Fine Jewels
Silver
and Antiques
For Sale or
Purchase
Speciality : REPAIRS
C. T. GILMER
(Charles T. Gilmer Limited)
LATE OF
MALLETT & SON
16, OLD BOND STREET BATH
BATH 3754

himself a painter who has exhibited for the last few years in the Royal Academy and the Pastel Society.

Continuing up Silver Street the name changes to Woolley Street where at Number 5 Mr. Robin Eden has a business of yet another character. He sells old English furniture, china, pictures, glass, iron and stone work. Many interesting articles at low prices in this shop have been gleaned from the wealth of antiques in Wiltshire around. Trade buyers are invited : indeed, all three dealers cater specially for the Trade, which is advised to make a point of visiting thistown.

There is a gem of a Saxon Church, a magnificent tithe barn, good hotels ; and we are very glad of the opportunity to bring Bradford-on-Avon to the notice of those who love history, fine architecture and domestic articles of beauty.

BATH

There is no need to bring Bath to the notice of our readers. No town in the British Isles, few in the world, has the special interest of this for the lover of olden things. It is itself a work of art, with many, many antique shops, among which we are inclined to recommend a few specially for certain departments.

Thus Messrs. Charles T. Gilmer, at Number 16 Old Bond Street in the centre of the town at the foot of Milsom Street, readily identifiable by the attractive bow-front, are first-class for antique silver and jewellery. The proprietor was formerly with Messrs. Mallett and Son and displays very good taste, also his staff can be entrusted with fine repairs.

Then a few doors down from Messrs. Gilmer at Number 13 Old Bond Street find the excellent antique furniture business of

Mr. Andrew Dando, occupying an 18th century building and selling only fine old English furniture, English and Oriental porcelain, silver and the like, to be regarded very much as a West Country aristocrat of the trade.

Now cut through opposite and inquire the way to Broad Street, another antiques quarter of the town. At the top end will be found Georgian Antiques (Number 21), a firm which claims one of the largest stocks of antiques, export and furnishing goods in the West of England, with a separate warehouse for trade items. Mr. John Goddard is the founder and proprietor.

After which proceed down to Number 31 Broad Street, where that young and enterprising dealer Mr. Charles Lake has a new business. He is very good for inexpensive chandeliers, but also English and Continental porcelain, silver and Sheffield plate, with large stocks of Georgian period furniture. Mr. Lake has newly opened this shop but is of course an expert and dealer of long standing. Prices are most reasonable.

Now ask your way to the famous old Theatre Royal and the home of Beau Nash. The street leading upwards from St. John's Place is yet another antiques area. There is, for example, the shop

called "The Chatelaine," at Number 11. This charming 18th century parlour is beautifully laid out with porcelain, pottery, *objets d'art* and jewellery.

Further up this thoroughfare—his address Number 1 Barton Street—is Mr. F. J. Symes with his most attractive antiques shop devoted to old furniture, porcelain, glass, silver and other items. Mr. Symes is nearly always busy with customers who come to him because he has a flair for finding lovely and interesting articles and selling them at highly competitive prices. This is a good target for the visitor.

Finally you will not leave Bath without visiting the fine old Abbey Church, and a short distance away, at Abbey Green, is the antique shop of Mr. Francis Christie, colourful with items of the 18th century as well as of local interest. This is an excellent shop for most of the items that attract our readers.

YEOVIL—SHERBORNE—DORCHESTER

From Bath take the road to Shepton Mallet, from thence to Sparkford, and so to Yeovil. Follow the direction signs in this town that point to Sherborne, and as you pass along Middle Street, Yeovil, look for the fine old firm of antique dealers, Edgar Vincent and Son, established 1900, whose leading speciality is silver and Sheffield plate, but who also carry much good antique furniture as well as out-of-the way items in antique clocks, table clocks, pewter—all kinds of things.

Continue now to Sherborne, delightful old town, where we recommend Messrs. J. H. & G. Elliott in Newland (turning to the left as you come to the beginning of the main shopping area). They not only sell interesting antiques, but carry on a long tradition as master wood-carvers and cabinetmakers, with skilled craftsmen able to undertake all classes of fine work.

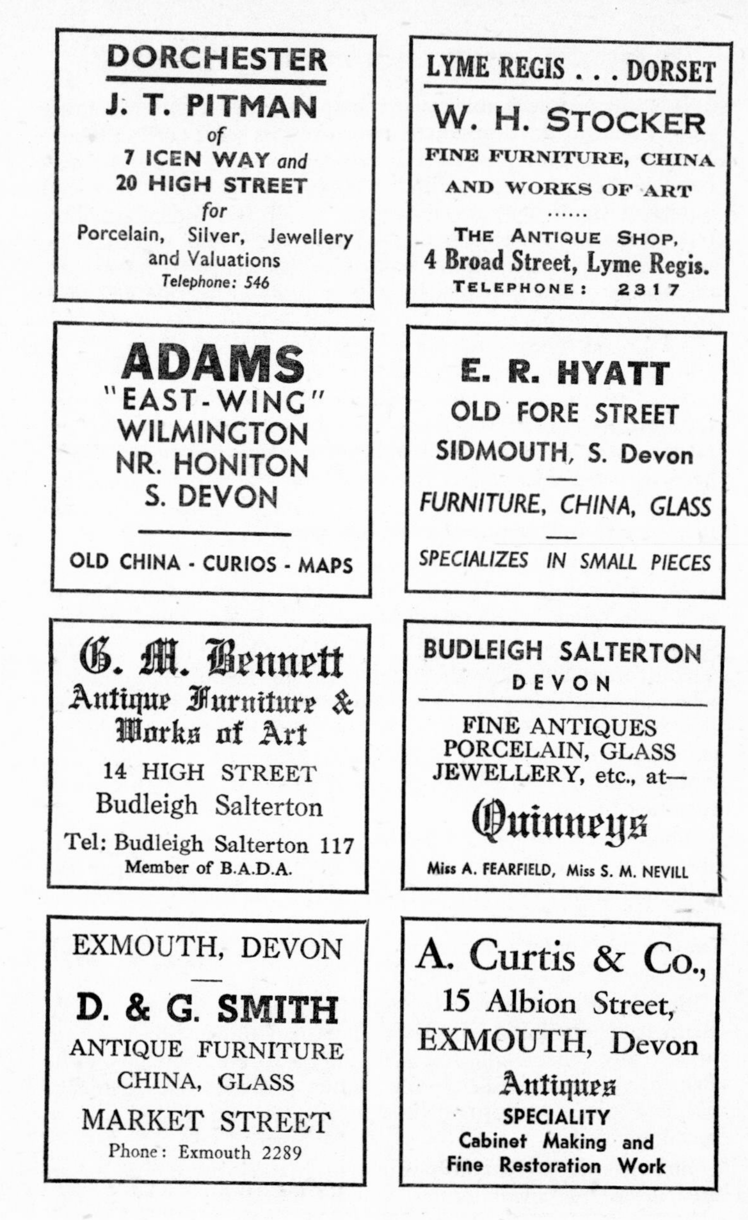
DORCHESTER
J. T. PITMAN
of
7 ICEN WAY and
20 HIGH STREET
for
Porcelain, Silver, Jewellery
and Valuations
Telephone: 546
LYME REGIS . . . DORSET
W. H. STOCKER
FINE FURNITURE, CHINA
AND WORKS OF ART
THE ANTIQUE SHOP,
4 Broad Street, Lyme Regis.
TELEPHONE: 2317
ADAMS
"EAST-WING"
WILMINGTON
NR. HONITON
S. DEVON
OLD CHINA - CURIOS - MAPS
E. R. HYATT
OLD FORE STREET
SIDMOUTH, S. Devon
FURNITURE, CHINA, GLASS
SPECIALIZES IN SMALL PIECES
G. M. Bennett
Antique Furniture &
Works of Art
14 HIGH STREET
Budleigh Salterton
Tel: Budleigh Salterton 117
Member of B.A.D.A.
BUDLEIGH SALTERTON
DEVON
FINE ANTIQUES
PORCELAIN, GLASS
JEWELLERY, etc., at—
Quinneys
Miss A. FEARFIELD, Miss S. M. NEVILL
EXMOUTH, DEVON
D. & G. SMITH
ANTIQUE FURNITURE
CHINA, GLASS
MARKET STREET
Phone: Exmouth 2289
A. Curtis & Co.,
15 Albion Street,
EXMOUTH, Devon
Antiques
SPECIALITY
Cabinet Making and
Fine Restoration Work

It is worthwhile to run down now to Dorchester, partly because we get near to the desired coast road in this way, partly because Dorchester is still Thomas Hardy's homespun town, and partly because there are antique shops there, among which we would ourselves single out for our readers Mr. J. T. Pitman's modest but interesting businesses at 20 High Street and 7 Icen Way, with silver, porcelain, antique furniture and small items at very reasonable prices. Our readers will be grateful for this introduction.

LYME REGIS INTO DEVON

Next recommended port of call is lovely old Lyme Regis, reminiscent still of the Four Georges, and Jane Austen and Hardy—with a truly tasteful and excellent antique shop at Number 4 Broad Street, where the main street falls to the sea. Here Mr. W. H. Stocker, a London expert, sells fine pieces of small furniture as well as porcelain and works of art.

Now travel via Axminster and the inland road temporarily to Wilmington (near Honiton and inquire way carefully), where at " East-Wing " the firm of Messrs. Adams sell old china and curios as well as *antique maps*. This is an interesting new target.

And from Honiton drop again to sun-favoured Sidmouth, whose special charm for visitors is always notable. There will be real Devonshire cream here, as well as a small shop with an attractive Regency bow window in Old Fore Street (called " The Antique Shop," with small pieces of good quality 18th century furniture, etc.)

For scenery the best road to Exeter now is along the coast via Budleigh Salterton, and it is a road that may also repay the collector. He will find in Budleigh, down the main street on the left, a pleasant little shop known as " Quinneys," most charmingly run by two young ladies, who deal mainly in small *objets d'art*, porcelain, glass and jewellery.

But the main dealer of the town is undoubtedly Mrs. G. M. Bennett at Number 14 High Street farther down. She has built up a really reliable shop of standing, with membership of the British Antique Dealers' Association. Her stock, genuine, old and nice, would not be out of place anywhere, and is recommended.

So onwards to Exmouth where in Market Street (facing an area devastated by bombing) will be found the very pleasant

Phone: Topsham 8551
Closed Wednesday afternoon
(except by appointment)
Gee's of Topsham
(EXETER)
ANTIQUE PORCELAIN FIGURES
and
SMALL FURNITURE
TRADE and OVERSEAS
BUYERS WELCOME
5 FORE STREET
TOPSHAM
Close to Exeter, Devon
CURTISS &
SONS LTD.
13 CLARENDON ROAD, SOUTHSEA
3 THE AVENUE, SOUTHAMPTON
13 BRAMLEY ROAD, LONDON, W.10
offer their services for
Packing, forwarding, or
shipment of large or small
quantities of effects.
More than 80 years' experience in the packing and removal of antiques and household furnishings.
Agents in all parts of the world.
EXETER
FOR RESTORATION
WORK TO : : :
Antiques
F. G. MANSFIELD
& SONS LTD.
NORTH STREET
(Phone : Exeter 3216)
Fine Stock of Antique Furniture
Valuers

antique shop of Messrs. D. and G. Smith. This lady and gentleman have established themselves firmly by fairness and discriminating taste, offering much of interest to the average collector.

After leaving Smiths proceed to Parade Corner, then turn up Albion Street. The antique shop of Messrs. A. Curtis and Co. will be found at Number 15 some 50 yards up on the right. They sell a variety of antiques but are themselves specialist cabinet-makers and restorers, whose name is worth noting.

TOPSHAM

Now on the way into Exeter enjoy an interlude in charming Topsham. Be careful as you enter this village to turn sharp left where the road to Exeter turns right. This left turn will take you into the quiet backwater of Fore Street, where at Number 5 will be found (opposite the old Tudor House) an excellent antique shop known as " Gee's." Here Mrs. M. E. Grave sells porcelain—often some very interesting figures, as well as pottery, *objets d'art* and small furniture. We called ourselves just after a Royal personage had honoured the shop with a visit. Mrs. Grave is, of course, a lady of taste and such charm as makes friends for her everywhere. She buys what we all want and sells at prices which we can afford. Do visit her.

EXETER FOR ANTIQUES

Exeter itself is one of the foremost cities of Britain which *must* be starred in an antiques itinerary. It is lovely and quiet with Devon content, yet live with riches, as will be found immediately by seeking the brave cathedral and entering opposite, at St. Peter's Galleries, Cathedral Close, the real old antique shop of the renowned Messrs. Sellicks.

This is superficially a curiosity shop of considerable proportions, with a tremendous stock at the front of china and small objects—the sort of shop that attracts the bargain-hunting browser. But behind and below and above it is far more than that.

In the basement is farmhouse and cottage oak furniture, whilst on the ground floor are well-filled cabinets displaying fine Chelsea, Bow, Derby and Oriental porcelain, and even at times the rare Plymouth and Bristol figures so much sought after. On

the first and second floors is a collection of antique furniture in mahogany and walnut of all periods, and what is possibly the largest stock of tea, dinner and dessert services in the provinces. Note, moreover, that Messrs. Sellicks are export specialists, doing a very large business with American clients, whose requirements they understand.

A splendid Charles II building now awaits, decorated with four white urns, opposite in the Cathedral Close after passing the Clarence Hotel. Enter an archway and see the very ancient structure of the Annivellars College (so named after the Cathedral Chantry priests appointed circa 1350, who built their dwelling-houses and refectory there in 1410). This is the home of " Murray's Antiques," one of the most sober and reliable firms in the country. In the Refectory and other rooms are displayed choice pieces of Elizabethan, Stuart, Queen Anne and Georgian furniture—a wonderful sight. " Murray's Antiques " is indeed an outstanding business, and is strongly recommended to the visitor, whether from home or overseas.

This Cathedral Close is perfect, and the shops are in keeping with that perfection. There is, for example, a delightful old bookshop, that of Mr. James G. Commin, at Number 16. His name is known to bibliophiles everywhere—he has in small compass one of the outstanding stocks of fine old books in the country: also books to illustrate and explain *antiques*.

Now walk through to the main street, turn left, and find on the right the descending hill of North Street, with the firm of F. G. Mansfield and Son, Ltd., a little distance down on the right. The Mansfields are excellent people, with a strong feeling for antiques. They sell old furniture and other items, but stand out undoubtedly for restorations and repairs. Many a wise American has sent his valuable antique furniture all the way to Exeter so that Mansfield's staff of old, careful craftsmen can repair it for him. Note this name and address.

Returning to the main street you will find at the corner Messrs. Brocks' large premises (182 Fore Street). They fit into the picture nicely as experts in packing and removing antiques, also in the export of antiques, while they have a department where all kinds of antiques are sold.

Proceed now down South Street opposite Brocks, and continue into Holloway Street where at Number 82 opposite the " Valiant

Soldier" Inn will be found Mr. R. Bradshaw Smith's excellent display of antique silver and jewellery (shop in an 18th century house with fine staircase and double-dome Adam ceiling).

BLUE SEAS: RED CLIFFS

The journey west becomes lovelier and warmer every hour as the road to dainty Dawlish by the sea is taken. At Dawlish itself there is an old established business in a nicely-arranged small shop, that of Mr. Arthur West, The Strand (turn right when you come to the sea and proceed up the shopping area, finding this shop on the right). Small period furniture and rare china and glass are sold.

After which comes Teignmouth, where at Number 2 Wellington Street in the centre of the town Mr. Thomas Extence stocks English and Continental porcelain, glass, interesting small pieces of furniture, and pictures (including some by his very talented children, both artists of considerable promise). His son is also a skilled woodcarver and restoration work can be undertaken.

Instead of travelling across the bridge from Teignmouth strike up the short six miles to Newton Abbot and journey through to the centre of the town and the Clock Tower, beneath which at Number 3 Wolborough Street in a fine black and white building scheduled as an Ancient Monument will be found the really attractive antique shop of Mr. and Mrs. C. Waite. They recently acquired this business—being well-known before in Exmouth—and have enlarged the premises to fill their showrooms with much exciting new stock, from small pieces of fine antique furniture (a speciality), to porcelain, English and Irish glass, and items of unusual interest, such as children's antique furniture and historical pieces. The attractions of Newton Abbot are added to by this newly-garnished shop.

But Newton Abbot has a very fine establishment indeed, that of Mrs. M. Sellick at Forde House a mile or two out on the Torquay Road, lying back in spacious parkland, a magnificent Elizabethan mansion visited by Charles I in 1625, and the first lodging place of William of Orange when he landed in Tor Bay, 1688. Mrs. Sellick, "mother" of the famous Exeter shop, preserves Forde House to-day as a home of antiques for sale. It

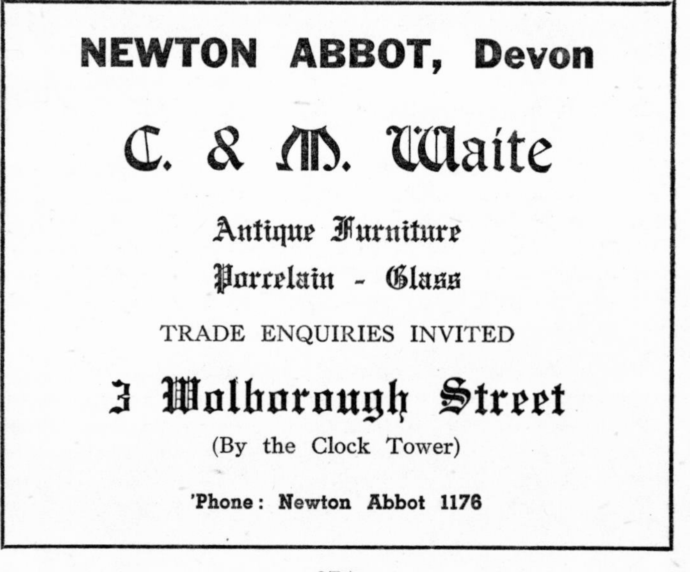

(By Courtesy of Messrs. Phillips, Odiham.)

Fine Pinewood Mantelpiece.

Lovely Setting for Antiques—Woolstaplers' Hall, Chipping Campden, Glos.

One of the Fine Showrooms of Messrs. Quinneys of Warwick.

Through the open door of HAYWARD'S of CREDITON, on the main Exeter-Barnstaple road, where may be found a variety of goods for those of discerning taste but modest means.

Telephone: CREDITON 2136 TRADE WELCOMED.

Small Bow-fronted Sheraton Sideboard with Tambour Shutter
Set of three Colebrookdale Vases
Pair of 18th Century Chelsea Figures

Fine 18th Century Furniture and Porcelain

(MR. & MRS. R. E. MARTIN)

ANTIQUES

Dartmouth

Devon

Telephone 145

TRADE AND EXPORT BUYERS WELCOMED

is furnished almost exactly as in 1688 when Dutch William walked in. You can have tea there, and wander through the past, and find the furniture or china that you have long been looking for.

Torquay—through which you must pass next—is lovely and modern: Brixham, a few miles the other side of Torquay and Paignton, is lovely and old, old with memories and fishing smacks and fine furniture such as will be found in the shop of Mr. W. J. Courtney Beer, at 48 Fore Street on the left as you run down to the fascinating harbour. Mr. Beer has a most comprehensive stock, offering fine furniture, silver, porcelain and pottery. He is a connoisseur of the beautiful in cherished antiques, and stands out as a leading dealer of this area.

DARTMOUTH—SMUGGLERS—PLYMOUTH

It has already become a question which is the loveliest of these Devon towns. Run across from Brixham and take the ferry from Kingswear over the mirrored Dart to Dartmouth and, if the day be fine, you will probably remember Dartmouth always for its placid beauty. The little town has an atmosphere all of its own. Even the antiques shop is "different." You will find it in Hauley Road, a turning off the waterfront. This firm of Messrs. Richard occupies an ancient cottage, one of the oldest in Dartmouth, and, besides good antique furniture, sells particularly some fine porcelain and pottery. It caters specially for the trade, who are recommended to call, this road and route being altogether more interesting than that which runs inland and carries the heavy main road traffic.

From Dartmouth follow the directions to Kingsbridge, a most intriguing run through Devon lanes, and a mile or two before reaching Kingsbridge look carefully for " Boffins Boft " on the left, just at the turning over New Bridge. Here Mrs. Angela Halsey has a new antiques business with the accent on interesting china and pottery, as well as fine small furniture, particularly of the French and satinwood schools. Here is already a most popular port of call—which was once a smuggler's haunt. (They will show you the tunnel by the quiet river where *it* was landed.)

Now pass through Kingsbridge (thinking maybe of poor Cookworthy who made his hard paste here) and continue to Plymouth. The principal antique shops of interest will be found to be those of Messrs. Alvin, at Number 51 Union Street, Stonehouse (actually on the way out of the city) and at Number 24, New Street, Barbican. The proprietor, Mr. A. V. H. Gamble, sells

antique furniture, porcelain and glass. He has been honoured by royal patronage.

(And an interesting note: When at the Barbican, whence the Pilgrim Fathers left for America, visit the unusual shop of Messrs. Lethbridge at Island House. They sell nautical antiques, but also adapt such items as old leather cartridge cases and lamps from ships to make excellent furnishing items, with very good discounts to the trade, who should write mentioning *Antiques Yearbook*.)

CORNISHMEN—AND MORE DEVON

We shall not cover Cornwall thoroughly this year, only indicate some leading dealers, leaving many antique shops in smaller towns and seaside villages for later inspection.

Stop first after Plymouth at St. Austell, where Mr. J. Morland Coon, of 4 Market Street, is a first-class dealer, among the best in the Duchy. You will find the shop opposite the church and convenient car park. Three generations of Mr. Coon's family are still engaged in purveying fine furniture (accent on Georgian),

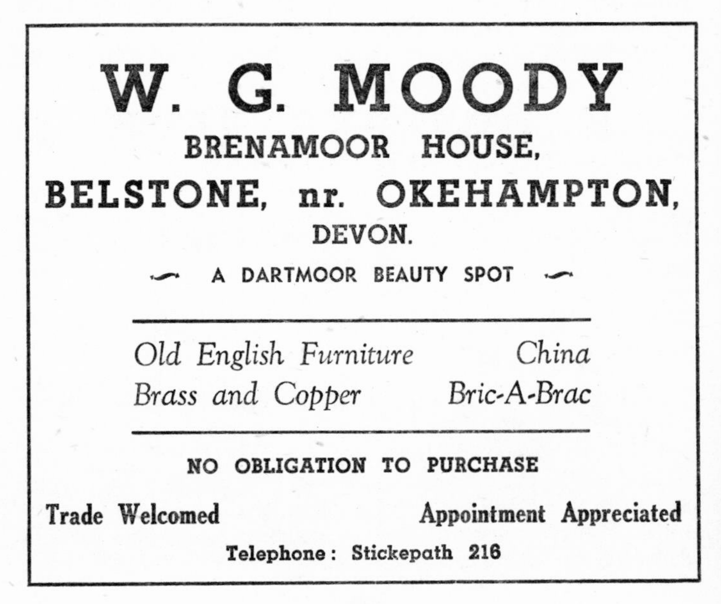

W. G. MOODY
BRENAMOOR HOUSE,
BELSTONE, nr. OKEHAMPTON,
DEVON.
A DARTMOOR BEAUTY SPOT
Old English Furniture China
Brass and Copper Bric-A-Brac
NO OBLIGATION TO PURCHASE
Trade Welcomed Appointment Appreciated
Telephone: Stickepath 216

porcelain, silver, Sheffield plate, glass, pewter, indeed all kinds of antiques.

Then for another sober and reliable business, much to be recommended, visit The Antiques Galleries at Truro (most convenient town for reaching other Cornish beauty spots). Conducted by Mr. Michael Chesterman, the Galleries occupy an elegant Georgian house at Number 20 Lemon Street, the thoroughfare leading out to Falmouth. The speciality is fine furnishing pieces, but a wide variety of lovely antiques are sold.

After which proceed to Falmouth, quaint port, where there is an old-established business known as John Maggs, in narrow Church Street. The lovely Georgian bow-front premises have been scheduled as a building of historic and architectural interest. Inside, collected over a period of 50 years, are fine stocks of furniture, porcelain, prints and glass.

Now return through St. Austell to Liskeard but branch left there to ancient Tavistock, the most genuine of Devonshire country towns. Herein at 5 King Street Mr. F. N. Dann (successor to Mrs. V. E. Norman-Dann whose unfortunate death last year was a sad loss to the antiques trade), sells old furniture, china, silver and glass, with the accent on authenticity and a welcome always to trade and overseas buyers.

After which a unique experience can be promised if the reader takes our good advice to return to Exeter via Okehampton. Situated on the edge of Dartmoor, 1,000 feet up, three miles the other side of Okehampton and only 20 from Exeter, is the village of Belstone. This will be found three-quarters of a mile from the main road at the Tongue End turning signposted Belstone. When almost in the village you will see on your right Brenamoor House, where resides Mr. W. G. Moody. Pause awhile, and inspect his stocks of antique furniture, china, glass, copper and brassware. You will be welcomed, without the slightest obligation to purchase. This visit will not be regretted, as the antiques are good and the scenery magnificent.

CREDITON—TAUNTON—NORTH DEVON

It will be a good idea now to run back the short distance to Exeter, perhaps spend some more time with the shops there, and, at leisure, drive out the eight miles to Crediton, ancient market town. The great age of the town is shown by the fact that the cathedral for the diocese was established in A.D. 909, when

Exeter itself did not exist. At the Barnstaple end of the town and immediately opposite the Queen Elizabeth Grammar School is the new antique shop of Messrs. Hayward. Although there are some fine pieces of a purely decorative character, the stock consists largely of good antiques and works of art calculated to be of real use to the discerning home-maker at moderate cost. Mrs. Hayward is a charming guide to her treasures always, and caters specially for the trade.

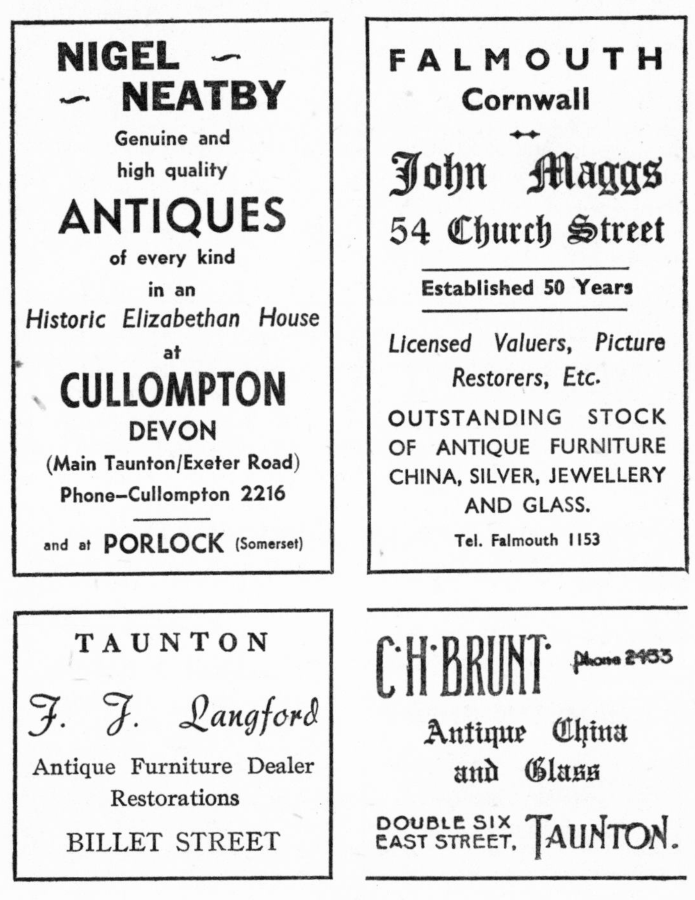

ROUND THE ANTIQUE SHOPS

The road to Taunton from Exeter passes through the old town of Cullompton, wherein will be found in a fine old house on this road known as The Walronds the antiques business which Mr. Nigel Neatby has transferred from Chumleigh in North Devon. The house is of considerable architectural and historical interest (dated 1605) and is itself worth a visit. Mr. Neatby, as is well-known, is most dependable for excellent antiques of all kinds.

Taunton, next on the road, offers only two antique shops which we would like to describe, but they are both unusual. The first is at Number 66 East Street, which at first sight appears to be merely a tobacconists' shop of unusual distinction for these parts. It will be found inside, however, that Mr. C. H. Brunt the proprietor is a personality of the old school who sells in addition to his fine cigars quite a notable array of antique clocks, china, glass, ivories and other items. We feel this is quite an important little discovery. After which turn right up Billet Street and find about half-way up the premises of Mr. F. J. Langford, a young but enthusiastic dealer who always has some interesting furniture and is a first-class restorer to the public and trade.

From Taunton take the road leading to Minehead, into some of the most beautiful country in the world, and at Minehead go at once to the spacious Park Street shop where Mr. John Bullivant has carried on a high-class business for nearly twenty years. He has had lifelong experience in the trade, is an expert on fine furniture, and makes a speciality of good furnishing pieces for the home at surprisingly reasonable prices. In addition he holds a fine stock of metalware, English, Continental and Chinese porcelains, and other *objets-d'art* of interest to trade buyers from overseas.

Neither should one overlook two other excellent antique shops, The Old Curiosity Shop of young Mr. John T. White, 6a The Parade—right in the centre of the town—where all kinds of interesting small articles in china, glass, silver, copper, brass and pewter may be found ; and the establishment of Messrs. Cracknell and Roberts at 19 Friday Street (under an archway) where there is a large stock of excellent furniture—and craftsmen who can undertake restorations reliably at reasonable prices.

Nor should the short further journey be omitted to Porlock—whence came the " person " who interrupted the poet—since Mr. Nigel Neatby of Cullompton already mentioned has another antique shop here, in the High Street.

BRIDGWATER TO CASTLE COMBE AND CIRENCESTER

Return through Minehead and lovely country again to Bridgwater, pausing at the shop of Mr. F. Harding in Cannington on the way, but certainly making for Mr. Harding's main business at 28, High Street, Bridgwater, a romantic antique shop of the kind usually found only in fiction—excellent stock from warming-pans to furniture—and then visiting the fine shop of Mr. J. Blake Camp at Number 67 High Street. Mr. Camp sells good period furniture as well as English and Continental porcelain among which may always be found some unusual pieces, displaying always most meticulous taste.

Then in Bristol, do not forget Christmas steps. This was traditionally the haunt of antique dealers. It is worth visiting today for the shop of Mr. Herbert W. Smith (Number 7), which teems with porcelain, glass, silver, miniatures and small pieces of period furniture. This, indeed, is the kind of shop that the experienced buyer values, with a constant changing stock, skilled management, and a very high standard of commercial morality. Mr. Smith is always glad to purchase antique jewellery and the like.

Bristol has been covered so thoroughly in previous years that this time we would additionally draw attention only to a newcomer, Mr. Gordon Frederick at 42 Park Street—the hill leading up to the University from the Centre. This careful shop is

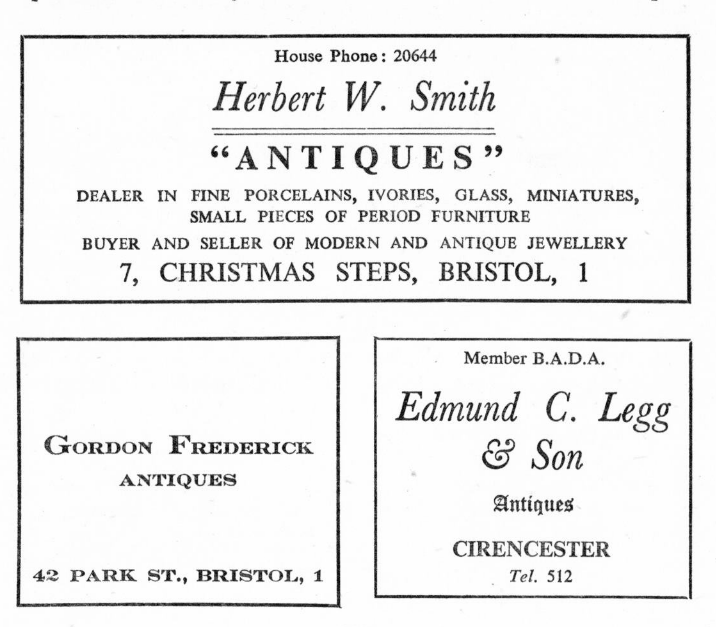

notable already for small pieces of furniture and tasteful kindred items. Do make the acquaintance of Mr. Frederick.

Now from Bristol take the road to Chippenham, and at West Yatton a short distance from Chippenham turn left and carefully find the way to Castle Combe. It is worth the care, because Castle Combe is perhaps the fairest village of all England, utterly sequestered, stone-built and prettily grouped—with the very charming antique shop therein of Mrs. J. M. Watson, most tasteful items at very reasonable prices.

From Chippenham the recommended route is via Malmesbury to Cirencester, wherein will be found the very old established antique shop of Edmund C. Legg and Son, who may be relied upon to offer only the most authentic early English furniture, English and Irish glass, also rare keyboard instruments: at 29 Castle Street.

GLOUCESTER—CHELTENHAM

Gloucester must be visited next if only for the Cathedral which is among the finest of all in England. You find the Cathedral entrance by turning left down Westgate Street from the cross-roads in the centre of the town, and taking a turn to the right in Westgate Street. This is College Street—and immediately you see the attractive black and white antique shop of Mr. and Mrs. Frith, with all kinds of antiques for sale, but especially some interesting silver (accent on *spoons*, and 17th century Exeter Apostles are urgently wanted) also glass, maps, and Gloucestershire topographical and genealogical items of all kinds.

So to Cheltenham, prime town of these parts, with the silver spoon in its mouth again, for the delightful tree-lined Promenade has both Messrs. Martin and Co., Ltd., at the beginning, and Mr. Eric Scott Cooper at Number 52.

Mr. Scott Cooper is worth visiting not only for silver but also for Sheffield plate, antique jewellery, Battersea enamels, and, in fact, for *objets-d'art et vertu* generally. We recommend him too for gold and silver snuff boxes, vinaigrettes and nutmeg craters, also Bilston and Continental enamels. The personal touch in this business is very noticeable, and Mr. Scott Cooper is both skilled in his trade and helpful.

The firm of Martin and Co. itself was founded as long ago as 1806 by a Mr. Martin, and bought in 1889 by Alderman G. Dimmer, J.P., C.C., the owner of similar businesses in Southsea and Liverpool. On his death in 1927 he was succeeded by his son Mr. L. G. Dimmer, and his grandson Mr. M. A. Dimmer is now on the Board of Directors. The Dimmers have made of this business an establishment of Bond Street standard which always carries a large stock of antique silver, early Chinese jade and *objets d'art* including pieces by Paul Lamerie, Peter Archambo, Eben Coker, the Hennels, Hester Bateman, and other famous silversmiths.

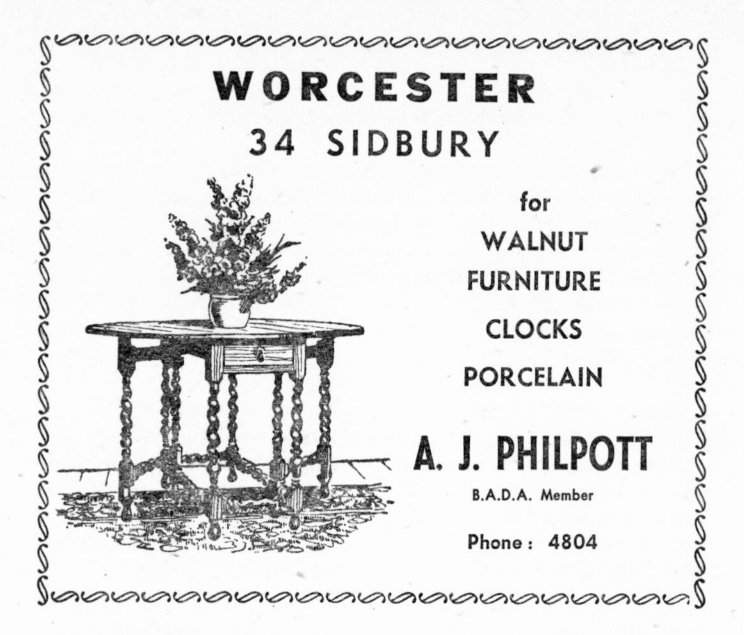

Remember also that at Number 62 to 64 The Promenade is the Cheltenham branch of Asprey & Co., Ltd., the Bond Street salon described in another place. Here will always be found much lovely antique silver, porcelain, and kindred items.

How pleasant to drive a fine car under the spreading trees of the Promenade up to the elegance of the Rotunda and Montpellier Walk, where, at Number 22, is found the dainty shop of Georgina Ashwell! She sells a wide variety of the most delightful and genuine antiques, small pieces of furniture a speciality, old china, glass, curios ; and both the proprietress and her husband are very charming cicerones round this display.

After which proceed to Royal Well Place between the bus park and the Station and just behind the magnificent Royal Crescent. Here at Number 7 Audrey Bull inexpensively sells small items including antique jewellery, and is especially interested in china and glass (wine glasses).

Always Travel With ANTIQUES YEAR BOOK

THE FINEST PORCELAIN

The road runs from Cheltenham to Tewkesbury, an historical, quiet town of subtle charm. No doubt there is an antique shop—a country antique shop—here. Behold, there is a shop which stands with only a very few others in the world as a gallery of the finest porcelain. This is a great surprise (unless you have already been told of it) the Old English Ceramic Galleries of Mr. T. Leonard Crow at Number 10 Church Street, Tewkesbury, in the centre of the town on the right.

Mr. Crow himself is a prince among antique dealers, warm of heart and much admired in the trade, whose customers of consequence across the globe come back to him again and again because his taste is unerring and he treats them so fairly when they buy his rare English porcelain of the best periods. He is outstandingly good for Worcester. We recommend him with stars! with stars and stripes, indeed, considering the number of cars with flags of that ilk that so often stop outside his shop.

MALVERN—WORCESTER—PERSHORE

Yet another interesting town is near : Malvern clinging to its splendid hills, and with a very pleasant and long-established antique dealer, Miss M. W. Price, at Holland Cottage, on the right at the foot of Church Street as you enter the main part. Here you will find nice, small pieces of furniture, together with china, pottery and glass.

The Cathedral of Worcester lies but a few miles ahead, and after visiting it proceed along the road a little till you suddenly see the most attractive old black and white shop of Mr. A. J. Philpott facing you at a corner—Number 34 Sidbury. This is a thriving business thanks to the excellent position and to Mr. Philpott's extremely dependable taste in walnut furniture, clocks and porcelain—with a particular interest in scale-blue Worcester, as is right and proper with the famous Works situated only a short distance to the rear. (Visit it. You will be very welcome.)

Then continue a short distance down Sidbury to the extremely quaint shop of Mr. Thomas Tolley at Number 46. This always contains many small items of interest, but we recommend Mr. Tolley particularly because he is a first-class picture restorer, one of the best in the West. He is always very busy on important

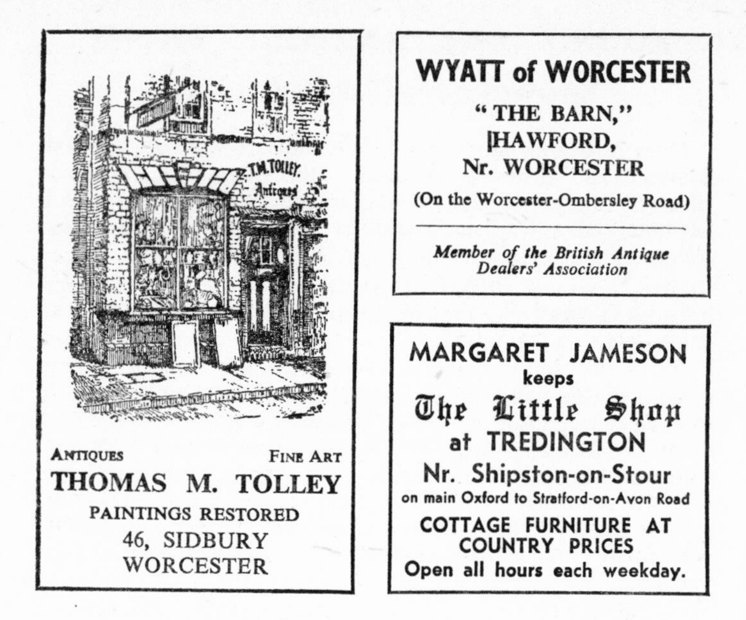

contracts, and recently restored a Canaletto, a Gainsborough and a Murillo. Write to Mr. Tolley also for details of his *monthly antique auctions*.

If after Worcester it is desired to proceed to the Midlands proper, then take the Wolverhampton road, and at Hawford only four miles from Worcester find the picturesque Old Barn on the right, which partly houses Mr. T. Wyatt's large stock, based on 50 years' experience, of furniture, Oriental and English porcelain, Staffordshire pottery, silver, needlework, tapestries, ironwork, and *garden figures*.

We then recommend returning to Worcester and taking the road to Evesham via Pershore—Pershore, lovely, unspoilt old town of superb architectural interest with Perrott House therein, a mansion built in 1760 for a Baron of the Exchequer. During 1951 it is to be opened as an antique business, those lovely Adam rooms to be stocked with the delicate French and satin-wood furniture, and the excellent porcelain and pottery, the mirrors and clocks for which a certain well-known dealer is famous. We strongly advise ringing Pershore 41 and arranging to visit this abode of beauty if and when it is opened.

SHOWPLACES OF ENGLAND

Then Broadway is not so far from Pershore—straight ahead to Evesham and a few miles more: Broadway, the showplace village of England indeed, catering splendidly for the visitor with fine hotels but still a place of country charm and superb domestic architecture in warm Cotswold stone.

Here, moreover, is Mr. H. W. Keil's lovely establishment, "Tudor House," a building with few equals of its type which we deliberately illustrate again elsewhere in our book, and to be found on the right just after proceeding through the centre of the village. Within will be found perhaps the largest and most distinctive collection of fine period furniture and other antiques of the entire Midlands area. Mr. Keil is among the great dealers, with very high standards. 17th and 18th century furniture is his speciality, but he also sells much else, such as panelling, silver, armour and weapons; and we congratulate him upon his success with a new stand at the Grosvenor House Antique Dealers' Fair, London.

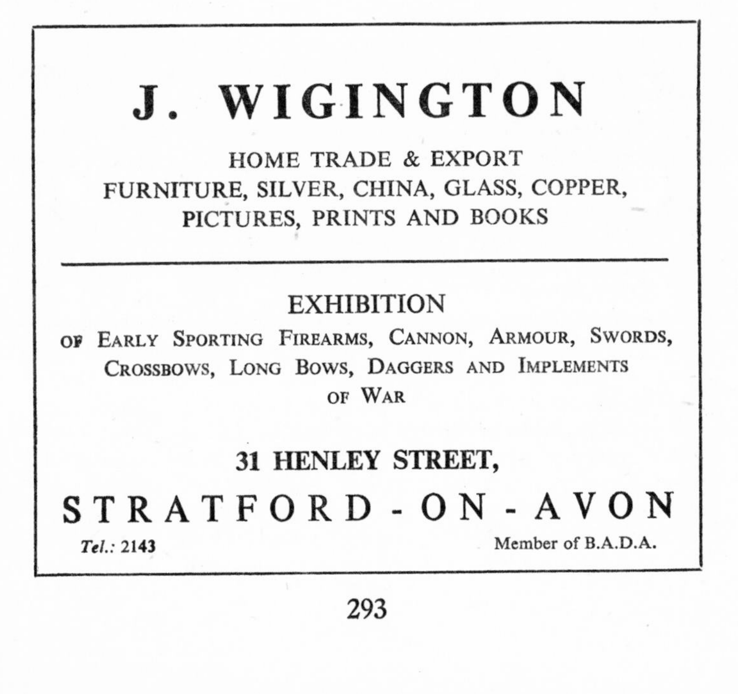

Opposite and a step farther down the road will be found two other shops, one of them a subsidiary of Messrs. Keil devoted to more everyday antiques, and the other that famous " Christie's " of Broadway which is connected with Woolstaplers' Hall in Chipping Campden (to be described in a moment). Do visit " Christie's " for all kinds of intriguing antiques at reasonable prices. But really there is no need for this injunction as the shop is justly patronised by everyone who visits Broadway for antiques.

Then we have to report a recruit to the Broadway ranks, Messrs. R. Halford Bailey, Ltd., who at Grey Gables, up the road and opposite the turning you are about to take for Chipping Campden, have their " House of many treasures that covers all branches of the Arts from early Renaissance times through the ages down to the late 19th century." You are welcome to these spacious galleries, and whether you are looking for a simple gift or a rare piece for your collection you will find it here. Fine clocks are a speciality.

Take that road marked " Stratford-on-Avon " opposite Halford Bailey's and proceed along it a few miles until a direction to " Chipping Campden " indicates the road to that exquisite

Member of British Antique Dealers' Association
ROGER
WARNER
BURFORD
OXFORDSHIRE
Telephone:
Burford 2114
Doll, circa 1780
Antiques of Character

MEMBER
THE BRITISH ANTIQUE DEALERS' ASSOCIATION
ARS NON HABET INIMICUM NISI IGNORANTIAM
BENVENUTO CELLINI

Cotswold town. Here the visitor who wants at once to learn something on the spot of England's past and at the same time buy antiques, can achieve both desires by visiting Woolstaplers' Hall, the ancient meeting-place of the merchants whose prosperity once built this most stately of districts. Mr. and Mrs. Pritchard of " Christies " in Broadway, run this fine antiques business of Woolstaplers' Hall, where may be found all kinds of byegones in natural habitat at country prices.

From Campden proceed into poetry's Warwickshire and Stratford-on-Avon. Here you will go at once to " The Birthplace," which is in Henley Street—where the best antique shops are also to be found. Nearly opposite Shakespeare's house is the local branch of a fine antique business, Mr. Grainger-Brown's of Warwick (which is described in Tour 5). There is a comprehensive stock, but fine antique silver and Sheffield plate particularly strike the eye.

Now look down to the far end of Henley Street, where the bold sign " Antiques " dominates the valuable block of old buildings there, property of Mr. John Wigington, antique dealer. (Somebody will make Mr. Wigington a bold offer for that block one day and build a fortune thereon.) Mr. Wigington has a most interesting shop, with all kinds of antiques from furniture to silver. He also runs at Poet's Arbor opposite the Post Office in Sheep Street a museum of antiquities and old books—thousands of old books—but his outstanding interest is antique weapons, upon which he is a leading authority. Mr. Wigington has a passion for this subject, which he knows from the beginning : and his stock of weapons is most comprehensive.

COTSWOLD CHARMS

Take the road to Tredington (signposted to Shipston-on-Stour and Chipping Norton and Oxford). Notice on the left as you run into Tredington a side road which has a fine house of Cotswold stone only a short distance up, garnished with the sign " Antiques." There is a story behind this beautiful house, because it was built only recently, almost with their own hands, by Mr. " Shirley " Brown and his son to satisfy a lifelong ambition. Mr. Brown, called " Shirley " in the trade because of his associations with the district of Birmingham, is a splendid type of antique dealer, largely a wholesaler of fine antiques to the trade—furniture, glass, china, old ironwork and garden ornaments—but with showrooms here that will delight the wayfarer.

Also in Tredington, a little further on, is the charming small antique shop of Miss M. Jameson, always with many small items of the type to interest those who go motoring in search of inexpensive antiques.

Now be exceedingly careful *not* to continue on the road to Shipston, but to return to the beginning of Tredington and there take the road to Moreton in Marsh, continuing afterwards to secluded, rare Stow-on-the-Wold, where you may pause with profit at the Cotswold House of Mr. T. Pritchard. Part of this business has been converted into a museum of articles used locally and traditionally in crafts and agriculture. The antique shop proper offers interesting old items of many kinds.

Then continue to Bourton-on-the-Water, a gem of unspoilt architecture, with elegant stone bridges across an ever-present brook that babbles through the streets. Here Mrs. D. J. Dawkes, at Portland House (over 300 years old) sells old English china and figures, glass, Oriental porcelain, brass and copper. Have tea in a miniature hall of ancient times complete with minstrel gallery as adapted by Mrs. Dawkes' talented artist husband.

After which return on the Stow road till a signpost indicates an abrupt swing to the right on to another road leading to Burford.

And on entering Burford join the controversy at once as to which is the most beautiful of these Cotswold towns. The Burford main street rising to the hill certainly has few architectural equals. On the left half-way up are the exquisite premises of Mr. Roger Warner, an antique shop of distinction and charm, devoted to excellent 18th century furniture and the like, but specialising most attractively in early dolls, needlework and costumes. This is to be carefully noted by the wise.

Now the main Oxford and London road is attained, and next Cotswolds town is Witney. There is no need to pause in the centre of this, but proceed out towards Oxford and note on the right a very attractive antique shop with some fine articles in the window. This is the business of Mr. L. O. Castle, 108 Newland, and the repository of much good furniture, porcelain, pottery and glass.

OXFORD

Oxford awaits. On entering the city proper keep a very sharp look-out for the narrow thoroughfare on the right called Little Clarendon Street, for here at Numbers 1, 2 and 7 will be found the famous old antique business of Messrs. H. W. Jones and Son. The emphasis is on prime 18th century furniture and nearly always a really choice and unusual piece is in stock. Our readers have often thanked us for this recommendation. Known to generations of undergraduates and dons, Messrs. Jones have the quality of reliability, not only in the furniture aforementioned but also in china, silver and works of art.

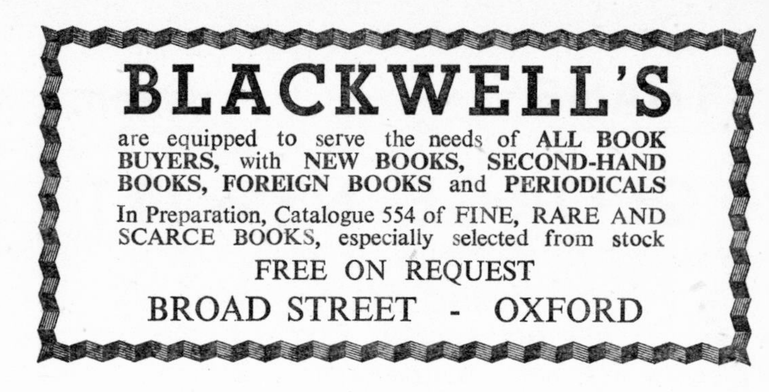

Outstanding also in the antiques world of Oxford is the personality of Mr. A. H. Goodban. He has two fine antique shops—" Hallidays " at 86–7 High Street, turning to the left at the central crossroads of Carfax—and " The Antiquary " at 50 St. Giles Street. Much fine old furniture is sold particularly at " Hallidays," with silver and other items. " The Antiquary " has similar pieces but also much interesting china and silver. These are both very flourishing businesses, built up by skill, probity and a flair for the discovery of antique rarities in which all can share. Mr. Goodban can offer good facilities for repairs and restorations.

It should be worth noting, by the way, that Oxford, home of fine books, has one of the finest antiquarian booksellers in the world, Messrs. B. H. Blackwell in Broad Street—who might well be visited while you are here for works on collecting subjects. Or write.

THAME

After which—Thame. The village is a few miles from Oxford on the London road. Watch for a direction sign on the left before you come to a railway bridge over the road. Thame is a pleasant small town or village in a district where collectors abound, and so it possesses interesting antique shops, such as the " Witch Ball," a beautiful establishment with a large witch ball hanging outside as a sign, centre of the town at Number 2, Cornmarket.

Here Mr. and Mrs. T. Evelyn Swain specialise memorably in the provision of old pieces for old houses (as they would themselves put it.) The facade of this shop is a model for modern antique businesses, decorated in exquisite taste. The interior more than fulfils that promise, and the stock, with much of the

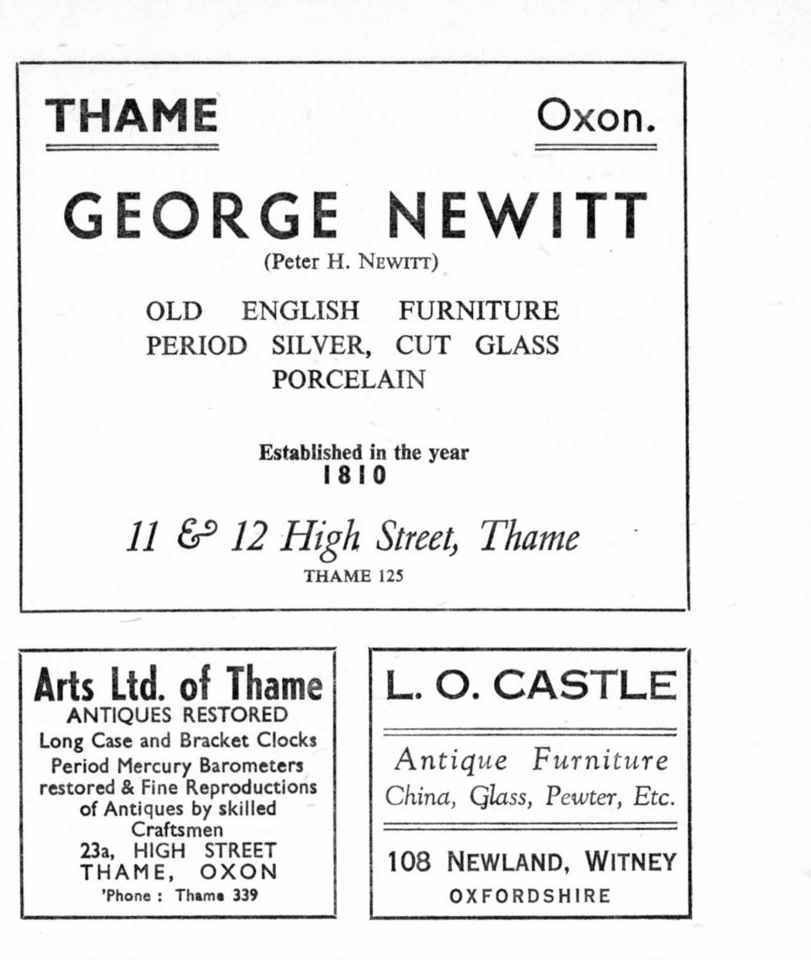

better kind of old cottage furniture, glass, pottery and porcelain, clocks, is a scintillating and yet always homely array, designed to please all kinds of purchaser.

But Thame has a very old business—one of the oldest in the country—the firm of Messrs. George Newitt, further up the High Street on the other side. Do call here, because a great variety of good but inexpensive antiques is offered, and, for the connoisseur some rare items, particularly in Windsor chairs, which are the personal interest of Mr. Peter Newitt, a personality indeed among modern antiquaries. Leading film stars, famous people in all walks of life, assemble from time to time at Newitts to browse, talk, and buy.

Further down on the left at Number 23a High Street is the firm of Arts Ltd., restorers of antiques in whose hands can be safely placed work of all kinds with the speciality of restorations to long case and bracket clocks and period mercury barometers.

BUCKINGHAMSHIRE

Take the London road from Thame and continue to West Wycombe, charming village at the beginning of High Wycombe. On the left is Miss Irene Donald's "Apple Orchard," attractive tearooms with, at the back, considerable showrooms of English and Continental furniture, porcelain, pottery, glass and bric-a-brac. Trade buyers are specially catered for.

Then proceed through High Wycombe, pass the Cricket Ground bus stop on the right, and be very careful not to miss Bassetsbury Lane on the right. (There is a large sign "Antiques"). The Mill is a short distance down the lane, worth visiting for its historical interest alone, being a fine old specimen of a water-driven flour-mill, with much of the apparatus preserved. Bassetsbury Manor is itself mentioned in Domesday Book, and the 16th century, half-timbered mill is scheduled as an Ancient Monument. The three capacious floors with gigantic beams and good oak boards carry what must be the most extensive stock of antiques in these parts, every kind of period furniture but only genuine pieces, and many sidelines in which Mr. G. A. Turner specialises such as pewter and horse-brasses.

After which it will be necessary to return to the centre of the town and take the road via Great Missenden and Wendover, a lovely road, to Tring, that most pleasant town in real, unusual Buckinghamshire country. And for over half a century monosyllabic Tring, for lovers of antiques, has been associated with the equally terse name Bly, of which to-day there are two representatives each with a notable business, though both are different and need not be regarded as competitors. John Bly of Tring has his premises at 50 High Street, in the centre of the town; F. S. Bly is equally well-known (with his good wife) for his establishment "The Corner Cupboard," Brook Street, on the right a little farther on.

Do not think, however, that "The Corner Cupboard" is in any way small or just an old curiosity shop. Ask to be shown the great barn at the side with its huge stock of all kinds of antique furniture. Explore the premises at the rear with their wealth of garden ornaments, sundials, lead tanks. Mr. F. S. Bly is a specialist in these lines ; while in his main shop will be found small pieces of all kinds in the untouched condition beloved of collectors.

Similarly Mr. John Bly's showrooms at 50 High Street are far more extensive than would appear from the road. Possibly they are the largest in these parts, with a floor space of over 3,500 square feet. Here the object is to specialise chiefly in the very best kind of 18th and early 19th century furniture, and Mr. John Bly himself deserves to be regarded as a leading expert on mahogany, which is his great interest. Everything is in splendid condition, and the front shop is among the most delightful of its kind in the country. Do not omit to visit this establishment if you are interested in small mahogany pieces—the most sought-after in the antiques world to-day.

(Note here that Messrs. F. Weatherhead of Kingsbury Square in nearby Aylesbury are first-class antiquarian booksellers, members of the A.B.A., with one of the largest and most convenient showrooms in the provinces, all books carefully classified and including items that many collectors want. Write to them, mentioning us, for books on collecting.)

BERKHAMSTED TO UXBRIDGE

The London road from Tring soon enters interesting and polished old Berkhamsted, wherein you will find on the left a very lovely and attractive antique shop indeed, that of Messrs. F. E. Norwood Ltd., 146 High Street. Fine period furniture is sold here, and Georgian glass (amongst which a large number of interesting tumblers will be found), also Staffordshire copper lustreware, and—take special note—a really fine collection of pistols of the flint-lock era. This is the headquarters of the new business at St. Albans, described in Tour V.

Turn right in Berkhamsted and run down through Chesham to old Amersham, turning left at the foot of the town on to the

F. E. NORWOOD LTD.

146 HIGH STREET
BERKHAMSTED, Herts.
(Tel.: 361)

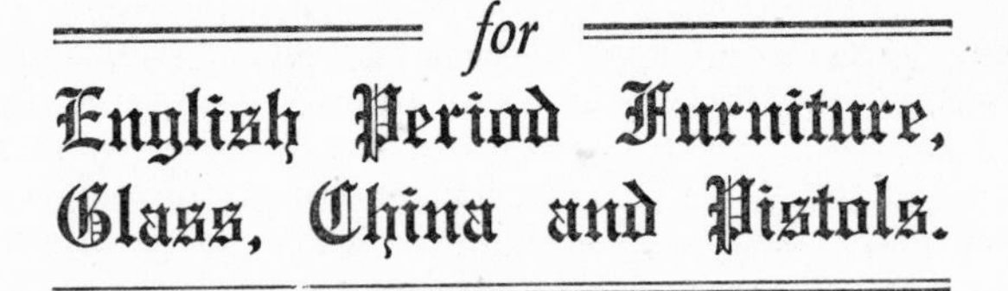

Also at 23 HOLYWELL HILL, ST. ALBANS.

Period Furniture
Old Pottery & Porcelain
Paintings & Prints
Old Glass
Antique Copper,
Brass & Pewter

W. & D. Bruton

125 HIGH STREET
RICKMANSWORTH
HERTS.

Telephone:
Rickmansworth 3264

WEST WYCOMBE,
BUCKS.

Irene Donald

Apple Orchard

Antiques M.B.A.D.A.

AYLESBURY, Bucks.

F. Weatherhead & Son Ltd.

New & Second-hand
Booksellers. A.B.A.
58 Kingsbury Square.
Phone: 153
Personal calls invited.
Catalogues on application.

London road and finding a short distance along on the left the well-known "Mill Stream" of Captain Vyse Millard. This ancient structure, with an old mill house which is one of the few of its kind left, covers not only a leading antiques business (represented at the Grosvenor House Fair in London each year) but also a first-class restaurant. Capt. Millard specialises in the small piece of walnut or mahogany, and he has a very pretty taste in the most desirable unusual examples: for the connoisseur a delight, and for the trade buyer an essential port of call.

Turn left now and then eventually right on to the road to Rickmansworth. Half-way along the High Street on the right in this town is the excellent antique shop of Messrs. W. and D. Bruton, Number 125. The stock comprises furniture, glass, copper, pewter and the like, but Mr. Bruton's personal interest is porcelain, especially Worcester of the Dr. Wall period. Moreover, he usually has interesting items of Victoriana, catering for American buyers at very reasonable prices.

By following the signs to Uxbridge you can run down from Rickmansworth to the main London-Oxford road, and we highly recommend proceeding back towards Oxford on this a few pleasant miles to Beaconsfield, which is a beautiful old town with two splendid antique shops. On the right as you enter are Mrs. Florence Helen Wood's generous showrooms, and, a little further on the left, Mr. H. L. Brown's ("Louis Brown's") famous establishment, 26 High Street.

Mr. Brown is one of the most respected antique dealers we know, with a great knowledge of his speciality, old English furniture. He is highly recommended.

So with Mrs. Florence Wood, who sells fine furniture, china, glass and works of art generally in rooms furnished exactly as they should be under domestic conditions. She does a large export business, having a branch in the United States.

Beaconsfield is indeed worth visiting specially from London for these two shops at any time, quite apart from the inclusion in this tour.

And the last port of call—Uxbridge. This is a busy town astride the road into London, but possesses an antique shop that many a storied cathedral city might envy. This is the establishment of Mr. H. R. S. Turner, which you find in Cross Street, an oasis by an old churchyard reached by a side turning from the main street as you pass through. The premises were formerly the historic "Catherine Wheel" Hostelry, of 15th century origin. Mr.

Turner has converted quaint old rooms into beautiful, intimate abodes for his lovely stock-in-trade. Here are fine antiques, furniture, porcelain, glass and *objets-d'art*; and the firm was established as long ago as 1863.

We entrust you confidently to Mr. Turner at the end of a long, and, we hope, memorable journey.

Always Travel With ANTIQUES YEAR BOOK

ROUND THE ANTIQUE SHOPS

TOUR THREE

BRIGHTON AND THE SOUTH COAST

THIS will not only be an easy and profitable but it will also be an extremely fascinating tour, especially if made this Festival year of 1951, when Brighton is holding its own Antique Dealers' Fair amid true Regency surroundings.

It is advised that the journey from London be done quickly —an hour or two—and headquarters be established in Brighton, where it will be possible to roam around for several days. Probably no town in the country outside London has exactly the character of Brighton for antique shops—or so many of them. Tortuously interweaving the quaint old buildings by the sea at the centre is the famous district known as The Lanes, given over to antique shops almost alone, and with an atmosphere recalling French and other Continental market centres. A book could be written about The Lanes, a film made. There is the ancient antique dealer who sits amid piled treasures; there is the up-to-date porcelain specialist from London; the cap on head junk merchant; the languishing lady: they are all there.

But primarily The Lanes to-day is a revived area, infused with much new and enterprising blood. And do not think that Brighton for antiques is The Lanes alone. Many of the best dealers are just outside or even far outside that particular focal point. An association of them was formed last year, The Brighton and Hove Antique Dealers' Association. Others are members of the British Antique Dealers' Association. Some are quite independent of any grouping: so that the district is a microcosm of England for antiques as a whole.

OLD LACE—ANIMAL BANDS—PORCELAIN

Apart from the romantic character of the Brighton and Hove antique shops, there is a special atmosphere which derives from the type of antiques sold, which tend to be small and with a leaning towards *objets-d'art* and porcelain. Furniture is not the feature, though of course it is often offered. One can, for example, speak at once of—and pay a just tribute to—the charming doyen of the local trade, Mrs. A. M. Hirst, whose shop " Shann's of Harro-

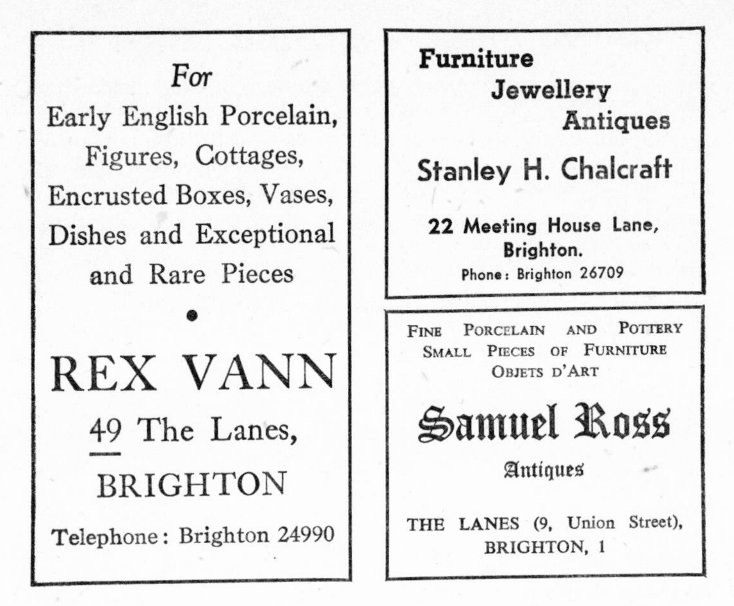

English Porcelain: A Chronological Table

Factory	*Dates*
Bow	1744-1775
Chelsea	1745-1770
Longton Hall	1752-1758
Worcester	1751
Derby	1756-1849
Lowestoft	1756-1803
Plymouth	1768-1770
Chelsea-Derby	1770-1784
Bristol	1770-1781
Caughley	1772-1814
New Hall	1780-1825
Coalport	1790
Pinxton	1796-1812
Spode	1800
Nantgarw	1811-1822
Swansea	1814-1824
Rockingham	1820-1842

gate," has such a distinctive, petite frontage in fashionable East Street (Number 73).

Mrs. Hirst and her mother before her have had the honour of supplying exquisite specimens of old lace to successive Queens of England. Their lace, their lovely and genuine Venetian mirrors, their fans, ivories, jewel-like specimens of old furniture, priceless *objets-d'art* have frequently attracted Royalty to that distinguished shop with the fine gallery above : and here is a find at once for our readers whether they visit Brighton or not, for it is possible they will not find a more reliable dealer, particularly in old lace, anywhere in the world.

Or wander into The Lanes immediately and pause at one of the brightest shop-fronts therein, that of Mr. Geoffrey Van (also of Beauchamp Place, London), whose number is 47. You will find excellent porcelain of the kind most in favour at present. Within this speciality Mr. Van has another—monkey-band porcelain figures, of which several delicious groups are always available. Then Mr. Van has sections devoted to Dresden, Meissen, and shipping goods generally. He is a most energetic and helpful personality with a big future.

Continue to Number 49 and the wholly individual establishment of Mr. Rex Vann, wholly individual because famed already for unusual items of porcelain, such as encrusted boxes, vases, dishes—*and cottages!* Mr. Vann is strongly recommended for such items, also for figures and exceptional pieces.

Porcelain and shipping goods : this is undoubtedly the area. Emerge from The Lanes again and call at 25 Ship Street, the shop of Margaret Cadman who is an expert and export porcelain dealer *par excellence.* It is a liberal experience to examine the delightful and extensive stock : still more so to visit the private headquarters of the firm at 12 Marine Square along the Regency front towards Rottingdean and the white cliffs. Here are gracious rooms laden with porcelain both English and Continental, together with some fine pottery of the best periods. Mrs. Cadman and her associate Major Stewart-Browne (President of the local Antique Dealers' Association) have had long acquaintance with the needs of visiting collectors, and ship porcelain regularly to many parts of the world.

Then nearby to the Cadman shop is that of Mary Russell, (15c Prince Albert Street). Again two charming specialists in porcelain and pottery purvey unusual wares, but the accent is on old English pottery here, all the best from Whieldon to silver resist, with tempting sidelines such as unusual pieces of furniture and some lovely musical boxes, whose tinkle, carried away in the mental ear, will always recall a pleasant rencontre for discriminating visitors.

Porcelain again : You proceed from Mary Russell's a few steps on to Number 9 Union Street, yet another entrance to The Lanes, and find between two others the starred shop of Mr. Samuel Ross, a young dealer of the most discriminating taste and fine historical judgment who buys and sells Bow, Chelsea, Worcester, all the fine porcelains, who usually has some interesting Wedgwood, and who also is equipped for shipping business.

CERAMICS CONTINUED—AND SILVER

Wander into The Lanes once more. (You cannot help it!) But some sort of system is necessary, some sort of *discrimination* among so many, and we choose for you carefully the tiny shop of Margaret Trevor at Number 52, tiny but deceptive, because this is merely the *pied a terre* of a really extensive export business

Shann's
(of HARROGATE)

Member of the British Antique Dealers' Association

OLD LACE
FANS

China & Bijouterie

Established 1887

Telephone 21494

73 EAST STREET AND
83 MARINE PARADE

BRIGHTON

Margaret Cadman

25 SHIP ST.

Brighton

Telephone : 29627

Porcelain Pottery
Enamels
Furniture

I give Best Prices for the above

MEMBERS OF THE BRITISH ANTIQUE DEALERS ASSOCIATION
W. WILLIAMSON & SONS
F. H. BOYS
Old English Furniture
VALUATIONS FOR INSURANCE
& PROBATE
Castle House, 49 Quarry Street
GUILDFORD
Telephone 5019
SURREY.

ONE OF OUR THREE LARGE SHOWROOMS

Journey's End—at the Lovely "Witch Ball" Antique Shop in Thame, near Oxford.

A Corner of Showrooms in a very Attractive Antique Shop, that of Messr. F. E. Norwood, Ltd. (Specialists in Weapons), Berkhamsted.

conducted by Mr. Michael Trevor-Venis. He has a large warehouse at 15A Ship Street Gardens, and specialises in direct export of all types of fine porcelain and pottery, also Victoriana.

Or proceed to Number 22 and meet Mr. Stanley H. Chalcraft who is the genuine antique dealer among his five showrooms (deceptive, these small shops!) of antique furniture, and especially antique jewellery, also porcelain and pottery. This will be a very pleasant call.

And continue a little farther along to the extensive establishment of Hannington's, branch of the big Brighton store in North Street, where the accent is on period furnishings and the appurtenances to antique interiors (much valuable advice will be given, and mention *The Antiques Year Book*).

But enough—and let there be for the meantime a silver ending. At 5 Prince Albert Street will be found Messrs. Ward of Brighton, the dealers in antique silver and plate. Mr. Ward is an expert with a profound feeling for the fine articles he sells and nearly always has something really unusual to offer. It will pay to visit and browse with him.

THE HOVE SIDE

And silver it shall be for a little while longer—silver, glass and jewellery, which in their finest antique manifestations are to be found at Messrs. Evershed and Sons, 121 Church Road, Hove, the spacious thoroughfare that extends from the west end of Brighton. Eversheds are among the leading silver firms of the provinces, having been established as long ago as 1858 and yet retained in the same family since. You may see a superb silver centrepiece of 1794, or a lovely pair of Georgian ship's decanters. There is the unusual speciality of George III Twopenny Pieces—about which a note appears elsewhere in this book—and also, dare we whisper it ? fine porcelain.

Which does certainly seem inevitable in these parts. Brighton is going to be as famous for porcelain as is Edinburgh for silver. Proceed to Portland Road, Hove, and find at Number 156 opposite St. Peter's Church in a long wide thoroughfare with no parking worries the shop known as " The Cabinet." Here Mr. and Mrs. Towner seek to display only the finest porcelain, and usually have a unique piece for exhibition. They have a flair for finding what is so seldom encountered in these days, the unflawed

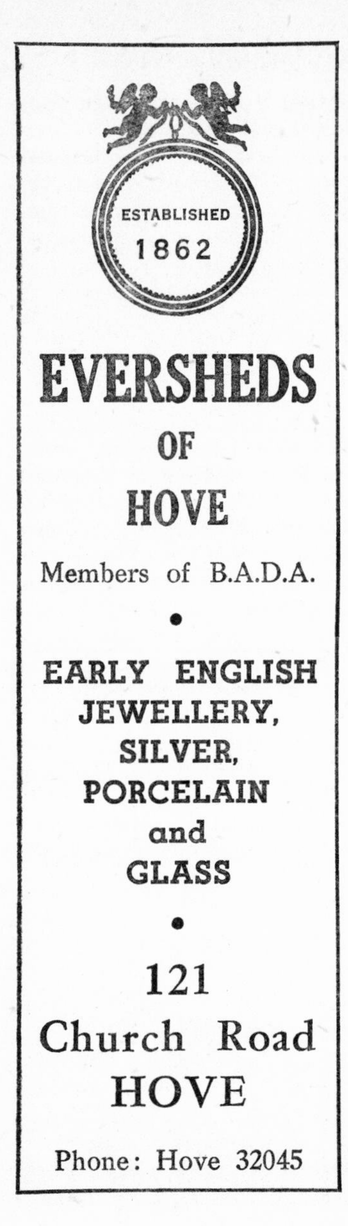
ESTABLISHED
1862
EVERSHEDS
OF
HOVE
Members of B.A.D.A.
EARLY ENGLISH
JEWELLERY,
SILVER,
PORCELAIN
and
GLASS
121
Church Road
HOVE
Phone: Hove 32045

best, and must indeed be carefully noted by all who take their porcelain collecting as seriously as it should be taken.

Or for silver again—and porcelain—return to Church Road and at Number 146 enter the shop of Messrs. Ward of Hove, who can always offer antique silver and plate, often unusual pieces, at very reasonable prices, with years of good reputation to recommend them.

From which the return to Brighton should be made via Church Road, and if you love architecture, be careful to turn right towards the sea into Lansdowne Place.

At number 42 will be found the charming shop known as Ashleys, where Mr. Strawbaum who had a good business in Huddersfield for many years offers American export goods, also tasteful schemes for furnishing and decoration in period style, lamps, antique jewellery, porcelain. He should not be forgotten by the visitor who likes to spread a net wide, so please make a point of calling at this shop—and afterwards, proceed down Lansdowne Place, and journey eastwards along the front, eyes dazzled alternately by the bright sea and the superb, continuous hotels and squares of that elegant long ago.

SEAFORD—EASTBOURNE—PEVENSEY

Brighton is certainly an excellent centre. A very pleasant excursion can be made along the superb coastal road to Seaford, Eastbourne and Pevensey.

When unusual little Seaford is reached ask for the narrow old High Street, wherein it is impossible to miss The Old House, a genuine black and white structure which was the residence during the reign of Queen Anne of Thomas Tufton, Bailiff of the Cinque Ports. This is a good antique business with a very large stock covering most interests. It is the sort of shop where you can browse around and maybe find the rarity or the bargain.

Then climb the clean downs behind Beachy Head and enjoy the sudden panorama of Eastbourne, a large town which has a few antique dealers worth visiting, such as the lady at "Quality Corner," 55 Gildredge Road, turning to the right off the main

Always Travel With ANTIQUES YEAR BOOK

Terminus Road opposite the railway station. She sells porcelain, *objets-d'art* and antique jewellery at very moderate prices, together with small antique furniture.

Proceed along the Grand Parade by the sea till Devonshire Place is reached on the left. This leads to Cornfield Road and, at Number 11, the very attractive Eastbourne shop of Messrs. Byrne of Camberley. The specialities are china and ornamental items, and trade buyers are recommended to call.

Now turn left into Terminus Road and continue till Grove Road is reached on the left again, and at Number 40 find the shop of Seldon's Ltd. Enterprising Mr. Seldon is here building up an extensive stock of low-priced antiques, ranging from good early porcelain to cloisonné enamels, from pictures to clocks. He caters for American export business, and should always be visited.

After which leave the town and run a few miles further east for the highspot of this particular trip, Messrs. Allens' Old Mint House at historic Pevensey, just under the Conqueror's Castle, a "must" for all visitors to England. The Mint House, itself 600 years old, is one of the world's leading authentic settings for antiques, with no fewer than twenty-eight rooms rich in well-preserved oak beams and with much fine panelling. King Edward VI stayed here; there is a traditional ghost and a room that *feels* haunted: also a very large selection of antiques of all kinds and a great deal of fine oak, all chosen and priced with the needs of the present-day small collector in view.

(It might be worth mentioning that a firm of auctioneers at Lewes, county town behind Eastbourne and Brighton, specialise in antique weapons, in coins, and in books on weapons. This is Messrs. Wallis and Wallis, 200 High Street, Lewes. They will gladly send catalogues of their regular sales, and will execute postal orders from all parts of the world.)

Rimington Beeson

at

13 Marine Court,

St. Leonards-on-Sea, Sussex

Phone: Hastings 4000

buys and sells

The Finest Quality Porcelain

(Continental a Speciality)

ANTIQUE CHESSMEN

Old Clocks, Specimen Glasses, Old Paperweights and Pottery

(Elers ware a special interest)

BOUNTIFUL BEXHILL

Continue now the few miles to Bexhill, more of an attraction in many ways than the larger coastal towns, and look carefully as you enter the Old Town for Forge House, an interesting building of the late 17th century recently modernised and turned into an antique business. Three rooms are used for the display of furniture, porcelain and pottery, the type of furniture displayed being old oak, walnut and yew tree wood.

Then in the seaside town of Bexhill itself prepare for a surprise at Number 13 St. Leonard's Road, where the severely-tasteful establishment of Mr. Malcolm Anderson is devoted to—rare Chinese works of art, together with old prints, such as aquatints and mezzotints, especially sporting prints. But it is as a natural connoisseur of Chinese porcelain and jade that Mr. Anderson is outstanding. He is a very enterprising and scrupulous young dealer for whom we predict a considerable future, and whom we wholeheartedly recommend to the cognoscenti.

Another interesting recommendation is to Messrs. Mayfair Antiques of 37 Sackville Road, because young Mr. Heathcote the proprietor similarly knows his antiques through and through—and because there are provided here what yet another class of customers want, small inexpensive antiques of all kinds : and some fine reproductions in old mahogany of chests, writing desks and bureaux. Write to Mr. Heathcote for his catalogue of these.

And lastly—the climax of the run probably for many of our readers who know that these notes sometimes recommend a long-remembered wine. On the great promenade of St. Leonards, a few miles further along, is a large block of flats, Marine Court, and in a shop, Number 13, of this building is : Mr. Rimington Beeson, and his porcelain and pottery, clocks, glass, old paperweights, and *chessmen*. We know of only one other dealer in the British Isles who sells and repairs chessmen in Mr. Beeson's way. (Needless to say they are close friends!) Do, therefore, visit this lovely shop beside the sparkling sea and make a lasting friend. (Meissen and Continental porcelains are an added interest.)

Always Travel With ANTIQUES YEAR BOOK

ROUND THE ANTIQUE SHOPS

WORTHING

A visit to Worthing is now strongly recommended, not only because this very elegant seaside town on the other side of Brighton has an atmosphere all of its own, but also because some good antique dealers are to be found there, including one who is outstanding perhaps in the entire country as a business devoted wholely to export and wholesale trade.

This is the remarkable firm known as Godden of Worthing, situated at Number 17, Crescent Road (telephone Worthing 5958), a turning to the right along Montague Street. Here Mr. Leslie Godden, Vice-President of the British Antique Dealers' Association, and upholder of a family business established in the middle of last century (brought to Worthing as long ago as 1900), applies himself as a specialist entirely to the buying of export antiques of all kinds, and to smoothing the way of customers, trade and overseas, who require the minimum of trouble after making their purchases.

It is a revelation to go through this firm and see how the goods are handled from start to finish by experts in packing, customs regulations, and shipping. You can make your bulk purchase and walk out without further worry of any kind. And the selection of goods offered—it is as if the cream of available export antiques in the country, particularly in china goods, have been specially assembled here by the salubrious sea for your delectation!

But Worthing also has good dealers who cater for the general public, pre-eminent among them Mr. Hugh Williams at 126 Montague Street. Although he handles some very important antique furniture on occasion—pieces that go to the London Fair and to museums—Mr. Williams caters also for the ordinary man and woman, offering them moderate-priced stock in exceptionally good condition.

Now continue along Montague Street till it becomes Rowlands Road, wherein at Numbers 101–3 Mr. Lionel Waldron has his antique shop, the type of shop where you may equally find a Louis XIV commode or the missing Georgian silver spoon for your set. Mr. Waldron does a considerable business with the trade, and offers always a wide variety of good, genuine antiques.

Onwards west to Number 28 Goring Road, a new shopping area with at least one business that deals only in the old and beautiful, Messrs. Christophers, a considerable firm who offer

in these premises attractive antique furniture, china and glass, also Oriental rugs and carpets. They are worth visiting, but still more their other establishment at Selden Manor, Patching. This is half-way between Worthing and Arundel, a fine old English country house with six show-rooms of antiques in their natural habitat, old oak, walnut and mahogany furniture, also a very fine and comprehensive range of porcelain. Mr. and Mrs. Curzon, the proprietors, give personal attention and really valuable advice to all customers.

After which we recommend a run down to Bognor Regis, pleasant seaside town with a very useful little address at 2, Goodwood Place, West Street, for those who want a wide range of porcelain and pottery of excellent quality. Miss Ursula Sichel's standard is high for all her stock and her prices are moderate. She always carries American export goods.

And while in this area it might be helpful to note that Messrs. Farr's Depositories Ltd., of St. John's Street, Chichester, have developed a most efficient service for the packing, carriage, storing and shipping of antiques. They have a branch at Brighton, and really understand their job.

BACK TO LONDON

We now suggest an interesting journey back to London from Brighton which comprehends some beautiful scenery and some worthwhile antique dealers. Take the inland road from Brighton to Old Shoreham.

Reaching old Shoreham look for Georgian Cottages on the left, a picturesque collection of period buildings where Mr. and Mrs. Winter of Worthing run an antique business combined with a first-class restaurant (coffee recommended, also the chicken luncheons!) They offer all kinds of antiques, and bargains can often be found, the appeal being especially to those who wish to furnish in period style at moderate cost.

Then take the main London road north through the downs to the charming village of Steyning, showplace of this area, wherein will be found a lovely Georgian-lined green and also a house reputed to be 1,000 years old and another mentioned in Domesday Book. Here Mr. Hugh Williams of Worthing has another shop, 29 High Street, in which he sells some important furniture as well as genuine Sussex oak and byegones. This is a pause well worth making.

Proceed onwards now some six miles to the village of Storrington and carefully turn left for another seven miles to a main road. Turn right along this a short distance and find in the village of Bury a charming and most unusual establishment known as The Barton, where two knowledgeable ladies set themselves an extremely high standard as antique dealers, having always some rare and lovely stock.

Now follow the main road onwards to old-fashioned Petworth, unspoilt town clustered round its great house. If you are interested in furniture at trade prices—this firm is deservedly well-known to the trade—visit Messrs. C. Denman and Son in East Street. They have many showrooms, have been established over forty years, and their furniture is offered untouched.

Then proceed up to the fine church and Petworth House, finding opposite these the shop of Messrs. Ernest Streeter and Daughter. Mr. Streeter was an expert on old clocks of very wide reputation. His daughter carries on the tradition, selling antique clocks, silver and jewellery—a personality whose acquaintance is well worth making. Many kinds of finds for collectors lurk in this friendly establishment.

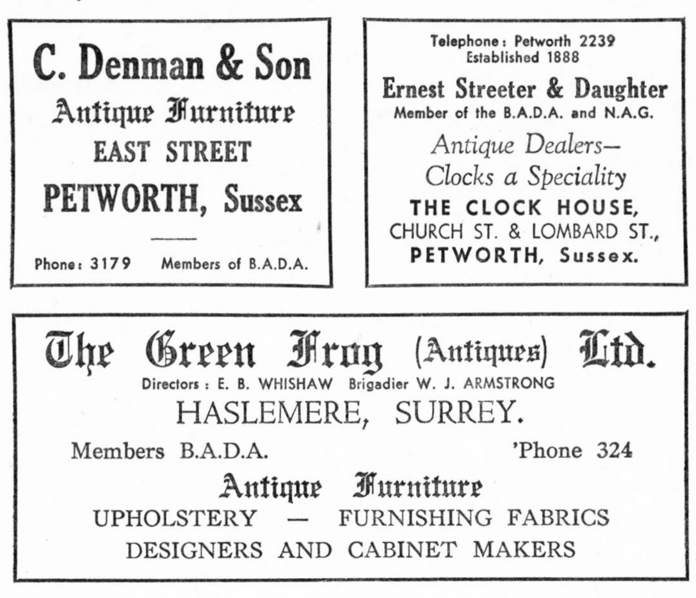

Now take the road leading via Midhurst to charming Haslemere. Just as you enter on the right will be seen The Green Frog antique shop. This offers attractive small pieces of furniture and a variety of things old, rare and beautiful.

Eight miles farther north along the Surrey-scenic road is Godalming, and, on the right as the road leads out to Guildford, the establishment of Messrs. A. J. Brooker (8 Meadrow), another good shop with a high standard.

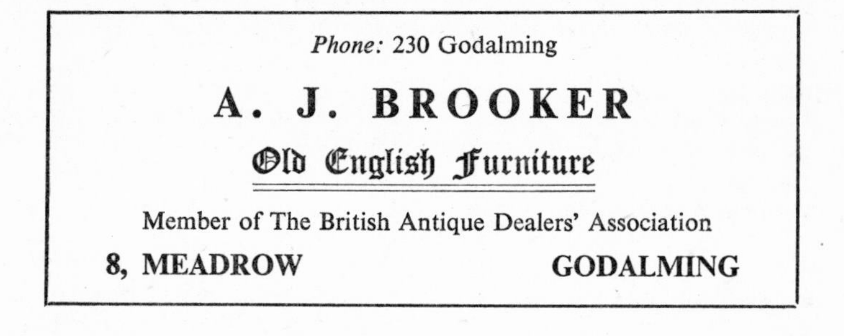

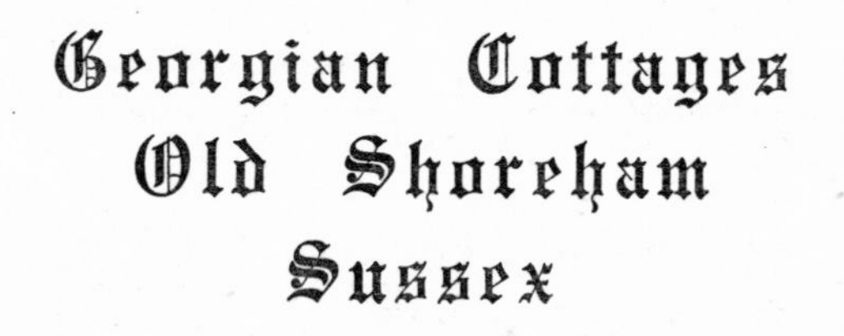

ROUND THE ANTIQUE SHOPS

HOROLOGIST EXTRAORDINARY

Now before entering Guildford on the road from Godalming look carefully on the left for St. Catherine's House, an Elizabethan mansion built on a mound, which was taken as a burnt-out shell in 1946 by Mr. R. G. A. Wells, the well-known horologist, and has been converted since into a remarkable headquarters for his extraordinary business—an antique business probably without an equal in that it is concerned with one item alone, the preservation, repair and sale of old clocks and watches. Mr. Wells himself is an outstanding personality of the trade, famous for his television broadcasts and talks to America, and, with his helpmate wife and staff of some twenty expert workmen, devoted to the task of giving customers exactly what they want. This establishment is highly recommended, especially to overseas visitors. Mr. Wells' London branch, in Beauchamp Place, is dealt with elsewhere.

GUILDFORD

So to Guildford where the rest of the day can be profitably spent before the final run straight up to London in less than an hour. There are several interesting establishments, but we present for our readers an outstanding firm.

We refer to Messrs. W. Williamson and Sons, whose Castle House, an interesting old place incorporating remains of Guildford Castle, will be found by turning right at the traffic lights at the foot of the High Street into Quarry Street and proceeding upwards to Number 49.

The point about Messrs. Williamson is that they are really good, having a reputation second to none, and offering only perfect pieces (particularly in furniture of the 18th century). This description need not, however, alarm the modest collector, as good pieces are offered at moderate prices over a wide range.

It should in any case be a valuable experience to visit Messrs. Williamsons—and to meet the proprietor Mr. F. H. Boys—as this firm was established towards the end of the 18th century and is probably among the oldest in its class. It has received visits from various members of the Royal Family including Her Majesty Queen Mary, and extensive dealings have been had all over the world. Personages who have passed through these famous galleries have included Cecil Rhodes, Lord Kitchener, William Ewart Gladstone, Lord Rosebery, Lord Wolseley and Lord Northcliffe—to mention but a few.

ROUND THE ANTIQUE SHOPS

TOUR FOUR

AROUND LONDON AND KENT

WE now suggest one or two easy runs from London, particularly east of the city and to Kent, the first being to Epping in Essex, where a branch of Charles L. Nyman & Co.'s Camden Town business will be found at Number 178 in the High Street of that excellent old town amid the great forest which is still not fully appreciated for its beauty so close to grime. You can run out there very quickly and inspect some of the Webb cameo glass—or the many other items of glass, china and old furniture which this typical country antique shop can offer.

RATCLIFFE OF ESSEX

After which continue via Ongar to Chelmsford, finding there at Number 24, Duke Street, the first of the several businesses in these parts of Messrs. G. T. Ratcliffe, Ltd., who, at Durwards Hall, Rivenhall, some miles further on along the Colchester Road, have no fewer than thirty-three showrooms of antiques. The old Hall is a landmark on the right as you proceed, undoubtedly the largest antiques establishment in the county, with some very interesting sidelines such as armour, wrought ironwork and period architectural fittings.

Then proceed onwards to the village of Kelvedon itself, where there are two more Ratcliffe offerings, a very dainty antiques shop on the left (once featured in a film) which is especially good for pottery, porcelain and small pieces with a French atmosphere; also " The Old Queen's Head," an old inn with a skittle alley in the cellar which has recently been acquired and converted into many showrooms.

And hereabouts we suggest what should be a very pleasant experience, namely that you continue to Colchester, then journey via Sudbury to Lavenham in Suffolk, there spending the night. Why ? Because the village of Lavenham is one of the loveliest in England, still comparatively untouched by modern development and right in the heart of the Constable country, with Long Melford nearby. And also because Mr. R. McCausland-White of Folkestone has an excellent antique shop here, Number 4, High Street, in a beautiful old building and with some very interesting stock, from furniture and china to *pictures.*

On the way back to London next day follow direction signs that lead the main Southend Road to the North Circular Road, and ask at the point where the North Circular Road begins for *old Wanstead* wherein, at the picturesque Old Cottage, High Street, Messrs. A. McClure and A. H. Barns sell some interesting antiques at very reasonable prices. The little pilgrimage is worth making because Wanstead contains the Manor House where Penn of Pennsylvania lived, also the house where Sheridan wrote *The School for Scandal.* Maintaining its reputation for famous men, it is to-day a leading part of the parliamentary constituency of Mr. Winston Churchill, who owes a lot to its unfailing loyalty in time of crisis.

THE ROAD TO KENT

The mention of Mr. Churchill comes usefully here, because we are about to suggest another quick tour, this time into Kent, which will take the interested reader as an early port of call to Westerham where this outstanding of modern Englishmen has his country residence.

On the way out a very good antique shop can be visited at Blackheath, found by proceeding over the river to New Cross and then taking route A2 (to Rochester) to Deptford and then Blackheath Village. At Number 23, Tranquil Vale, will be found this shop, the establishment of Messrs. E. A. J. and M. H. Parker (also twenty minutes from Charing Cross by Southern Railway). Here is a varied stock of antique and reproduction furniture, china, glass, pewter, brass and copper. Pictures and jewellery are also offered—and the business is undoubtedly one to which customers return. Mr. Parker was many years with Harrods and Maples, while his wife has long had a smaller business in the village. After Blackheath ask the way to Bexley, where Christy's of Kent have an interesting shop at 52 High Street, and then to Petts Wood, where at 181, Petts Wood Road, will be found a further branch of this excellent Mayfair establishment.

Now continue to Bromley and there proceed by the main road to Westerham. In Westerham will be found three famous old half-timbered houses.

First to be noted is " Pitts Cottage," once the home of William Pitt, Earl of Chatham, now known to tourists all over the world

Pitts Cottage

XIII CENTURY

Once the Home of William Pitt

Well-famed for its Old World atmosphere. Here for your pleasure, in surroundings that charm can be had—Morning Coffee, Home-made Cakes, Afternoon Teas and Luncheons too.

Arts and Crafts.

WESTERHAM, KENT.

'Phone 125

AND JUST

" OVER-THE-WAY " a Guest House with much to offer for an enjoyable and restful holiday. 600 years old—yes—but modern in its Comfort and Service.

'Phone Westerham 125 or 268.

WESTERHAM ANTIQUE SHOP

(J. B. WILSON)

OLD-RARE AND FINE MODERN BOOKS, FURNITURE - GLASS - CHINA, ETC.

99 High Street, Westerham, Kent. 'Phone 125.

as a delightful tea house, where the best of good food is provided. Besides its wealth of oak, it is furnished with choice antiques.

For those who wish to tarry peacefully for the night there is a large half-timbered house just " Over the Way " with superb old-world garden. Space forbids detailing the infinite charm of this old house, except to say the comfort of visitors is the first consideration of Miss Elsie Wilson, the proprietress. It is 600 years old, but 1951 in appointments and service.

A short distance down the road at Verralls Corner (mentioned in Domesday Book) is the antique shop, where Mr. J. B. Wilson is always pleased to show early printed, rare and fine books, glass, china and furniture, which are displayed on three floors of different levels in one charming gallery—at the far end of which may be had teas served in the " Pitts Cottage " tradition amid old-world surroundings.

TUNBRIDGE WELLS–MAIDSTONE–CANTERBURY

Tunbridge Wells is an interesting town to visit next, and we choose from among the several antique shops there one which

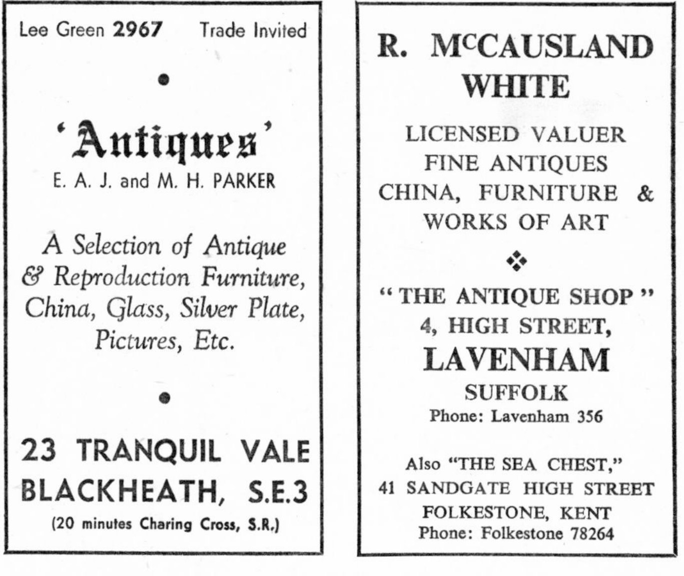

we are convinced will specially interest visitors. This is situated in the famous "Pantiles," quaint 18th century thoroughfare where the dandies once walked, and the number is 18B, the name S. A. Gardner, Ltd. The shop might appear very small, but leads to an intriguing series of underground galleries, wherein will be found not only a large stock of excellent antique furniture, porcelain, pottery and glass, but also novelties like musical boxes, unusual clocks, and *Tonbridge Ware*. This is a good dealer to contact for anything off the beaten track and highly recommended by us for the interest of his wares.

It is now suggested that the road to Canterbury be taken via Maidstone, because you will find in Maidstone, on the right as a narrow road leads out of the town—Number 52, King Street—the good antique shop of Mrs. W. Draycon, good for furniture, silver, porcelain—and wine-glasses! Many American friends have visited her at our recommendation and have always found some interesting old pieces.

So to Canterbury, chief Kentish centre for the lover of antiquities, and we can point to an excellent antique shop therein, that of Mr. W. H. Stringer at Number 45, Palace Street, part of the former Palace of the Archbishops of Canterbury (where Thomas A'Beckett once lived). Here will be found fine old furniture of all kinds, and other period items.

Are you interested in old spinning-wheels and looms, or have you a period piece of this kind which requires restoring? If so you will be very glad to have the address of Douglas Andrew, Summerhill, Harbledon, Canterbury. Here is not only a specialist in spinning wheels and looms but also a school for hand weavers, unique, flourishing, and recommended.

After which a rest might be indicated by the sea, in the finely-appointed holiday town of Folkestone not so far away. And you would like to visit here " The Sea Chest " of Mr. R. McCausland-White at Number 41, Sandgate High Street. English and Continental porcelain and pottery, furniture, paintings and prints are sold by an artist and student of history with the knowledge that leads to good buying and much wholesale and overseas business. It is a real pleasure to meet this gentleman.

From Folkestone and Canterbury the road back to London follows the historic Dickens way via Chatham and Rochester—Rochester where will be found at Numbers 12, 18 and 19 the original antique galleries of Charles Woollett and Son, the fine London firm, established 1889, and outstanding in all this area for the best furniture, china, silver, glass and bric-a-brac. We conclude the tour on a fitting note, for undoubtedly at Woolletts will be found in epitome the best of Kent.

(As a postscript to this trip it might be suggested that the reader remembers the New Caledonian Market—more than a hundred stallholders in antiques assembling every Friday in Bermondsey Square, Tower Bridge Road, via Waterloo Bridge, south of the Thames.)

Always Travel With ANTIQUES YEAR BOOK

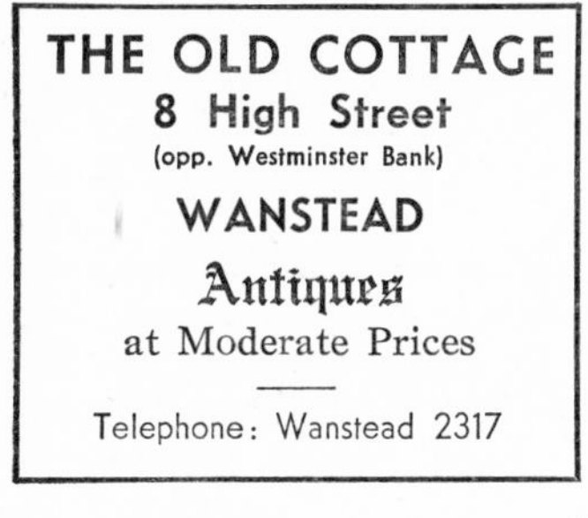

TOUR FIVE

LONDON TO THE NORTH-WEST

AN excellent route to the north and if necessary Scotland from London is via the north-west—Birmingham, Potteries, Manchester, Lake District—and begins with the Finchley Road from London, then Barnet, and next St. Albans, where there are some good antique shops.

In the centre of St. Albans turn left at the traffic lights and proceed down Holywell Hill to Number 9 and the establishment of Mr. W. J. Lomas. This was formerly an old coaching inn, the "Dolphin," and is maintained by its public-spirited young proprietor as a repository for fine pieces of 18th century furniture, particularly mahogany, and especially *chairs*, in good condition. It is always noteworthy, moreover, that Mr. Lomas has a penchant for the original brasses on his furniture. There is a subsidiary establishment at 26 George Street which was once the "Old George" coaching inn, built as a hostel for pilgrims.

Now opposite to the ancient Abbey in Holywell Hill, St. Albans, at Number 23, find the new and very attractive shop of Messrs. F. E. Norwood, Ltd.—a branch of the well-known Berkhamsted business. It is well worth a visit if only to see the fine pine panelling just uncovered. (The building was used by the monks of the Abbey in ancient days as a resting house.) But Norwoods yield much more than just a sight of pine panelling. They stock fine period furniture, but specialise in Georgian glass, Staffordshire copper lustre ware, and *pistols of the flintlock era.*

THE WEALTH OF DUNSTABLE

The next antiques stop, and a remarkable one, is Dunstable, a long town which seems to cater for our kind almost exclusively, having several really good businesses for its small population. On the right as you enter is the famous old firm of Harry Rixson, occupying an attractive building known as " Ye Olde Retreate " (part of the historic Dunstable Priory). You can rely on fair treatment and no profiteering here. The Rixsons are experienced dealers who wish to retain their customers, and do so from all

parts of the world. There is an excellent display of old English furniture, panelling, fireplaces and works of art generally; and *trade business is a speciality.*

Near to Rixsons, on the same side of the broad street (at Number 57 High Street South) will be found the shop of Mr. Alexander L. Podd. This gentleman had much to do with the introduction of the Regency vogue in London. He sells small, reasonably-priced furniture for the average collector, especially Queen Anne, has antique clocks, and caters for the American market also.

Proceed up the road and turn right into narrow Church Street, finding at Number 26 the premises of Mr. William Rixson. This young dealer is rapidly expanding a very old business, because he has a flair for giving callers what they want, genuine antiques of all kinds not too expensively priced. A few doors away is a subsidiary warehouse always stocked lavishly with antiques of every description, something for everyone, including china, clocks and prints.

Return to the High Street—for that is your road north—and proceed up High Street North some considerable distance,

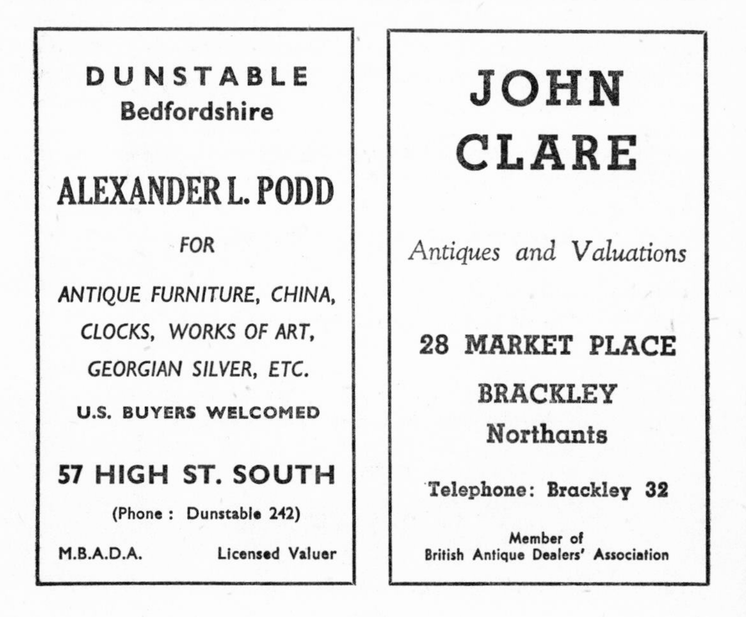

watching for a house on the right, Number 152. This is the premises of Blaise Preston, Ltd.: and indeed, you may think, Dunstable has been bountiful. Here you will encounter one of the most interesting of modern antique dealers, Admiral Sir Lionel Preston, K.C.B., author and antiquary. With his son he has always to offer at least something which will be quite unique, and often something which not even London can show. Very rare Old Master paintings are usually the outstanding feature, but also fine furniture, porcelain, enamels, clocks: and antique needlework and materials.

BRETT—TROLLY HALL—BRACKLEY

Continue on the fine northern road for some more outstanding experiences, as at Stony Stratford, lovely red-brick Georgian town with a secluded Market Square (turning off main road to left in middle of town) where the premises of "Michael Brett" will be found. The name Brett has long been famous in the antiques world, and this representative, Major C. A. Brett, will be found a singularly interesting personality with a penchant for the unusual—see the remarkable Regency piece on the first page of this book—and also for giving our American friends what they want. He is highly recommended for porcelain, and for novelties such as musical automata, also for all kinds of shipping goods, and his name should be on every overseas visitor's list.

A short distance past Stony Stratford is a turning left, to Buckingham, and Buckingham is a fine old town with a shop of great interest known as Trolly Hall (in Castle Street) wherein Brigadier Lake, connoisseur and friend to all his customers, has a large stock of old furniture, china, silver and *objets-d'art*, charmingly laid out in just the right setting in this beautiful Georgian house. Brigadier Lake's prices must be "right," as he sells so much to the trade. (He has a large selection of fabrics and rugs, also, and specialises in the making of curtains and coverings for furniture.)

Take from Buckingham the road to Brackley (famous for its associations with Sulgrave Manor and the Washington family) and at Brackley, Number 28 Market Place, call on Mr. John Clare, who is a really first-class specialist in 18th century furniture, a modest shop but one that often houses the piece of your dreams.

Now proceed up the road till Chester House is seen on the

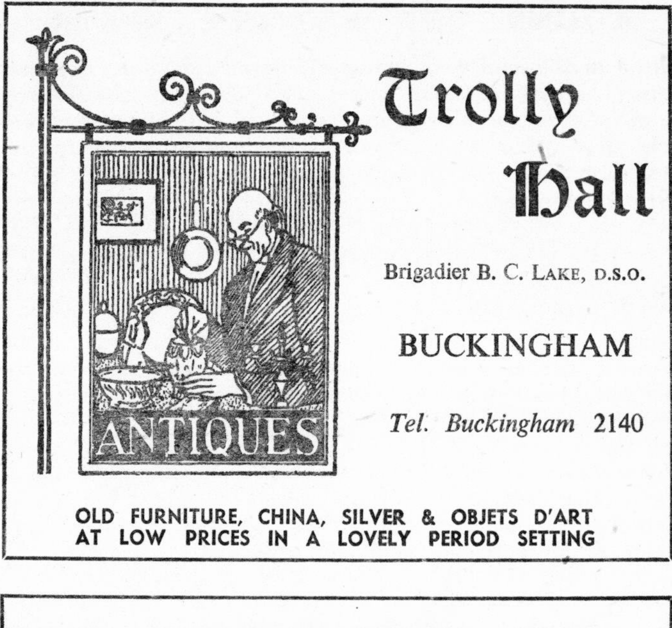

LEAMINGTON SPA

FOR ANTIQUE

ENGLISH, CONTINENTAL & ORIENTAL

POTTERY & PORCELAIN, IVORIES,
ENAMELS, JADE & GEMSTONES,
JEWELLERY, CURIOS, WORKS of ART

Collectors and Ornamental Pieces

A. GREENLEY,

86 WARWICK STREET

left, a most useful combination of antiques shop and excellent café. The premises were once an old Georgian inn. As well as period furniture, old coloured prints and early oil paintings are sold. This will be a pleasant call. The proprietors cater for the American trade also, and can usually offer some English and Dresden porcelain.

LEAMINGTON—AND FINE WARWICK

The road to follow from Brackley is that passing through Banbury to Leamington and Warwick. The distance can be covered without stop to Leamington, as Banbury has yet to develop the antiques interest it could well support. Leamington Spa, beautiful and stately, could also be disappointing, were it not for the enterprise of Mr. A. Greenley, who at 86 Warwick Street has a remarkably good stock of pottery and porcelain, curios, enamels, ivories, hardstone carvings, jewellery, bric-a-brac and small antiques generally. He has among his customers many curators and collectors, some with quite large and well-known in another tour, also an interesting museum for collectors down the narrow street opposite towards the Castle wall—known as Oken's House. Visitors throng these establishments and are invariably satisfied with their finds of good furniture, china, glass, needlework, antique jewellery, silver and plate. Yes, Warwick is a star town.

AROUND BIRMINGHAM

The environs of Birmingham sometimes yield pleasant surprises to the searcher after good antiques, and one can be offered right away. As the road from Warwick enters Birmingham, ask for Moseley, and in the centre of the shopping parade (152 Alcester Road) find the charming shop of Messrs. Abbot & Attwood Antiques. This is a most unusual shop, with interests ranging from antique dolls and Nailsea glass to Welsh dressers. Small inexpensive items are always sought-after by the energetic proprietors, and the reader is strongly advised to call.

It is worth remembering, too, that Moseley has an expert furniture restorer, Messrs. W. Nightingale at 154 Alcester Road. There is skill in the hands of these Birmingham craftsmen, who are enterprising people, ready always to take on work from any distance.

On the main road north to Derby and Nottingham from Birmingham lies the ancient Borough of Sutton Coldfield, and this possesses similarly a most interesting antiques establishment, Vesey Manor, on the left at a corner as you enter the main part of the town. Run along very efficient lines by Mr. and Mrs. T. W. Coulborn, the firm is increasingly developing its interest in fine Dr. Wall period Worcester, as well as Chelsea, Bow, old Derby and Dresden porcelains. There are all kinds of antiques, but the porcelain is a feature and those interested (to sell as well as to buy) should contact Mr. and Mrs. Coulborn mentioning *Antiques Year Book*.

Pass through the shopping centre and on the right leaving the centre stop at the Vesey Galleries of Mr. Norman H. English, Numbers 30a and 30b High Street. Mr. English is an artist who sells modern pictures—and everything which has artistic interest, whether modern or old. Framing of pictures is a speciality.

Always Travel With ANTIQUES YEAR BOOK

collections, and supplies a considerable amount to the trade for export.

From Leamington it is but a mile or two to ancient Warwick, fascinating historic town with two excellent antique shops, those of Messrs. Grainger-Brown, Number 2 High Street, on the right in the centre of the town, and of Messrs. Quinneys, a short distance on the left up quiet Church Street from Messrs. Grainger-Brown's shop. (While here it is suggested that the visitor enters fine St. Mary's Church opposite, with its exquisite Beauchamp Chapel).

At Messrs. Quinneys, Number 9 Church Street (and with a branch at Number 7 High Street) it will be found that Mr. A. G. Robinson and his son are truly excellent dealers of the old school, with a wide stock of English and French furniture, as well as porcelain (including Oriental), pottery, paintings and clocks. An unusual sideline is antique barometers (which they can repair and restore). Famous people know "Quinneys" and the firm is highly recommended.

As indeed is Messrs. Grainger-Brown on the corner of High Street. This firm have a branch at Stratford-on-Avon, mentioned

WOLVERHAMPTON

Then again Wolverhampton, next big industrial town on the recommended route (turn left after Sutton Coldfield and proceed through Walsall) has surprises for the discerning, notably in the establishment of Mr. E. J. Morris at Chapel Ash (proceed from Queen's Square at the centre of the town down Darlington Street, and the shop is found on the right at the foot of the hill round the corner). Mr. Morris is an authority on Staffordshire and Ralph Wood. His pottery, ah, those sturdy greens, blues and browns! is absolutely right, and you can rely on this dealer if you contact him from any part of the world. More than that, he has floor after floor and great barns at the back filled with low-priced antique furniture of all kinds, and his business is one of the oldest in existence (established by the first Morris in the year of Waterloo!)

Proceed a little further down Chapel Ash and on the right still will be found " The Little Gallery," yet another business conducted by Mr. Cecil Whistance of Hampshire—with a uniquely small frontage, but fine rooms upstairs with antiques, period furnishings and products of local artists and craftsmen.

Now continue on the main road towards Shrewsbury and pause in the suburb of Tattenhall, one mile from the centre of Wolverhampton, where Mr. Charles Davis's shop in Newbridge Crescent has some interesting porcelain, antique furniture—and miniatures. Here is a conscientious young dealer, recommended to collectors and the trade.

POTTERIES—BUXTON

The visitor will now wish to cover the miles quickly northwards to the Potteries, home of so much in which he is interested —and will find in this smoky but strangely romantic region just what he hopes for, several small dealers of character who always have interesting Staffordshire items for sale at modest prices. Enter Newcastle-under-Lyme and proceed up Merrial Street on the right to Number 4, where Mr. R. A. Chadwick, son of an old dealer whose shop is seen first, usually has in stock Wedgwood medallions and basalt, as well as early Staffordshire (and pot lids), together with general antiques of all kinds.

Then proceed to a busy crossing and take the road bearing right to the Potteries proper. This is Brunswick Street, and a distance up on the right will be seen the unusual small shop of Mrs. H. E. Little, a most enterprising and knowledgeable young woman who specialises not only in Staffordshire pottery (Wedgwood particularly), but also in brass and copper.

The ovens and smoke-stacks now crowd around as the road proceeds to Hanley, best of the five towns. One of the main streets is Piccadilly, and at Number 49 Mrs. D. M. Broughton-Thompson is again most conveniently a Wedgwood specialist, also selling other pottery and porcelain, as well as general antiques, jewellery and glass. She already has many friends in the United States as a result of care taken over special orders, and can be recommended for this purpose.

And before leaving this fruitful Piccadilly in friendly Hanley, visit or note the address of the antiquarian bookshop run by Messrs. Sanderson & Son, Ltd.—because they are one of the few booksellers in the world who specialise in usually unobtainable works on pottery and porcelain for the collector and manufacturer.

Visit them or write to them for your needs, mentioning *The Antiques Year Book.*

You may well require a short rest now or at least a soothing relief from industrial landscape, so take the road to Buxton, famous spa of Derbyshire, traversing magnificent hill scenery—and finding in this superbly-appointed tourist town at least three first-class antique dealers, Mrs. A. Hockenhull at 6 Cavendish Circus, and Messrs. Walter Salt, 42 High Street, and Plant and Sons, 6 Hall Bank. All three, by the way, specialise in trade business.

MANCHESTER

Take the main road to Manchester from Buxton. Watch carefully on the left when entering Stockport (and first encountering the cobblestone roads), for here is the shop at 292 London Road of Mr. J. Milner, antique jewellery, silver and Victoriana of special interest to American trade buyers. This pleasant North Country personality has a branch at 63 Oxford Road, Manchester, 200 yards from the Palace Theatre on the road to Wilmslow.

Manchester itself contains some strange experiences for the antiques visitor. Maybe you would not expect to find any worthwhile dealers at all in this area, but ask your way to the Market Place and find triumphantly alone among the bomb-devastation an ancient half-timbered building, sole survivor of Manchester's distant past, and climb rickety stairs to a real genuine old curiosity shop, Messrs. Chas. Clark (Antiques) Ltd., 25 Market Place, run by a most unusual lady of outstanding character, who has many fascinating sidelines such as old theatrical relics, sporting and *railway* prints, brass and copper—everything.

Moreover Manchester has nearby a Cathedral, yes, and a quiet Cathedral Yard, in which will be found the shop of Mr. H. J. Neal, who specialises in *long-case clocks*, as well as selling brass, china and other interesting items.

And, believe it or not, there is an art dealer not so far away—Mr. Charles A. Jackson, 12 St. Ann's Square—who sells not only Chinese ceramics, but also has in stock normally at least half-a-dozen Sickerts and Steers and a few Epstein bronzes. He is an art dealer of the best old school, with roots firm in the New English Art Club, and is strongly recommended to connoisseurs.

Another excellent firm of art dealers in Manchester is Messrs. J. Davey & Sons, 70 Bridge Street, turning out of Deansgate. Not only do they sell Old Masters, paintings and drawings, and undertake framing and restoring, but they deal in *old maps*.

And on no account, if you are at all interested in antique silver, omit a call while in Manchester at the shop in Ashton-under-Lyne of Mr. Tom Kenworthy (226 Stamford Street) a great local character and expert on silver who is constantly in requisition as a lecturer. He has some really first-class silver, most of the great eighteenth-century makers, and the prices marked are as different from Bond Street as is smoky but friendly Ashton itself.

LIVERPOOL

So back into Manchester and across through the factories and over the Ship Canal to Liverpool, where to start with we have a good British Antique Dealers' Association member, Mr. John Maggs, whose shop will be found at 114 Bold Street. He is particularly good for Staffordshire and porcelain, for unusual pieces, and his workshop can effect repairs to your antique furniture. All kinds of antiques are sold and the firm is very highly respected in the trade.

Frederick Treasure Ltd.

Members of the British Antique Dealers' Association

PITT STREET GALLERIES
PRESTON.

TELEPHONE : PRESTON 4414

Famous Stand of The Old Pewter Shop, Harrogate, at Grosvenor House Antique Dealers' Fair, London.

One of the Eight Large Showrooms at the Fine Business of Messrs. R. P. Carmichael & Co., Ltd., Hull.

At the other end of Bold Street will be found Hanover Street, with the Hanover Fine Art Galleries (Number 37), where Mr. and Mrs. Smith conduct a very modern and pleasant antique business. The premises are furnished most tastefully; the antiques offered are chosen with care to meet all purses; and there is a predilection for interesting porcelain.

Indeed, porcelain and pottery are notable in this area, for Liverpool has, at 5 Exchange Street East, the old firm of auctioneers Messrs. E. Owens and Son, who have always carried

a stock of really fine Chinese antique wares. Mr. Owens is one of the few provincial specialists in the best Oriental and is well worth meeting or communicating with by letter (please mention *Antiques Year Book*).

Porcelain will again be found in the shop of Messrs. Leonard at 26 Tarleton Street, off Church Street opposite Woolworths. Good antique silver and *objets-d'art* generally are also sold—and the firm wants particularly to buy, while catering specially for the trade.

Nearby, in North John Street, are the well-known Boydell Galleries, established over 100 years, but as interesting today as ever, under enterprising management.- Please note for useful reference that they specialise in two items, 19*th century Old Masters*, and really first-class restoration of paintings.

And in Liverpool do not forget Messrs. Henry Young, the new and antiquarian booksellers of 15 and 15a North John Street. They carry a large stock of collectors' books, new and old, conduct valuations for probate, and purchase libraries. This is a very good mark for either the collector of fine books or the connoisseur who requires a rare work on a collecting subject.

ROUND THE ANTIQUE SHOPS

PRESTON

There is a good straight road north from Liverpool to Preston, and Preston is one of the best towns in the north-west for antiques, having two major dealers and several smaller antique shops.

It will be a very interesting experience to find the extensive galleries of Messrs. Frederick Treasure, Ltd., situated in the quiet oasis of Pitt Street, behind the main road. These unusual showrooms always contain a large stock of all kinds of antiques, ranging from furniture for home-makers to export goods bought wholesale by knowledgeable Americans. Mr. Leighton Treasure, a live personality, is always delighted to conduct visitors in his friendly North Country way round the assorted " treasures of Treasure."

Regain the main road and turn left at Corporation Street, proceeding down this thoroughfare till another famous series of antique galleries are encountered, those of Messrs. Edward Nield at Number 223. The firm is old and fine—exhibits at Grosvenor House each year—and Mr. Nield himself is another North Country friend : good for 17th and 18th century furniture, excellent porcelain (Dr. Wall Worcester and Chelsea in particular), as well as Oriental porcelain, pictures—and overseas trade business.

Back again to the main road (Fishergate) and at Number 50a find Mr. Miller in his interesting showroom down a passage-way with the word " Antiques " guiding you in the street outside. The wares are furniture, porcelain, glass and *objets d'art*, offered quietly and sincerely by a hard-working dealer of taste and discrimination.

NORTHWARDS

An unusual route north is now suggested, as the main road via Lancaster is uninteresting and can be very traffic-jammed in the towns. Proceed first to Blackburn. Here is an excellent shop, that of Mr. F. E. Tinker at 14 Mincing Lane—good for antique furniture, *objets d'art* again, pictures, miniatures.

Then you could if you like proceed to Skipton in Yorkshire for the night, Skipton because it is a charming old town, free from industrialisation. You would find there, in narrow Coach Street, a quiet abode of fine furniture, some old glass, even some rare porcelain at the shop of Messrs. R. N. Myers and Son. Also in Skipton—many would say principally in Skipton—is the establishment of Messrs. Frank Laycock, Water Street. You find this on leaving the town next morning, and Mr. Laycock, although averse to publicity, is one of the great antique dealers of old England.

The road recommended for scenic interest and quiet motoring from Skipton runs to Settle—where the shop of " Elizabeth Robertson " is to be found in 17th century premises (Bishop

Court House) in a quiet neuk almost opposite the Town Hall Clock. Collectors and lovers of antiques will find much of interest there.

From Settle proceed on the long run to the Lake District via Kendal, a town that has been described so often that we shall be content with noting this year two small antique shops where bargains may be found. The first is called " The Gateway," will be found on the left on entering the town, and the proprietor Mr. D. E. Wrathall sells (and proudly) both genuine horse brasses and pot lids as well as old maps and cottage furniture. The second will be found near the Railway Station in Wildman Street, is called " Raffles," run by Mr. N. R. Phillips, and offers some charming cottage furniture in a really quaint old shop, " The Old Farm House," one of Kendal's oldest surviving buildings.

LAKE DISTRICT

And so to the Lakes, in fair weather offering perhaps the finest scenery in these islands, and in foul—an ever-fascinating route north with some excellent antiques stops on the way. For ex-

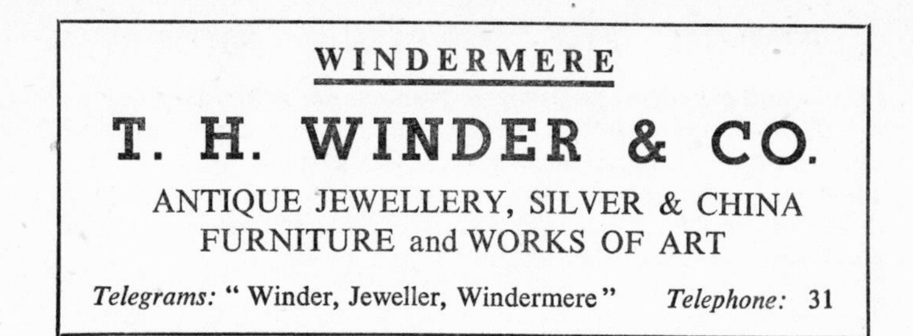

ample, in Windermere, or rather Bowness-on-Windermere down by the Lake, is the establishment on the left as you enter of Mr. and Mrs. T. H. Telford, largest dealers hereabouts, who sell a very wide variety indeed of always-interesting antiques ; and there is also the shop of Messrs. Winders, on the left towards the foot of the hill, where antique silver is sold primarily, but also good old furniture and other items. This is an unusual business and a call there is often well-repaid.

Now follow the fascinating motor road through the Lakes northward again, via Ambleside and to Grasmere, heart and soul of the region, with Wordsworth memories—and the second establishment of Mr. and Mrs. Telford next door almost to Wordsworth's cottage, a shop replete with furniture, silver, china, pewter and local items.

Continue afterwards to Keswick, looking at scenery, not antiques, save for a pause in the town itself at Number 16 Main Street, where Messrs. John Young and Son are very solid North Country antique furniture dealers, recommended for reliability.

AND THE BORDER

All of any recommended interest left now is in Carlisle, best reached as soon as possible for the night, a lovely city with its saffron stone and clean thoroughfares, at the centre of which, next to the celebrated Crown and Mitre Hotel, stands the antique shop of Messrs. James W. Clements (56 Castle Street). This shop is really " good for " the best in antiques of the kind that interest everybody, displaying excellent taste and always having some first-rate items of furniture, porcelain, silver, glass and jewellery to show.

At the other end of Castle Street next, in the interesting quarter of the town, will be found what appears to be a good silversmiths' and jewellers', the shop at Number 15 of Mr. E. Thompson. It is far more than that. Several galleries of antique furniture and the like will be found at the rear. In the shop itself Mr. Thompson offers *objets d'art*, enamels, jade, pictures—he is a dealer of unique quality and a starred recommendation. Also a good introduction to the Scotland which awaits.

Always Travel With ANTIQUES YEAR BOOK

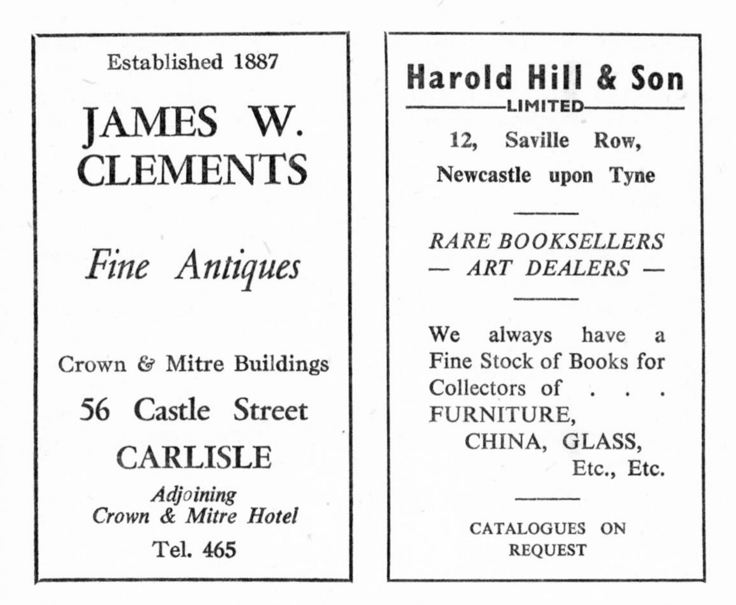

TOUR SIX

YORKSHIRE AND EAST MIDLANDS

IT is a sensible idea to take Northumberland, Durham and north Yorkshire in the course of a journey back to London from Scotland—and then to return to Yorkshire for a more prolonged investigation from a single centre such as Harrogate or York.

The first stop after crossing the Border south must be Newcastle on Tyne, a friendly city which has some antique dealers, among whom two may be mentioned here, Mr. J. J. Russell Agnew, of Numbers 3 and 34 St. Mary's Place, and Messrs. Harold Hill and Son of 12c Saville Row.

As you enter the city from the north you come to fork roads. At this point St. Mary's Place is a sharp turning to the left. Mr. and Mrs. Agnew sell principally antique furniture, china, armour and weapons, together with interesting sidelines such as mirrors, Toby jugs and gate-leg tables. They have a large warehouse, always well-stocked.

Saville Row is another turning on the left from the main road (Northumberland Street) to the city centre, and the firm of Harold Hill and Son are not only among the leading antiquarian booksellers of England, with an outstanding section of books on collecting subjects, but also general antique dealers, with the speciality of *bookcases*. You can write to Harold Hill from any part of the world for the rare bookcase you want.

After which proceed southwards to Durham, the outstanding town of historical and æsthetic interest in these parts, and turn abruptly right after passing the caged policeman in the centre to nose up the narrow street, Saddler Street, leading to the Cathedral. Here are two interesting antique shops. The first, at Number 58, is kept by Mr. Hugh B. Edwards, son of that respected doyen of the Yorkshire trade, Mr. Edwards of Harrogate. Mr. Edwards guarantees all his goods as genuine—17th and 18th century furniture and silver.

The second establishment, at Number 55, is kept by Mr. Michael Appleton, who has a good stock of fine quality period furniture at reasonable prices, together with pictures, china, glass —and a home and overseas trade connection.

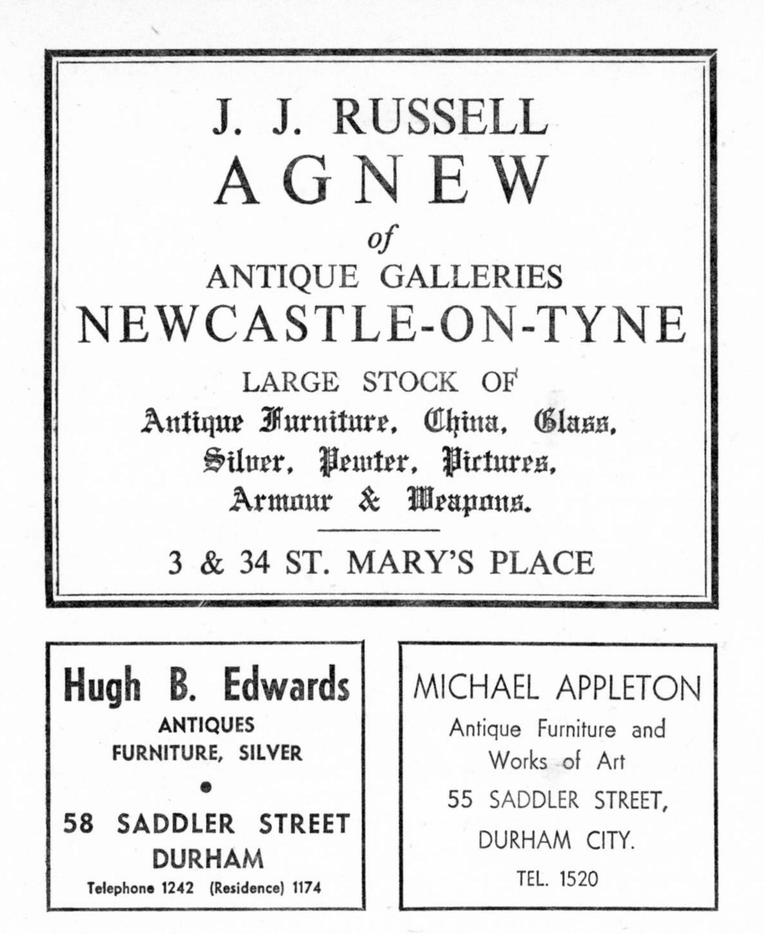

SCARBOROUGH

Alas, we now have a long journey before us, all the way to Thirsk, and then across to Scarborough, not too fruitful along the way, but necessary if we are to get south, and certainly ending most pleasantly at Scarborough itself, which is among the most comfortable resorts in these islands, catering for the visitor, and providing him with much of antiques interest.

There are many, many antique shops, but we shall guide the busy visitor to the few that he would probably thank us the most

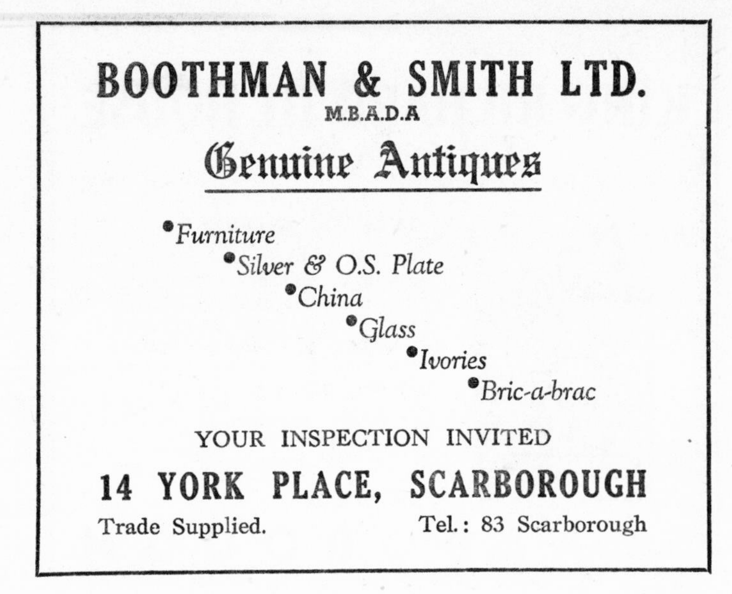

for recommending. The outstanding shop as such is that of Messrs. Boothman and Smith at Number 14 York Place, a turning off the central shopping street. These are dealers of taste and probity, stocking particularly some fine antique furniture and good silver, also porcelain, antique jewellery, ivories, *objets d'art* generally.

We would suggest particularly that the visitor asks to be taken by Mr. Boothman to Number 3, Belvoir Terrace, The Crescent, where a lovely Georgian house built remarkably of stone brought from distant Bath by the architect of the Quadrant at Bath is stocked with excellent antiques in their exact period setting. The neighbourhood, made famous by Osbert Sitwell in his autobiography, is most interesting; the view to the sea is magnificent; and Mr. Boothman is delighted always to show and explain his exquisite furniture and porcelain.

But Scarborough also has a very remarkable institution indeed, the famous King Richard III House down on the Harbour Side. This wonderful 14th century building, wherein the Yorkist King stayed, has been carefully restored by Mr. E. H. Burrows and opened to the public, on the one side as an unique museum of antiquities, on the other as an antique shop. Thousands of visitors regularly examine the three large floors of rare articles from man traps to lighting implements, from horse pillions to prisoner of war bone work, from early glass to old oak ; and the shop sells a very large variety of antique furniture, china, glass, pewter, brass and copper. This is certainly a highspot in our antiques tour of the country.

Indeed, between Messrs. Boothman and Smith and King Richard III House the visitor will have sufficient to occupy him—although he might care to find in the street between the Royal and Grand Hotel (7 Marine Parade) the shop of Mr. Angus Graham, whose china, pottery, silver and antique jewellery are calculated to appeal to many visitors.

ROUND THE ANTIQUE SHOPS

HULL

The run down to Hull is now well worth making, as this city has some good antique shops and one large establishment which has a very large stock of all kinds of antiques, suitable not only for the ordinary, modest collector, but also for the attention of export buyers. The firm is Messrs. R. P. Carmichael and Co., Ltd., of 53–63 George Street. There are departments for modern goods, but the antiques departments proper, under their own expert manager, are sufficiently large to absorb nearly a whole day of attention.

A feature of Carmichael's is that all prices are marked, are worked out to a flat rate of profit, and remain unaltered. Much good antique furniture is sold, but also porcelain, and the silver and antique jewellery departments are as large as most to be found in London, with a big stock always of interesting early articles.

Always Travel With ANTIQUES YEAR BOOK

YORK

We now come to the real antiques centres of the great county, and would suggest that the first run be made direct to York, which is of all cities what the overseas visitor hopes to find in England, beautiful, ancient, threaded with medieval thoroughfares lined with lovely old buildings, the superb Minster—and several of the most fascinating antique shops imaginable.

Perhaps the loveliest premises and the finest stock are those of that great personality among antique dealers, Mr. Charles E. Thornton. Petergate just under the Minster is a superb medieval street. The Adams House therein, Mr. Thornton's headquarters, is replete with antiques of quality, ranging from (on our last visit) a gigantic partners' desk that would enhance the largest board-room in the country to magnificent French commodes, from Tompion clocks to repeater watches, from the best Old Master paintings to Cries of London prints, from numerous sets of the best early porcelain to good 18th century silver. In Blossom Street, York, is another Thornton establishment, "The Georgian House," and between the two you have an antique dealer's fair in itself.

But York caters for all tastes, and if yours be the finest antique silver, then return from Petergate to the opening that leads to the Minster and opposite enter the delightful old premises of Mr. Henry Hardcastle the noted goldsmith and silversmith. This business (31 Stonegate) goes back to the year 1770, has a remarkable panelled room inside which is itself a show piece ; and Mr. Hardcastle is the most charming of expert guides to his fine stock (especially of flatware, knives outstanding) which ranges over the best periods of silver. The firm, by the way, are export specialists, and used to handling complicated business from all parts of the world.

Proceeding down Stonegate now you will come to two interesting businesses, the first being that of Mr. William Lee at Number 39. He is another outstanding York personality, who exhibits at the London Antique Dealers' Fair, having first-rate pieces only, both in furniture and silver ; but Mrs. Lee's shop a step further on, known as the Stonegate Furnishing Company, offers all kinds of antiques for the average man and woman, at low prices, and interesting both for ordinary visitors and for trade buyers. The connoisseur should see Mr. Lee : Mrs. Everyman will be grateful for our introduction to the Stonegate Furnishing Company.

So York could go on—for several days of delving—but there is a limit, and we cannot do better than advise the reader, after these experiences, to return to Minster Gates—the narrow opening referred to before—and find therein at Number 3 the very excellent small shop of Mr. Ron Hope, a craftsman himself (City Guildsman) who always offers some pieces of great interest, including porcelain and glass. York will then have proved very satisfying indeed.

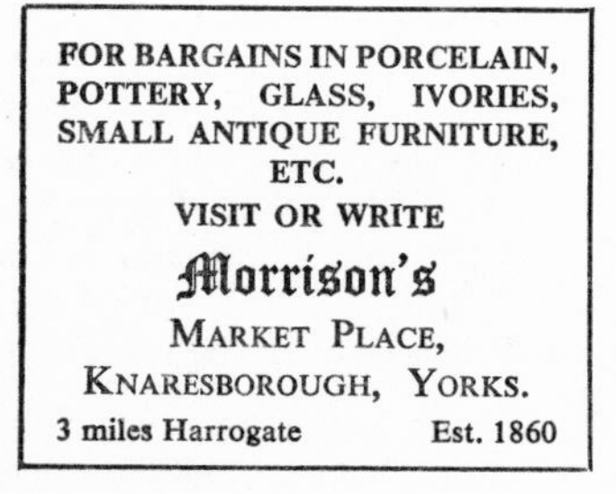

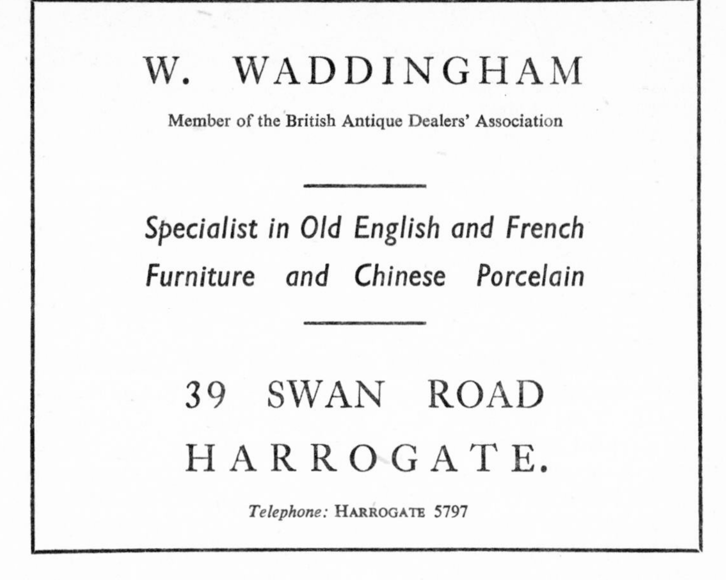

(In Stonegate at Number 15–18, nearly opposite the Lee establishment, is an antiquarian bookseller who carries our very hearty recommendation. This is Thomas C. Godfrey, excellent for early, rare works, fine bindings, and books of York and collectors' interest.)

KNARESBOROUGH INTERLUDE

The obvious road now leads to Harrogate, but proceed via Knaresborough, a most interesting old town famed for associations with such a diverse company as Eugene Aram, Blind Jack, and old Mother Shipton. What's more, it still runs true to type. You will find in the ancient market place, so often thronged with farmers, a little old antiques shop called Morrisons, where one of the greatest characters of all in the trade, Mrs. Watmaugh, displays an amazing knowledge of porcelain and glass, and has a really considerable stock among which you might find anything. She is a friend to all and the introduction will never be regretted.

Then in the High Street look for the exquisitely beautiful shopfront of the business known as " Ann Driver." Here another wide variety of good "bread and butter" antiques are sold. Indeed you may enjoy a stay in Knaresborough as much as anything, and the town is most conveniently situated for Harrogate and York.

HARROGATE FOR ANTIQUES

The climax of the Yorkshire tour will certainly be Harrogate, lovely holiday town with fine manners and excellent facilities, home of another regional Antique Dealers' Fair to be, and with as interesting an array of antique shops as any centre in the land.

For example you can proceed at once to Montpellier Parade and find the lovely showrooms of Messrs. H. Blairman and Sons, famous London name, where only the best antique furniture and works of art generally are offered, reflecting exquisite taste and invariably in the most distinguished mode of the day.

Or you can walk on to the Royal Baths and enter opposite, at Number 39 Swan Road, the establishment of Mr. Walter Waddingham, outstanding among Yorkshire antiques experts and a name of great trust in the trade whose work *for* that trade cannot be honoured too much. He offers the finest furniture, particularly French, and carries the largest stock of Chinese porcelain in the provinces.

And next door, at Number 35, find Mr. Thomas Edwards, doyen of the Yorkshire trade, who founded his very solid reputation fifty years ago and is one of the most reliable dealers in the world : silver being his great speciality, then pictures, furniture, bijouterie and porcelain.

Harrogate is good. Walk over to Royal Parade, and there at Number 10 is the renowned Old Pewter Shop of Mr. Charles Casimir, probably the outstanding specialist concern of its kind in the world. Here you will see, say, the earliest known specimen of a pewter candle stick, or flagons circa 1610 and 1630, a rare James I wassail cup, rosewater dishes circa 1650, Charles II tankards. It is not for nothing that the period pewter at the Rockefeller Centre, U.S.A., was provided by this establishment. Yet there is also a unique array for the beginner at moderate prices. Mr. Charles Casimir always guarantees his wares as a matter of course.

Fine Antique Furniture, Silver & China

SHOWROOM No. 6 One of eight Showrooms

CARMICHAELS

45-73 GEORGE STREET HULL

'Phone: **31656 (4 lines)** *Grams:* **"Carmichael, Hull"**

The Original Home of Beautiful Antiques
and Superb Old Oak Furniture

ILKLEY
IN
WHARFEDALE

TEL. : HARROGATE 5558

The Old Pewter Shop

(Charles Casimir)

M.B.A.D.A.

10 Royal Parade,
HARROGATE, Yorks.

Collections Purchased

Stonegate Furnishing Co. (Proprietress : MRS. WM. LEE)

41 STONEGATE, YORK. TEL. 3871

Specialising in Old Oak and Mahogany Furniture

PRINTS—AND GENERAL

Or cross from the Old Pewter Shop to the tree-lined seclusion of Crown Place and the shop at Number 1 of Mr. Ernest G. Barnard, one of the few specialist dealers in prints whom we can recommend in all England. Mr. Barnard has sold fine coloured prints and old English sporting prints for a generation. His business has been established for forty years. Harrogate thus possesses yet another unique attraction.

And return to the Montpellier area, where at Number 6 Montpellier Gardens there is the antique shop of Mrs. D. A. Cooksley, a lady who sells interesting porcelain and silver as well as *objets d'art*. She may always be recommended to trade buyers, as well as to modest collectors who want to be able to rely on the dealer of their choice.

Then continue down Montpellier Gardens to Number 1 and the very well-known shop of Mrs. A. M. Beevers, who is again most reliable for antique furniture, china, silver and Sheffield

plate, also diamonds and jewellery. This business was established in 1880 and has an interesting speciality—old lace, to buy or sell. The recommendation to this shop is always appreciated by our readers.

After which mount steps before you, and reach Parliament Street, Harrogate's main shopping thoroughfare, with the antique shop at Number 29A of Mr. G. Shaw Bolam, an enterprising young dealer—one of the youngest in the trade—who has quickly developed a good business because he provides furnishing antiques of the kind so many people want for their homes at low prices : items such as wardrobes, usually so elusive : and a personal speciality, namely Sunderland lustre ware.

You can now walk through to Commercial Street—and if you like an unpretentious dealer who often picks up odd pieces of furniture and other items of an antique nature : an old shop where you can browse around : go to Number 17 and Mr. D. V. Shutt.

Meanwhile in the centre of the modern shopping area of Harrogate, quietly away from the bustle, at 13–15 Market Place,

Always Travel With ANTIQUES YEAR BOOK

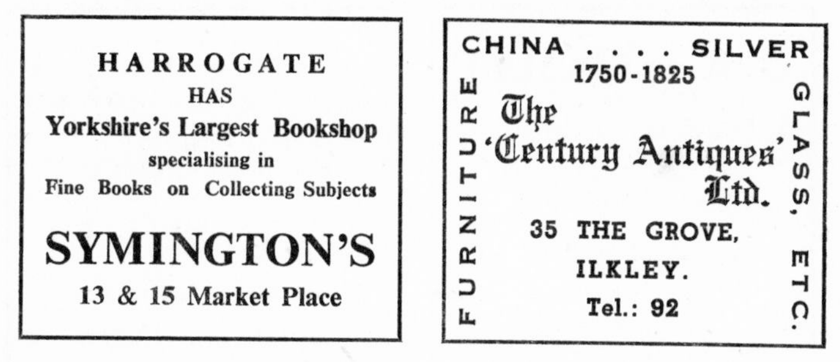

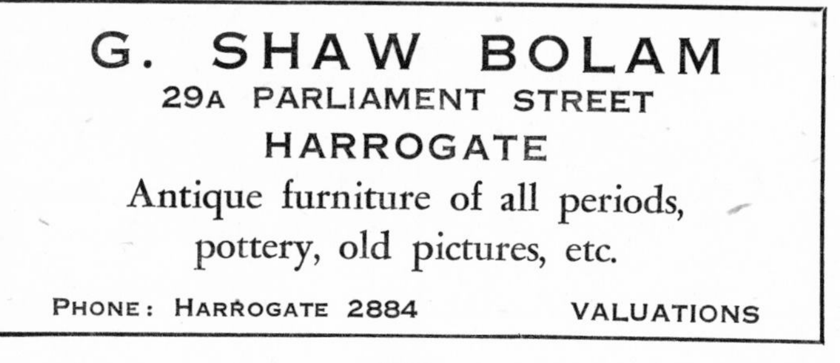

is the fine antiquarian bookshop of Messrs. Symingtons, mentioned here because it is really very good for collectors' books—visit or write, and be assured of satisfying service.

(And if you are interested in silver do not omit to call at the Harrogate branch, 15 Princes Street, of Mr. Henry Hardcastle the York expert. There is a splendid stock, with jewels also in abundance.)

COUNTRY CHARMS

A most pleasant tour is now suggested from, if you like, Harrogate as a base. First proceed to Skipton and visit the business of Messrs. Myers, Coach Street, and Messrs. Laycocks, Water Street, as described in Tour V. Then take the road to Ilkley. Keep a sharp look out on the right as you enter the town for the delightful establishment known as "Minton," Church Street. Here in the Old Box Tree Cottage, complete with original 16th century inglenook fireplace, Mrs. Kitty E. White (one of the most popular and charming of women dealers in the trade) sells—with the aid of her most courteous assistant—a wide variety of very pleasant and tastefully-chosen antiques, from fine pieces to good cottage furniture, and with all kinds of interesting china and glass : the kind of things most of us look for to-day in an antique shop, but all in good condition and reasonably priced. Mrs. White has her finger on the pulse of the public and most usefully provides what is really wanted by the majority. We feel sure that our readers who visit her will remember the occasion and be grateful for it.

Further along the road, at Numbers 33 and 35 Church Street, is a different kind of shop but one that will be equally welcome, Messrs. J. H. Cooper and Sons' show-rooms of moderate-priced antique furniture, with at the side the sort of exciting arcade where you may find a real bargain naked and unashamed on the open pavement. Messrs. Cooper are also restorers, recommended because of their high Yorkshire standard of craftsmanship.

But that is not all, and the visitor should not omit to seek The Grove, parallel with Church Street but at the top of the town, where Mr. Eaton-Smith at his " Century Antiques," Number 35, is very sincere in his endeavour to offer collectors' pieces in china and silver, as well as clean pieces of small furniture and inexpensive glass. This young dealer has high standards—and a future.

BRONTE MEMORIES—AND BRADFORD

Return on the Skipton road now as far as Addingham, then turn left to Keighley, and from Keighley make the very short pilgrimage to Haworth on the moors : Haworth of the Brontes and so representative of the true Yorkshire—where Mr. Lawson Hodgson has a choice selection of antiques in his compact shop

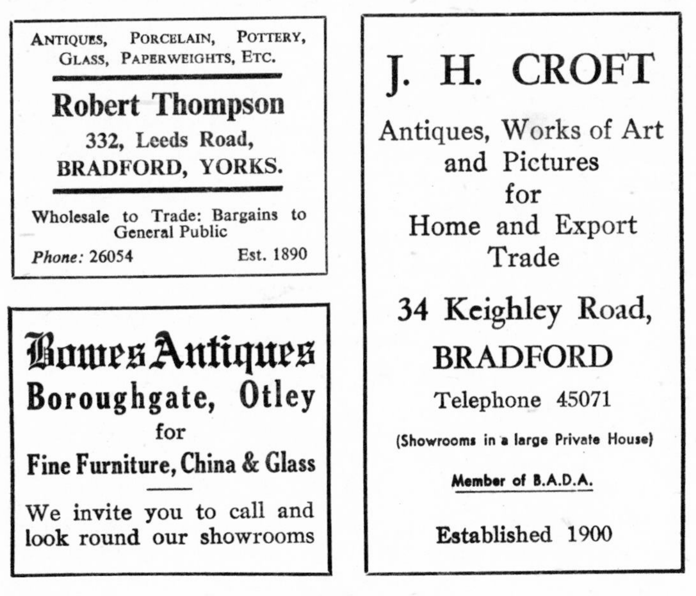

at Number 1 Main Street, next door to the Old Hall where several scenes were filmed for the picture *Wuthering Heights*.

After which run back to Keighley and down to Bradford, and, just before entering this homely but cultured city of woollen mills, make sure that you find the house on the left of Mr. J. H. Croft—Number 34, Keighley Road—because this young dealer, continuing a business established in 1902 and himself just made a member of the British Antique Dealers' Association, is good especially for the American market, and for the English trade in low-priced fine furniture, china, pottery, glass and pictures, all guaranteed (good idea to phone Bradford 45071 in advance for an appointment).

There are several small antiques and curio shops in Bradford but we would ourselves recommend Mr. Croft and also a dealer at Number 332 Leeds Road, Mr. Robert Thompson, who is very good for shipping goods particularly, a regular port of call for American buyers, with a good stock always of the pottery, porcelain, glass and Victoriana which is required.

Now take the road from Bradford back towards Keighley for four miles and turn right to Otley, interesting old market town, with a pleasant antique shop known as Bowes Antiques, recommended for inexpensive goods, and with some pleasant small furniture, china and old coloured glass tastefully chosen by the proprietress.

HOROLOGY—LEEDS

Take the Leeds road from Otley and after a mile or two carefully inquire for a road to the right which leads to Horsforth. In Horsforth find Lee Lane, and then the premises " Windy Lea " therein, where will be found Mr. George F. H. Hutchinson and his antique clocks. This will indeed be a discovery and the trip more than worth making. Mr. Hutchinson is one of the leading authorities in the country on antique clocks—organised the famous Antique Clock Exhibition at Temple Newsham—and has a most remarkable collection of early timepieces for sale.

In Leeds itself proceed to Number 30 Duncan Street, just across from the Corn Exchange, where the very old firm of antique dealers Messrs. W. W. Slee, Ltd., will be found. All kinds of excellent antiques are offered, and the trade is especially invited, prices being reasonable. Furniture, silver, paintings are shown in abundance.

While in Leeds the bibliophile might well care to call on Messrs. James Miles at 80–82 Woodhouse Lane, chosen as outstanding antiquarian booksellers, good especially for early printed and University literature, but also stocking many rare books on collecting subjects.

Then it is suggested that the visitor should aim for the bracing district of Moortown and interview at his residence (perhaps phoning first Leeds 62777), 154 Shadwell Lane, that well-known

specialist in overseas business, Mr. Gerald C. Dimery. He can be relied upon to produce much good period furniture and porcelain : a very good wholesaler.

From Leeds to Wakefield is only a few miles and the journey is well worth making to " Ye Merrie Citee." Beneath the shadow of the lovely Cathedral lies the old antique shop (11–13 Warrengate) of Messrs. Cooper and Launder, 50 years established, always with a choice selection of porcelain, furniture, etc., and a right Yorkshire welcome from " Tony " and " Peter " the two popular partners.

DONCASTER—ROTHERHAM—SHEFFIELD

The return could now be made to Harrogate. If it is wished to continue south, then take the road to Doncaster. At Number 36 Bennetthorpe—the main road south out of the city—is the very charming antique shop known as Peerage Antiques, most attractive to the general public with much pleasant porcelain, pottery and good furniture. Mr. L. Spero the proprietor is at the same

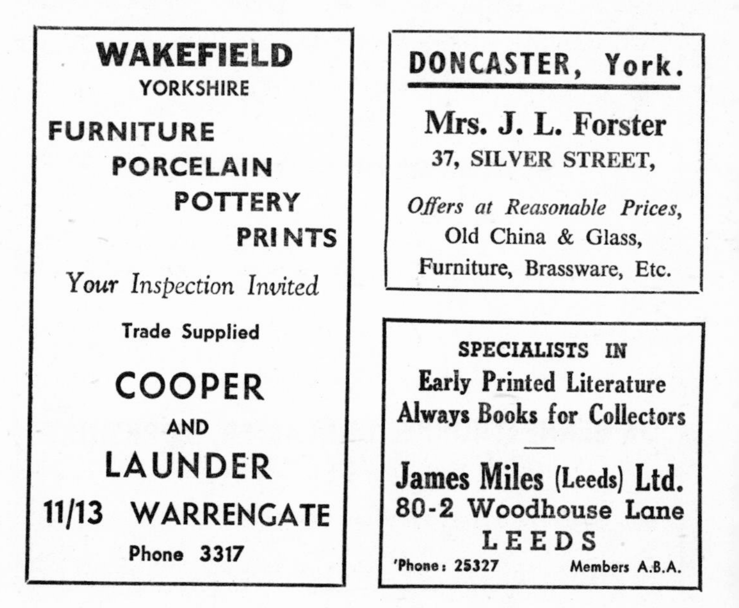

time a trade and export specialist on a large scale, whose warehouse premises here and elsewhere are always well-stocked with the kind of goods most in demand by American wholesale buyers, from Wedgwood to Victoriana and from Regency furniture to antique jewellery. This is a highly recommended business and should on no account be missed.

While in Doncaster, moreover, don't forget to look for Silver Street (turning off the main road from centre of the city), where Mrs. J. L. Forster continues her late husband's antique business, a pleasant lady who sells furniture, china (tea sets sometimes) and glass.

From Doncaster take the road to Rotherham and at Number 36 High Street in that town—where the road leads out to Sheffield—stop for sure at the silversmiths and clockmakers, Messrs. John Mason, Ltd., established 1695 and one of the early clockmakers, yet supplying the silver for the Royal Box at the St. Leger 1950 : with rare porcelain as well as Knibb, Tompion and Fromanteels in stock (long cases especially).

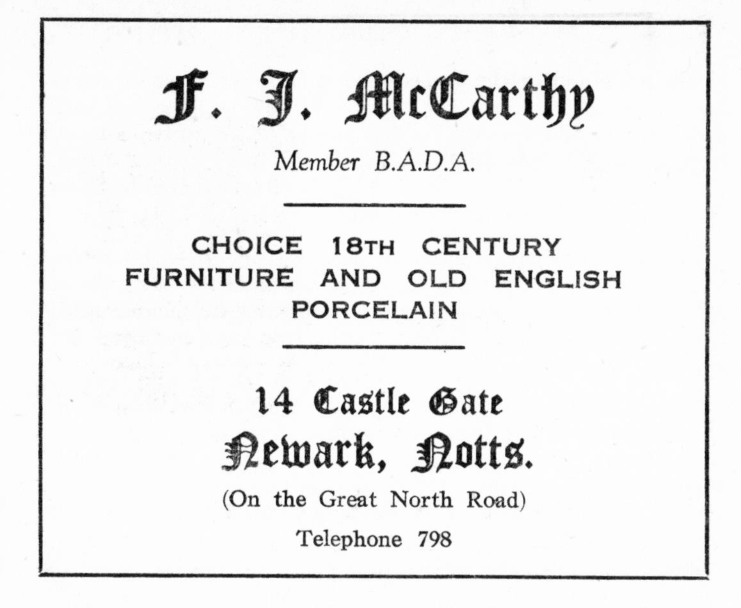

Now continue to Sheffield and proceed to Glossop Road, where at Numbers 288 and 290 is the fine antique shop of Messrs. G. W. Ford and Son. Fine furniture and china are stocked here, also Oriental and Persian carpets in extensive premises where there are facilities for the repair and restoration of both furniture and carpets by real craftsmen.

SOUTH TO NEWARK AND NOTTINGHAM

After Sheffield there is not much of interest for a considerable distance south, so it is recommended that the long run be accomplished swiftly via Eckington, and Ollerton to the excellent old town of Newark, excellent for the night and for a pleasant stay. Near the Castle on the Great North Road at 14 Castle Gate is a fine Georgian house to which Mr. F. J. McCarthy, very enterprising young Yorkshire dealer, has transferred his business. Mr. McCarthy is highly recommended for a call, dealing particularly in good mahogany and rosewood furniture, also porcelain and pottery at reasonable prices : and he can provide 19th century goods for the export market.

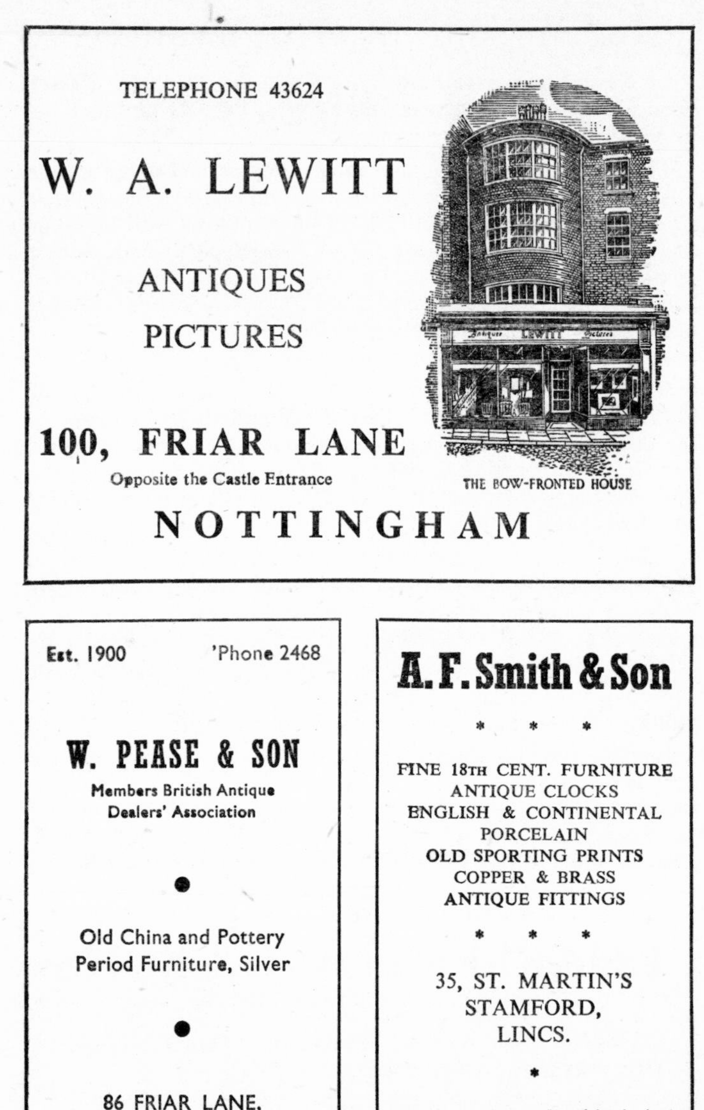
TELEPHONE 43624
W. A. LEWITT
ANTIQUES
PICTURES
100, FRIAR LANE
Opposite the Castle Entrance
LEWITT
THE BOW-FRONTED HOUSE
NOTTINGHAM
Est. 1900
'Phone 2468
W. PEASE & SON
Members British Antique
Dealers' Association
Old China and Pottery
Period Furniture, Silver
86 FRIAR LANE,
NOTTINGHAM
A. F. Smith & Son
FINE 18TH CENT. FURNITURE
ANTIQUE CLOCKS
ENGLISH & CONTINENTAL
PORCELAIN
OLD SPORTING PRINTS
COPPER & BRASS
ANTIQUE FITTINGS
35, ST. MARTIN'S
STAMFORD,
LINCS.
Trade and Export Inquiries invited
Phone: 2218

In Newark also is a branch, at 6 Market Place, of Messrs. Ford of Sheffield, exclusively for carpets, Persian, Oriental and English, with facilities for repairs.

The next stop is Nottingham, and proceed at once to the ancient Castle, under the walls of which, at Number 100 Friar Lane in an excellent Regency building with fine windows, will be found the old antique shop of Messrs. W. A. Lewitt, partly with modern pictures and the like displayed in front, but with a great surprise behind, where stairs lined with Old Masters and prints lead to many showrooms of interesting antiques.

Nearby at Number 86 Friar Lane is a very important shop indeed, that of Messrs. W. Pease and Son, the specialists in pottery and porcelain. Mr. Pease Senior might be described as the doyen of his trade, *most* reliable and with a truly profound knowledge of his subject: and in these modest showrooms will often be found Chelsea, Derby and Ralph Wood up to London standards—but at provincial prices.

Another interesting call in Nottingham can be made at Number 185 Mansfield Road. Here will be found a young dealer, Mr. Malcolm Cameron, whose works belie his years, in that he is specialising already in *pewter*, both for the collector and for the trade. He always has some interesting pieces to offer, also furniture. We believe that Mr. Cameron will become an important addition to the thin ranks of pewter dealers in this country.

Loughborough is the next town south after Nottingham, and here the wayfarer is invited to pause (after branching left from the Post Office) in the quiet sanctuary of Church Gate, opposite the noble 13th century church, where will be found the old antique shop of Charles Lowe and Sons, often new on the surface but with many fascinating antiques in the background.

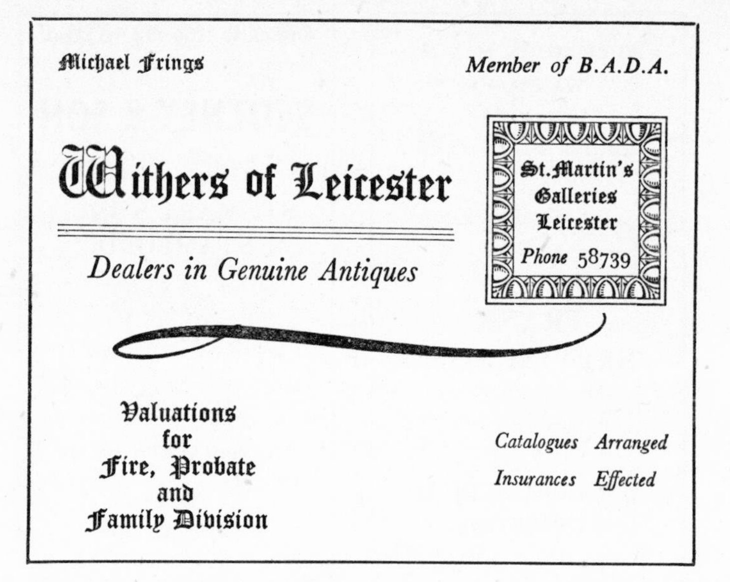

Just on the way out of Loughborough on the Leicester Road will be found the Lantern Galleries of Messrs. W. B. White and J. S. Oliver—with the unusual speciality of weapons and armour, both European and Oriental, also antique furniture, and excellent repair facilities.

The old village of Quorn comes next on the route, and has a good antique shop at Numbers 5, 7 and 9 High Street, known as Mercy Jeboult, lovely green front, and always offering very attractive items of dainty old furniture, china and clocks.

LEICESTER—STAMFORD—PETERBOROUGH

There are several antiques shops in Leicester but only one "Withers of Leicester." This fine old business, with its St. Martin's Galleries in Loseby Lane, is unique locally for standing and stock, and full worthy of the complete recommendation of this book. Mr. J. M. Frings, the young and energetic proprietor, is assured of a big future in the trade, and is good for 18th century furniture, particularly mahogany, for porcelain, silver, Sheffield, paperweights : and always at low prices.

A good plan now is to strike across to Stamford, not only one of the loveliest stone towns in England but also a famous centre for antiques, wherein, for example, are the excellent and always fascinating shops of Messrs. Scotney and Son (13 and 15 St. Mary's Hill). There is an ancient, finely-groined Crypt dating back to the 13th century under these premises, shown with pleasure to visitors ; but more than that, Messrs. Scotney have a really large stock of fine old furniture, works of art, mirrors, porcelain and glass.

Proceed down the hill to St. Martins, not only the main road but also a thoroughfare famed wherever architecture is cherished, and at Number 35 is the growing establishment of Messrs. A. F. Smith and Son, growing because young Mr. Smith knows what the modern searcher after antiques wants, and provides it in excellent 18th century furnishings, interesting country pieces also, chandeliers, fine copper and brass. Many of our readers will be grateful for this recommendation.

Always Travel With ANTIQUES YEAR BOOK

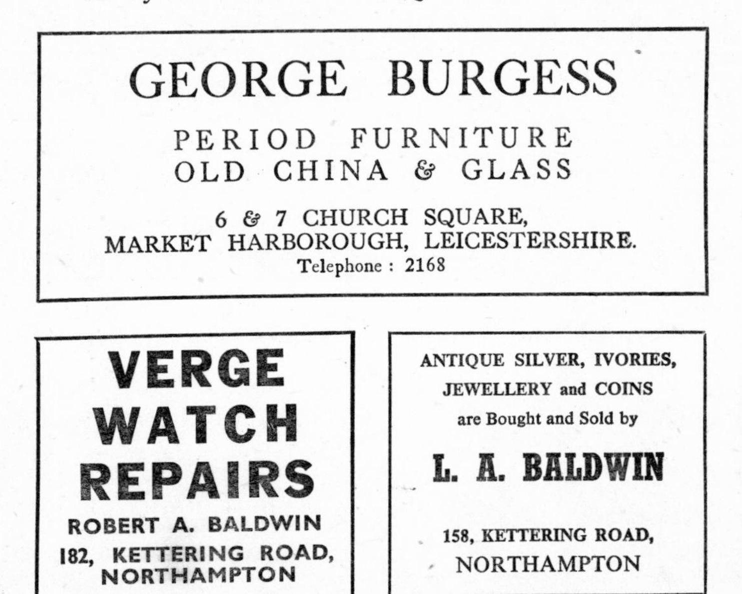

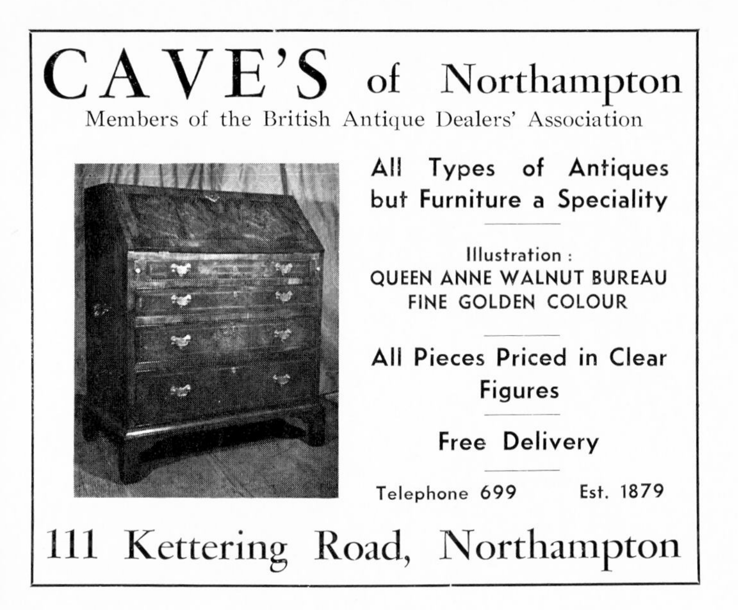

Always Mention ANTIQUES YEAR BOOK

The Reader's House, Ludlow, Unusual Museum of Antiques.

CATHERALLS of CHESTER
CATHERALLS Antiques and OLD MASTERS.
ANTIQUES.

A Fine Early Welsh Oak Dresser 4 ft. 4 ins., and a Collection of Blue, Yellow and Silver Resist Lustre

And now for an interesting experience.

Take the Great North Road 6½ miles south to Wansford and a short semi-circular lane which loops back to that road farther down. Signposted " Stibbington Only," the lane leads to Stibbington Manor, a delightful early Jacobean stone house with mullion windows, and with the notable collection of antiques of Mr. Frank Skevington. These range over fine period furniture, English and French clocks, old English glass, English, Continental and Chinese porcelain. Mr. Skevington's prices are reasonable and his goods represent the harvest of a lifetime's collecting experience. This will be a most valuable and interesting contact.

Regain the main road and continue to Peterborough—which we combed carefully to reveal—at Number 293 on the Lincoln Road—a most excellent small shop for china, glass, lustres, chandeliers, gleaned from all over the country by an enterprising couple, Mr. and Mrs. Potter. Lamps they make from Dresden groups are sold very reasonably—and this is worth noting by trade buyers.

NORTHAMPTON

An interesting cross country run now is via Oundle and Corby to Market Harborough. Find in Church Square (Numbers 6 and 7) the antique shop of George Burgess, solid and reliable for old furniture and interesting items from the past. This town can also be reached quickly from Leicester, should the traveller prefer to run south by a direct route.

After Market Harborough we would suggest making Northampton the final port of call before London—although Stony Stratford, Dunstable and St. Albans can be visited for antiques on the way if missed on the earlier trip north-west.

Northampton has some interesting shops. Aim for the Kettering Road, and at Number 111 on the left-hand side leaving the town find the old-established firm of F. and C. H. Cave, Ltd. Furniture is the speciality here, excellent antique pieces sold always in perfect condition, as skilled craftsmen working on the premises restore correctly where necessary. There is a modern department, so do not be misled by the windows, but walk inside and ask to inspect the very large showrooms which are packed with antique stock. Trade buyers are catered for and recommended to call.

Proceed up the Kettering Road and on the opposite side, at Number 158, find the shop of Mr. L. A. Baldwin, who sells antique silver, jewellery, and unusual items such as ivories and coins. Then at Number 182 farther up is his son Mr. Robert A. Baldwin, reliable horologist who has the almost unique speciality of antique watches, verge watches, old English levers. He is recommended for repairs to such items, as the making of new parts presents no obstacle to this fine craftsman.

Finally in the centre of Northampton, 50 yards from the Market Square, at Number 28 Newland, you will find the interesting shop of Mr. John Roberts, where you are assured of seeing many choice pieces of furniture and china, particularly mahogany and rosewood furniture.

But now the car boot, or the shooting brake, or the addled head will be filled : and the road to London is easy.

Always Travel With ANTIQUES YEAR BOOK

ROUND THE ANTIQUE SHOPS

TOUR SEVEN

WALES AND MARCHES

WE have planned this journey to involve the minimum of time and running, so that large areas with little antiques scope are omitted—and we have included English regions of the Welsh Marches, Shrewsbury, even Chester, Knutsford, so as to make a worthwhile tour.

It is suggested that Cardiff be visited directly, whether from the Cheltenham-Gloucester area, or from Bristol. There has hitherto been little between Gloucester and Cardiff, but an interesting specialist in antique silver, Mr. John Luddington, has recently come to the stately old river town of Newnham, and taken an old mansion there called Mount Severn (birthplace of the book *East Lynne*). Phone Mr. Luddington for an appointment (Newnham 296), and enjoy the perfection of his silver, also some fine porcelain : or write for the catalogues he sends to discerning collectors all over the world.

The antiques-minded traveller will find a number of shops in Cardiff, some of which are worth visiting. If, for example, you approach the city from the Gloucester side, bear right on the Cardiff-Swansea by-pass before entering the city. This is Albany Road, and at Number 131B on the right-hand side is the antique shop of Mr. G. E. H. Bents, a very live Londoner who usually has some good porcelain, with local specialities such as Swansea and Nantgarw, also interesting furniture, with Welsh dressers and the like.

Then proceed to the centre of the city and turn down High Street opposite the Castle. This is a city of arcades, and you will find at number 36 in Royal Arcade the shop of Alfred T. Philp and Son, good for Georgian furniture, Welsh oak, English and Continental porcelain, and Welsh lustre ware, also pictures, of which there is quite a gallery.

After which go further down the street to Morgan Arcade and the Wharton Galleries at Number 37. This is another good mark for small Welsh dressers, lustre ware, pewter, Toby jugs, and specialities such as Llangollen plates (we saw a Pratt dessert service with under-glaze scenes).

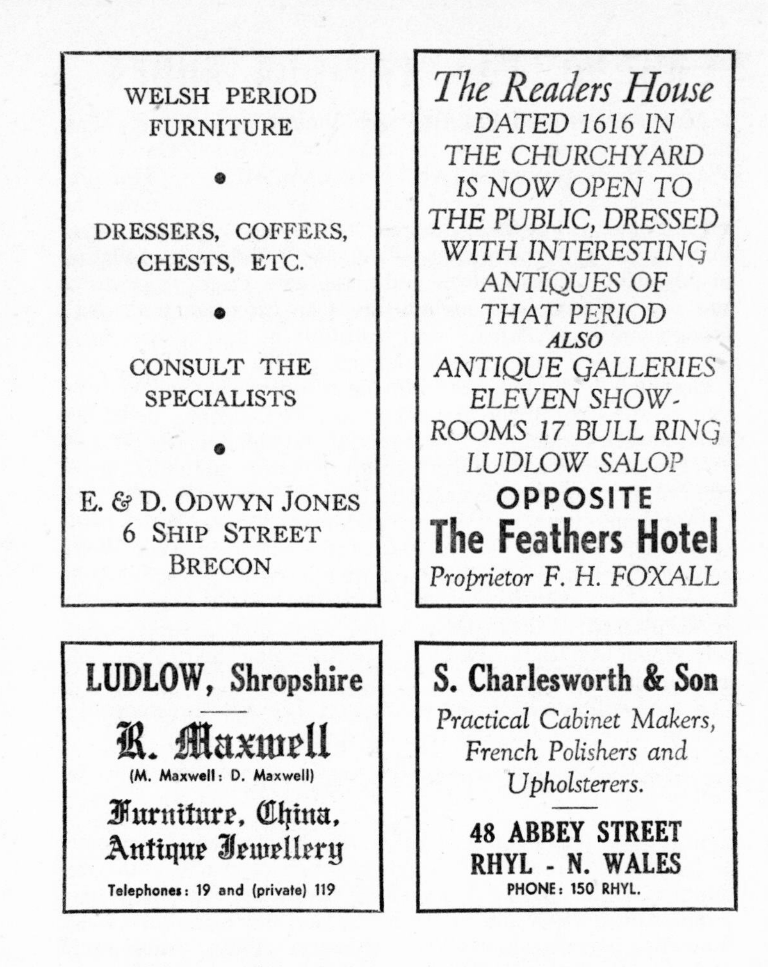

BEAUTIFUL BRECON

Now for a valuable experience take the road up through the Rhondda Valley—and past Nantgarw itself !—to Brecon. The value of the experience is that you will see the Welsh mining valleys as they are, neither so grim nor so compressed as expected ; and then you will emerge on the high ground at Brecon to savour country delights and the atmosphere of the real old-fashioned Wales.

Moreover, Brecon has two very interesting antique shops, doing a good trade as they are situated at this true " Gateway to Wales," the first conspicuously on the right, Mr. W. F. Hutchinson's just across the ancient Llanfaes Bridge as you enter the town. Popularly known in the trade as " Hutch " and a character for your gallery of interesting dealers, Mr. Hutchinson specialises in porcelain, pictures, silver and glass, with pieces at prices to suit every pocket. Although he does an extensive trade with foreign tourists, " Hutch " can truthfully be said to have built up his business on recommendations. He is one of those true " Quinneys " who believes in giving a square deal and his customers are accordingly his ambassadors. Travelling up to 800 miles a week searching for treasures, this dealer gets the goods.

Then continue a short distance up the street and cross on the right to the very charming shop frontage of Messrs. E. and D. G. Odwyn Jones. Enter and you will very probably hear Welsh being spoken between Mr. Odwyn Jones and a customer. True Welsh antique furniture is sold at the most reasonable prices, also old porcelain and pottery with a Welsh interest and books in the vernacular, Mr. Odwyn Jones belonging to that sensitive, scholarly school of dealers who believe in mastering their subject and aspiring high.

Brecon will indeed be left with regret. It is the ideal centre for a short, quiet holiday. But the road lies ahead.

HISTORIC LUDLOW

Run down the upper Wye Valley via Glasbury and Leominster to historic old Ludlow, with new experiences at once : the *real* antique shop of Mr. F. H. Foxall, 17 Bull Ring, redolent of byegones, famed especially for long-case and other antique clocks. Then Mr. Foxall will take you to Readers' House, a museum of antiques he has opened just behind the church, a wonderful early Tudor building furnished in contemporary style and always a main attraction of the town to visitors. There is a special collection of old domestic and agricultural implements, of ancient keys and locks, of too many items for catalogue here. Go and see!

Then adjoining the famous Feathers Hotel, one of the finest examples of Elizabethan architecture in the country, is the very tasteful shop of Messrs. R. Maxwell (22–3 Bull Ring). Here the specialities are Welsh oak, porcelain and pottery, and antique jewellery. This is another good mark.

SHREWSBURY

Then for Shrewsbury, perhaps the best " antiques " town in all these parts. There are two outstanding dealers, Mr. George Reynolds and Mr. W. G. Dugdale. Mr. Reynolds' establishment will be found at 4 and 5 Dogpole, an antique shop that has been in existence over forty years, and that has become refined by the years to the point when you can say : This is one of the good dealers. Mr. Reynolds really does sell exquisite furniture and other antiques, and is highly recommended. Royalty has bought from him.

The same applies to Mr. Dugdale. There is a small turning by the side of Messrs. W. H. Smith's, the booksellers, in the main street near the Castle. Down this turning, at Numbers 1–3 School Gardens, will be found the lovely shop and stock-in-trade of this solid, dependable dealer. He sells fine furniture, porcelain, paintings and prints, gives a written guarantee with all he sells, and is worth a long journey to meet and know.

Or proceed to the historic Square, where behind the 400 years' old Market Hall will be found that fine firm of goldsmiths and silversmiths, Messrs. Robinson and Co., Ltd. (established 1764), who under the discriminating direction of Mr. E. C. Plimmer sell excellent antique silver as well as jewellery, clocks, furniture, porcelain and glass.

BLACK AND WHITE COUNTRY

We are still proceeding north through the Welsh Marches, not actually entering the Principality—because the antique shops are on the English side—but increasingly encountering strangeness in the landscape, with a background nearly always of black and white, as shown in the perfect half-timbered " Olde Shoppe " of Mr. A. L. Wood in the High Street of Whitchurch, next town en route.

This building is no fake but probably the oldest in a very ancient little town. Formerly a Franciscan cell, it is gloriously apparelled with beam and plaster and black carving. That true old antique dealer Mr. Wood has much fine furniture and good silver.

NANTWICH

The next town is Nantwich and we are not only in Cheshire but possibly in its most interesting unspoilt repository of the past, especially if we ask the way at once to Churche's Mansion—everyone knows it—a truly magnificent domestic building in the elaborate black and white of the district. Restored carefully over a period of years by its public-spirited owners, the Mansion is appointed throughout with fine antiques for sale, furniture, jewellery, silver, china, the policy being "antiques have no value, only antiques of beauty."

The reader is strongly advised not to miss Nantwich, because there are several antique shops, such as that of Mr. Paul Smith at 12 Welsh Row—where the Welsh would once come down to harry these rich parts—which is a fascinating establishment, run by a young and most painstaking dealer whose knowledge of old oak and of old masters and prints is considerable, but who stocks all kinds of small antiques for everybody.

A little further up this street, moreover, is the famous Cheshire Cat Restaurant, worthy to be known to gastronomes and connoisseurs the world over (often serving recipes of Tudor days), but at the same time an Elizabethan building containing a unique collection of furniture dating from the 15th century.

Finally ask the way to Beam Street, next the Post Office, and find there at Number 20 the tasteful antique shop of Mr. A. H. Pearson, another young and most helpful dealer, who is principally interested in old furniture, oak and mahogany, but has more than that and is well worth a visit.

KNUTSFORD—CHESTER

Now we would suggest that the visitor travels via Middlewich and Northwich—these are the famous old salt towns—to Knutsford for the night, Knutsford the original of Mrs. Gaskell's "Cranford," still much as it was then, a quiet little town, wherein two good antique shops await you. The first will be seen immediately on the right as you enter the town. It is Mr. Arthur Lee's establishment, Hollingford House, an historic building originally the Church House mentioned in Mrs. Gaskell's unfinished classic *Wives and Daughters*. Mr. Lee himself is a first-class, independent type of dealer who has early oak and fine 18th century furniture—and who specialises in period wing chairs.

The second dealer will be found at number 72 in the quiet and prim King Street, by a house where Josiah Wedgwood used to stay when coming across to the Mersey to meet his shipments of kaolin. The dealer's name is John O. Curbishley (many readers, particularly Americans, will know it well); and he specialises in overseas and trade business. Should you seek early Victorian lustres or other strange nick-nacks of the period, you will find

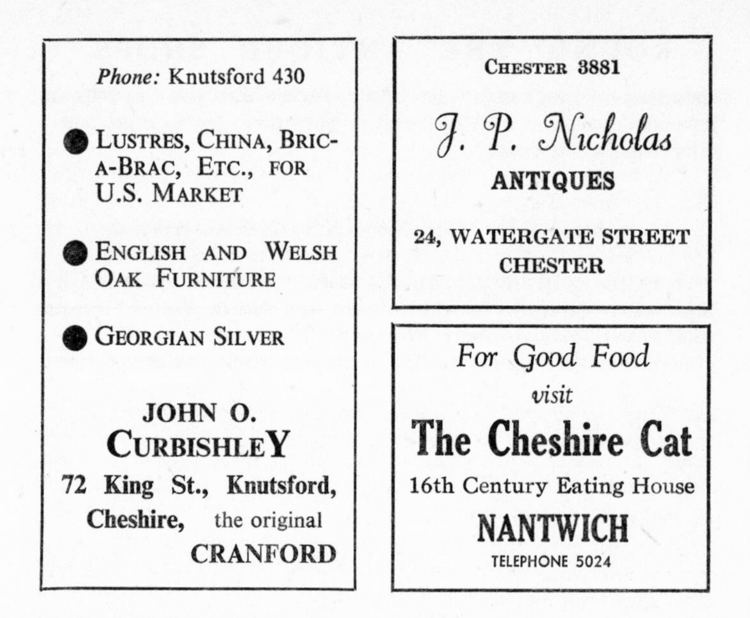

them in wholesale profusion here. This Knutsford is certainly not to be omitted!

CHESTER

And now Chester calls. It is a magnificent town, and has been famous for antiques. An interesting personality therein is Mr. A. P. Catherall, whose old antique shop and picture galleries occupy a section of one of the famous Rows—double-decker streets of early times—at Number 45 Watergate Row (from which may be found a car park). Mr. Catherall, a " Quinneys " indeed, has a large stock of old masters, the Dutch school being his speciality, and his reminiscences as an art dealer would be worthy of a book. He has recently purchased for Chester an historic house in the town that might otherwise have disappeared, and intends it to be used as a museum of antiquities and the basis of a Trust for the preservation of historic Chester. Do not forget Catheralls for pictures and also for all kinds of antiques.

Our readers will also appreciate the recommendation to call at Number 24 Watergate Street, nearly opposite Catheralls, where Mr. John Nicholas, the artist, sells good antiques, a quiet establishment for bargains of taste : the place where you can pick up an excellent piece of 18th century furniture, for example, at a surprisingly low price.

MORRIS OF FFYNNONGROEW

Take the road into North Wales from Chester towards Rhyl and watch carefully on the left for the North Wales Antique Galleries of Mr. Gilbert Morris at Ffynnongroew. This is a conspicuous building with half-timbered black and white front.

Mr. Morris is probably the leading antique dealer of the north-west, a homely, Lancashire man with an inborn flair for finding really first-class antique furniture, silver, glass, pottery, china, brass and pewter. He always has interesting oak, but all his treasures are not in that wood, and it is sufficient to say that Mr. Morris is one of the few northern dealers who have a large stand annually at the Antique Dealers' Fair, Grosvenor House, London, for it to be appreciated that he is worth visiting. He is, of course, a specialist to the trade, but has much for the private buyer, and is heavily starred.

Small shops will be found dotted round the great mass of Wales which have been investigated. The reader may care to go farther on his own volition, if prepared for the considerable distances.

(It might well be remembered, however, that Messrs. S. Charlesworth & Son, of 48 Abbey Street, Rhyl, are good restorers and repairers of antique furniture. Several generations of craftsmen have made their reputation. The panelling of rooms, the reproduction of fine pieces, indeed all the most complicated work is undertaken by this firm.)

Index to Advertisers

INDEX TO ADVERTISERS

INDEX TO ADVERTISERS

INDEX TO ADVERTISERS

Round the Antique Shops of Scotland

THE following tour is designed to comprehend Scotland as a whole within practical limits of petrol and time. Nearly every shop of standing is included—a remarkably high level of coverage and of probity.

We suggest that Edinburgh be the first target, reached at roughly equal distances either from Carlisle or Newcastle over a great tract of lowlands which is of little " antiques " interest to our readers.

THE CIVILISED CITY

And Edinburgh is every year more increasingly worthy of strong recommendation to the searcher after the best of the past. It is an excellent idea to go at the time of the Festival, when a most satisfactory holiday can be spent in a city which is to-day a second Paris in its civilised attractions for the visitor.

There are antique shops of all kinds, ranging from the impeccable salons of silversmiths who are sometimes even more imposing than their counterparts in Bond Street, to the many curious little establishments of the Canongate area. We have carefully chosen those which are good for all tastes.

Thus in silver first go at once to Shandwick Place at the western end of Princes Street, and find therein at Number 20 the establishment of George Cockburn. This fine business not only has the *largest* stock of antique silverware in Scotland, but is also the largest exporter of silver, which is sent to the U.S.A. and the Dominions.

In the hands of Mr. I. Rosenbloom, most charming and helpful of mentors, Messrs. Cockburns has become a rival in stock and taste to the leading London firms. The interior is compact like a jewel-case, but a-glitter with piled attraction. Here you can find silver of all periods, Sheffield plate, the most sought-after items of antique jewellery—and every item sold is guaranteed unconditionally.

Now proceed into Princes Street proper and to Number 139, the premises of Wilson and Sharp, outstanding dealers in fine silver for the last sixty years. Here is another most excellent firm

Telegrams and Cables:
Supergems, Edinburgh.
Telephone 25345
G. COCKBURN,
Established 1879. Member of the B.A.D.A.
Scotland's Finest Shop for Antique Silver, Antique Jewellery, Old Sheffield Plate.
20 Shandwick Place, EDINBURGH, 2.

Georgian Edinburgh—and the Premises of Messrs. Whytock & Reid, Royal-Appointed Cabinetmakers, at 7, Charlotte Square.

(By Courtesy of Messrs. John Bell of Aberdeen.)

An Example of Fine Old Scottish Furniture: Queen Anne Walnut Bureau. Circa 1710. One Rarely Finds a Bureau of this Period in such Completely Original State.

Example of Fine Modern Reproduction Work: Serpentine Mahogany Commode with Tambour Shutter Cupboard, Mahogany Cross-banding and Tulipwood Inlay, designed by Mr. E. R. Herrald, and executed by Messrs. Herrald of Edinburgh.

—at which the writer saw with especial interest a set of three Edinburgh octagonal castors by Patrick Turnbull, made 1713, and a set of decagonal Queen Anne candlesticks by Ambrose Stevenson, London, 1711. Mr. Wilson is himself a collector and most helpful friend. The stock is good, including some very interesting Highland items.

Down Princes Street the visitor slowly proceeds, slowly because there is so much to distract the eye, from the splendid scene of Castle, Scott Memorial, and Roman-topped hills to the cake shops, tartan shops : and for the discerning a quiet entrance at Number 90 to a resplendent gallery far within which is the wholely individual business of Mr. Gordon Small, an Asprey-type of business in which the best of old and new jostle together, but particularly some fine small furniture, porcelain, glass and unusual appurtenances to antique furnishings.

Next stop is inevitable—Number 80, where the notable antique business with the French flavour of Messrs. Wildman Bros. always detains knowledgeable visitors. The stock is very large, of interest alike to the trade buyer of, say, Dresden and Sheffield,

to the very serious and careful collector, and yet also to the beginner who wants small, inexpensive items of porcelain, silver, glass. There are always many fine items of furniture.

EIGHTEENTH CENTURY WAYS

Proceed now into the 18th century via St. David's Street, a turning to the left, carefully noting narrow Rose Street at the left again as you proceed. Pause here, for at Number 12 in Rose Street is the shop of Harry Chernack, another very good dealer in antique silver, who does a large export business, has friends across the world, and can be relied upon as they say in the trade " for a square deal."

The 18th century proper begins in the fine thoroughfares behind and leading from Princes Street, such as Hanover Street, wherein at Number 54 you descend steps to the true treasure house of Mr. Louis Henry, most enterprising of younger dealers with a famous name, good for porcelains, exquisite antique jewellery, silver, glass, and some fine furniture.

Next proceed to stately Frederick Street and walk down the hill revealing all the broad Forth to Fife, looking for the sober windows on the right of Messrs. Fairley and Co., Number 57, who have long been known to the best American collectors as purveyors of fine antique furniture, particularly the characteristic Scottish mahogany. A good firm.

And only a few doors on come to the imposing corner premises of Messrs. Herrald, again famous for furniture, patronised by Royalty, selling many items of antique interest in porcelain, glass and silver, but principally starred for that furniture. The writer happened to mention that antique wardrobes were always difficult to find for a furnishing scheme. He was immediately shown a selection of same, also hanging cupboards. Young Mr. Herrald knows his business very well, and brings to it a craftsman's intuition.

But these sensations are tiring. Why not repair to the noble bookshop of Messrs. Wm. Brown at 57 George Street just up the road and take refreshment there in the excellent coffee room, noting before or after what a splendid stock this firm has of art books and sumptuous volumes on collecting subjects generally.

Then proceed to Castle Street, yet another stately thoroughfare linking Princes and George Streets, where by happy chance is the other outstandingly good bookseller of these parts, Messrs. Douglas and Foulis, notable for Scottish fishing, sporting and topographical, early items, the fine antiquarian department being under that well-known expert Mr. John Orr.

But the 18th century still awaits, and is complete at the western end of George Street, which is Charlotte Square, wherein at Number 7 is the magnificent architectural abode of Messrs. Whytock and Reid, not only one of the few Cabinet Makers in Britain holding a Royal Appointment—they make magnificent furniture, design wonderful carpets—but also connoisseurs of the past who always show some excellent antiques. (Last year they lent their premises for the famous Exhibition of Rare Scottish Antiquities, one of the finest things of its kind promoted in Scotland. Do not miss it if it is held again in 1951.)

AULD TOON

The scene transforms—by a simple progress across one of the bridges from Princes Street to the truly ancient part of Auld Reekie, the Canongate, Lawnmarket and Grassmarket under the Castle and leading down to Holyroodhouse.

Strangely enough there is, quite near to Holyroodhouse, in Holyrood Square, and reached through a typical lowly wynd, a foremost furniture dealer, the noted George Neilson. He has a great warehouse packed with stock for trade and for public sale. His is an outstanding name in Scotland.

Wander back up High Street and peer in the dusty windows of many, many old curiosity shops. But enter for sure the excellent establishment of Mr. Lea Brown at 290 Lawnmarket, a continuation of High Street upwards. This is a very sound dealer's, especially for antique silver, coins, stamps and medals.

And, if you are " trade " or interested in export, do not miss Mr. George McNair a little further up on the other side at 503 Lawnmarket. He conducts a growing export business in English and Continental porcelains particularly, and has good facilities for packing and shipping—also welcomes the general public.

There are so many to see hereabouts, but we must be particular or lost. Ask the devious way then to the ever-fascinating Grassmarket farther on, scene of the Porteous Riots, of the signing of the Covenant, of public hangings in the bloody past, where at Numbers 52 and 60 will be found the shops of Mr. John McIntosh, personality and horologist. If you do not know Mr. McIntosh—and his wife—you will be grateful for the introduction. These are thoughtful, hard-working people, members of the Association, who are outstandingly good in all Scotland for unusual antique clocks and for repairs to same. Some wonderful musical boxes are also to be found.

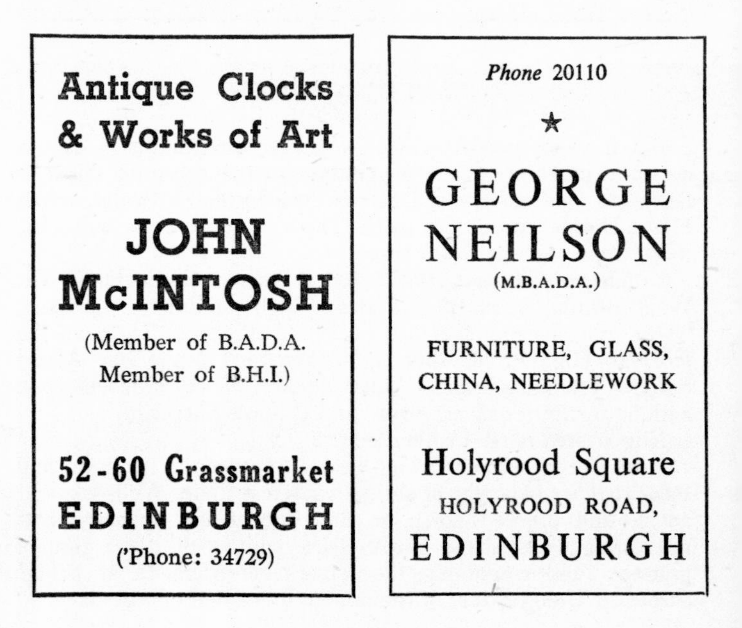

TO THE NORTH

But there is travelling to do and even an Edinburgh cannot detain us indefinitely. It is suggested now that the route north be taken via Queensferry and the spectacular Forth Bridge across Fife to Dundee, preferably by the Tay ferry route, as we will come to Perth on the way down later.

Dundee would be worth the visit if for one reason alone—Mr. W. S. Beaton, an excellent dealer of high standing in the trade, whose gracious premises will be found by proceeding from the ferry up High Street, then up Commercial Street into Albert Square. The number is 37 Albert Square. Mr. Beaton sells good antique furniture, silver, glass—and Chinese porcelain.

Now hasten north to Aberdeen.

It may seem a foolish thing to do. Aberdeen is far north and there *couldn't* be aught of antiques interest there. Well, take our advice and proceed north, to find one of the cleanest, most interesting cities in the British Isles, smiling with the glint of granite: and containing the remarkable premises at Bridge Street off Union Street of the famous John Bell of Aberdeen.

Mr. Bell sells his antiques from Aberdeen to half the world. His premises are as considerable in extent as any we know, but his immense stock is by no means beyond the common purse. There are items for all. Meticulous care is taken in the running of this business. The filing system contains 10,000 photographs of fine pieces that have passed through Mr. Bell's hands. Every good item is thus photographed and prints are available to inquirers anywhere.

But that is by no means all in Aberdeen. There is also the fine old firm of Wm. Young, at Number 1 Belmont Street, another turning out of Union Street. This is claimed not only to be the oldest established but also to have one of the largest stocks in Scotland of all kinds of antiques, and the visitor will be truly surprised at the array of items offered.

And at 16 Holburn Street, top of Union Street on the left, will be found the shop of Mrs. E. C. Edwards, good for small antiques, silver, china, export goods, the kind where even the biggest buyers often like to browse—and find their bargains.

Always Travel With ANTIQUES YEAR BOOK

A HIGHLAND GATHERING

It is well worthwhile for an interesting experience to proceed still farther north than Aberdeen, maybe across to Inverness (where there are one or two interesting shops) but certainly to stop at the fascinating town of Elgin, with its glorious Cathedral ruin—and the establishment at 48–50 Lossie Wynd (by the bus station) of Messrs. Anderson & England, who sell antique furniture, pottery and pictures, and had a fine set of Prince Charlie chairs when we were last there.

After which get to know the real Highlands by proceeding south via lovely Grantown on Spey to Tomintoul and Braemar where John Bell of Aberdeen has a good branch shop, packed with good old things : then enjoy the scenic road with the Devil's Elbow on the way to Perth.

Under the 13th century Kirk of St. John—in St. John's Place, Perth—will be found yet another very large Scottish antique business, that of Messrs. Love's, who have a remarkable organisation, ranging from a fleet of ten specially-constructed motor vans

for the conveyance of valuable pieces to all parts of the British Isles, to showroom after showroom of exquisite antiques.—There is, for example, one large salon for rare Continental, English and Chinese porcelain alone. The antique furniture department is large. There are rooms devoted to pictures, prints, miniatures. . . .

Or in Perth find at Number 15 Atholl Street, on the right as the road from the north enters the town, the fascinating premises (with painting of longcase clock outside) of Messrs. Fettes. There are several individualistically arranged showrooms of fine furniture, pictures, Scottish silver and Highland items. Mr. Peter Fettes the proprietor is a dealer of the kind that makes real friends of his customers.

The same applies to Mr. W. T. Graham Henderson at 5 Murray Street, turning off Kinnoul Street. Mr. Henderson was formerly an important figure in the London trade, and still, from far-off Perth, takes a stand at the Grosvenor House Fair. He is an authority on Oriental porcelain and jade, also regimental antiquities and Highland items.

Even yet Perth is not done. Yet another remarkable experience awaits the visitor who proceeds to the splendid Rose Terrace by the Inch and finds at Number 10 not only the well-known house of John Ruskin but also the excellent antique salons of Miss McLeish. It is a valuable experience to visit these fine rooms, and Miss McLeish can certainly be recommended for her lovely stock.

And now the road to Glasgow runs via Stirling, ancient, exciting gateway to the Highlands. Up beside the Castle at 56 Spittal Street is the shop of Mr. John Yates, famous old dealer, who impressed us particularly with his early and French furniture, his china, bronzes and pictures.

THE ARRAY OF GLASGOW

Glasgow in every way has a different character from Edinburgh, even in antiques. There are perhaps more large dealers with good furniture in Glasgow, though also much interesting silver and glass will be found, with a vast amount of what are termed " export goods " in the background, Dresden, Victoriana and the like. It is a happy hunting ground indeed.

Start if you like at Muirhead, Moffats, 132–6 Blythswood Street, a turning off Sauchiehall Street at the eastern end. This is one of the outstanding firms of antique dealers in Scotland, with a fine stock of furniture, silver, pictures, porcelain, weapons and armour, pewter. The directors are businesslike and scour the British Isles for their finds, which always include some interesting items of Scottish antiquity.

In Sauchiehall Street, at Number 398, will be found the Glasgow branch of Aberdeen's Mr. John Bell. This is a lovely shop (the adjective not being misplaced). There are several floors with many showrooms and the antiques are kept in perfect condition and are of uniformly high standard. It is possible to browse in this establishment almost indefinitely.

Further down Sauchiehall Street towards the centre of the city there is a turning on the left called Cambridge Street, wherein will be found the establishment of Mr. J. L. Kirkhope. This gentleman might justly be described as the revered doyen of the Scottish trade. In his establishment will be found only fine furniture of the 17th and 18th centuries, glass, clocks, pewter and porcelain—all " right " pieces but by no means at absurd prices. This is a good " trade " mark.

Now ask the way to Dundas Place, not so very far distant, and meet if possible Mr. Ernest Alexander, a very pleasant and reliable dealer who is justly proud of his recommendations and letters of thanks received from customers in all parts of the world. He does a large export trade, and has a warehouse usually well-stocked with export goods, but is for the general public also, being especially good for Dresden and Sheffield, also for *objets-d'art* generally and furniture.

Another member of the same family, Mr. B. Alexander, will similarly repay a visit to his shop at 134 West Nile Street, where he gives special attention to the North American market, and is good for early and Victorian china and pictures among much other interesting stock.

Established 1904
GLASGOW

ROUNDABOUT

While in the centre of the city stroll down to Trongate and at Numbers 27–9 you might find something to interest you at Messrs. Chisholm-Hunters, a remarkable, unclassifiable establishment—with furniture used by Queen Victoria in 1840, some silver and porcelain, bagpipes, sporrans—and indeed Glasgie begins to go roond and roond.

But the city does not by any means stop at the centre. Proceed to Woodlands Road, the main thoroughfare leading west, and at Numbers 220–8 find the business of Messrs. J. E. Rushmer, now controlled by Mr. David A. Barnet, who has long had family connections with the trade, knows it well himself from many years of experience in Glasgow and with Hamptons in London ; and offers interesting items of antique furniture as well as other good antiques.

Then at Number 188 in Woodlands Road do not omit to call upon Mr. A. Macdonald, whose real antique shop is supplied with treasures gleaned from all parts of the country by its indefatigable proprietor. Mr. Macdonald stocks all kinds of antique furniture, but usually has some very interesting pieces of oak, as well as china and glass. This is another Scottish member of the British Antique Dealers' Association who can really be strongly recommended by our book.

There are many other, smaller firms in Glasgow. There is also a first-rate antiquarian bookseller, Messrs. W. & R. Holmes of 3–11 Dunlop Street. They give prompt attention to lists of desiderata. Quotations for Burnsiana and important Scottish works are welcome and there is a rapid foreign and export order service.

Outlying areas of Scotland beyond the limits of a normal visit will not be covered this year and await the 1952 volume for investigation. When reaching the border on the Carlisle side, however, it is strongly recommended that a trip be made into Galloway, so lovely and unspoilt—and with the interesting shops (for furniture, china, silver, glass and prints) of Miss Stuart at 234 King Street, Castle Douglas, and 8 Arthur Street, Newton Stewart.

Round the Galleries

A GEOGRAPHICAL DIRECTORY OF DEALERS IN PICTURES SELECTED FOR THEIR SPECIAL INTEREST TO OUR READERS. UNUSUAL FEATURES ARE INDICATED IN BRACKETS.

XHILL, Sussex
Ialcolm Anderson, 13, St. Leonard's Rd. (**Prints**).

ACKBURN, Lancs.
. E. Tinker, 14, Mincing Lane (**Miniatures**).

URNEMOUTH
ictor Needham Ltd.,, 8, Lansdowne Rd.

RADFORD-ON-AVON, Wilts.
ohn Teed, Silver St.

ARDIFF
. T. Philp & Son, 36, Royal Arcade.

HESTER
. P. Catherall, 45, Watergate Row. (**Dutch School**).

ASTBOURNE
eldons, Ltd., 40, Grove Rd.

UNSTABLE, Beds.
laise Preston, Ltd., 152, High St. North.

ENMEAD, Hants.
. J. Radford, Robin Hood Cottage, Furzeley Corner (**Prints**).

FALMOUTH
John Maggs, 54, Church St. (**Prints**).

HARROGATE
E. G. Barnard, 1, Crown Place (**Prints**).

LAVENHAM, Suffolk
R. McCausland-White, 4, High St. Also : 41, Sandgate High St., Folkestone.

LIVERPOOL
Boydell Galleries, North John St. (**19th century Old Masters**).

LONDON
M. Bernard, 21, Ryder St., St. James, S.W.1. (**Old Masters, also drawings, prints**).
Francis Edwards, Ltd., 83, Marylebone High St. (**Prints**).
Leger Galleries, 13, Old Bond St., W. 1. (**Old Masters, Watercolours, Prints**).
Mrs. L. Loewenthal, 4, St. James's St., S.W.1. (**Glass and Silkwork Pictures**).

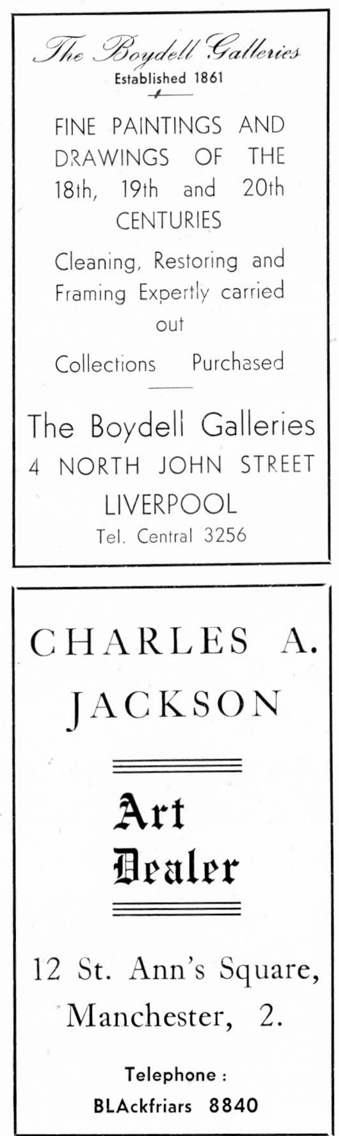

B. F. Stevens & Brow Ltd., 79, Duke St. (**Drawings and Literary Potraits**).

MANCHESTER

Chas. Clark (Antiques) Lt 25, Market Place (**Sporing and Railway Print**

J. Davey & Sons, 70, Brid St.

Chas. A. Jackson, 12, S Ann's Square. (**New Eglish Art Club picture Epstein sculptures**).

NANTWICH, Cheshire

Paul Smith, 12, Welsh Ro

OXFORD

B. H. Blackwell, Ltd., Bro St. (**Prints**).

SEAFORD, Sussex

The Old House, High S (**Prints**).

SHREWSBURY

W. G. Dugdale, 1–3, Sch Gardens (**Prints**).

SUTTON COLDFIEL

Norman English, Vesey G leries, 306, High St.

TEIGNMOUTH, Devon

Thos. Extence, 2, Wellir ton St.

WEYBRIDGE, Surrey

Lewis C. Lewis, 17, Bal St.

WINCHESTER

Philip King, 23 Southgate S

WORCESTER

Thos. Tolley, 46, Sidbu

YORK

Charles E. Thornton, Ada House, Petergate.

(By Courtesy of Mercy Jeboult, Quorn, Leics.)

Antique Giltwood Mirrors en suite in the Chinese Chippendale Style.

The Centre Gallery at " The Home of Daylight Saving "—Messrs. William Willett's Antique Salons, Sloane Square, London, S.W.1.